Afrique sur Seine

After the Empire:
The Francophone World and
Postcolonial France

Series Editor
Valérie Orlando, Illinois Wesleyan University

Advisory Board
Robert Bernasconi, Memphis University; Alec Hargreaves, Florida State University; Chima Korieh, Rowan University; Françoise Lionnet, UCLA; Obioma Nnaemeka, Indiana University; Kamal Salhi, University of Leeds; Tracy D. Sharpley-Whiting, Hamilton College; Frank Ukadike, Tulane University

See www.lexingtonbooks.com/series for the series description and a complete list of published titles.

Recent and Forthcoming Titles

Afrique sur Seine

A New Generation of African Writers in Paris

Odile Cazenave

LEXINGTON BOOKS

A division of
ROWMAN & LITTLEFIELD PUBLISHERS, INC.
Lanham • Boulder • New York • Toronto • Plymouth, UK

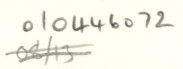

LEXINGTON BOOKS

A division of Rowman & Littlefield Publishers, Inc.
A wholly owned subsidary of The Rowman & Littlefield Publishing Group, Inc.
4501 Forbes Boulevard, Suite 200
Lanham, MD 20706

Estover Road
Plymouth PL6 7PY
United Kingdom

British Library Cataloguing in Publication Information Available

The hardback edition of this book was previously cataloged by the Library of Congress as follows:

Cazenave, Odile M. (Odile Marie), 1961-
  [Afrique sur Seine. English]
  Afrique sur Seine : a new generation of African writers in Paris / Odile Cazenave.
    p. cm. — (After the empire)
  Includes bibliographical references and index.
  1. African fiction (French)—History and criticism. 2. French fiction—20th century—History and criticism. 3. French fiction—Minority authors—History and criticism.
I. Title. II. Series.
PQ3984.C38813 2005
843'.91409920693—dc22
                                     2005006343

ISBN-13: 978-0-7391-1040-9 (cloth : alk. paper)
ISBN-10: 0-7391-1040-3 (cloth : alk. paper)
ISBN-13: 978-0-7391-2063-7 (pbk : alk. paper)
ISBN-10: 0-7391-2063-8 (pbk : alk. paper)

Printed in the United States of America

∞™ The paper used in this publication meets the minimum requirements of American National Standard for Information Sciences—Permanence of Paper for Printed Library Materials, ANSI/NISO Z39.48–1992.

For my father, Guy Cazenave

For Alex and Andreas

Contents

Preface

While working on my first book, *Femmes rebelles: naissance d'un nouveau roman au féminin* (1996), I had noticed at the time, but had not further elaborated on it, that African women writers from the continent wrote a different type of novel compared to the ones generated by their peers writing within France or in another European country.

This aspect continued to intrigue me and I started to think more about this. I looked at novels produced by male novelists and there, too, I came to the same realization, i.e., that the authors living in France were producing a different type of writing, in terms of themes and language, compared to the ones on the African continent. This sparked further my interest and got me started with this new project.

In particular, I wanted to address the following questions: Were these writers, men and women, part of a literary movement, part of a new diaspora, comparable to the previous one? Could we speak of a new generation that, beyond the relatively young age of the authors, all in their twenties and thirties, and their location of writing, France, brought together similar characteristics and let us think of a phenomenon of a new literature, of an autonomous body of literature that departed from the post-colonial novel written in the continent? Or were these authors simply multiple voices, who simply expressed their singularity?

As I went deeper in the topic, more questions came: What were these new voices interested in? What were they gazing at? Was their gaze politically committed? Can we still speak of an *engagé* novel today? What kind of new parameters do these new writings introduce? In what ways are they part of a post-colonial writing or identity? Does the question even make sense? In that regard, was gender a pertinent analytical category?

Besides, at a time when globalization affects both Western and third-world cultures, can the location of writing still have an impact on issues of writing, language and identity, the identity of the writer, and his/her characters? What role does displacement play in the fragmentation of identity/-ies? What kind of role may the readership play on these new voices and productions?

Does the fact that these writers migrated to France allow us to make the leap and think of their works as writings of new identities in France, and, beyond that, of a literature of immigration?

Looking at the dates of the first publications—the mid-eighties—I immediately made the link with what has been called the *Beur* novel, that is, the novel by children born in France from Maghrebi parents. I wanted to see if the characteristics of what has been defined as a literature of its own, separate from Maghrebi literature, could apply to the new African writings in Paris, in other words, if they belonged to a larger denomination and a phenomenon of the eighties in France.

Beyond that, I wanted to address the issue from yet another angle: whether these new voices corresponded to a phenomenon specific to France; or whether they should be considered within a larger scope, as emblematic of the new profile of European societies and their multicultural writings.

I would like to take a moment here to reiterate the thanks I extended to a number of friends and colleagues for their support in the original project. In particular, I want to thank Kenneth Harrow for his initial questions on the focus and objectives of this work; Michel Laronde for his reading of the first draft; Jacques Chevrier for his suggestions on the following versions; Mireille Rosello for discussing questions about literature, immigration, and post-colonial identities "under the baobab tree"; and Susan Andrade, Nathalie Etoké, Sonia Lee, Patricia-Pia Célerier, Boniface Mongo-Mboussa, and Ambroise Kom, for our frequent exchanges. I am also grateful to my fellow peers and friends from the Radcliffe Institute of Advanced Studies at Harvard University, where this project took shape and developed. Through their questions grounded in their respective expertise backgrounds—philosophy, sociology, history, literature, religious studies, but also arts and sciences—they enabled me not to get locked in one type of terminology, categorization, or critical reading.

All my thanks go to Maïmouna Coulibaly and Nocky Djedanoum as well, the directors of Arts et Médias d'Afrique, Fest'Africa in Lille, France. The many literary events and roundtable discussions that I have moderated there over the past few years have enabled me to further my understanding of the phenomena and writings that I examine in this essay.

I would like to thank MIT and the Department of Foreign Languages and Literatures, especially, for their generous support. I am also grateful to my MIT students for their questions through the different courses I have taught on postcolonial identities in France. My thanks go especially to Melissa Edoh and Jovonne Bickerstaff who worked with me during the summer of 2001 on a project on racism and minority youths in Paris.

I want to thank Melissa Edoh for her fine reading and translation of the first draft of *Afrique sur Seine*. It was a joy to work with her. My thanks also go to Susan Spilecki from the MIT Writing and Communication Center for proofreading and helping me edit this work.

Finally, my acknowledgments would be incomplete if I did not thank Alex and Andreas for their understanding and patience while I completed this essay.

Introduction

Ils sont nés à Yaoundé, à Brazzaville, ou Kinshasa,
mais aussi à Pithiviers, à Laveur dans le Tarn,
à Baccarat en Meurthe-et-Moselle, ou à Lausanne . . .
Ils vivent et écrivent à Paris.

Bernard Magnier

[They were born in Yaoundé, Brazzaville, or Kinshasa,
But also in Pithiviers, Laveur in the Tarn region,
in Baccarat in Meurthe-et-Moselle, or in Lausanne . . .
They live and write in Paris.]

The existence of an African diaspora in Paris is neither a new nor a recent phenomenon.[1] With the arrival of African-American writers and other artists in Paris in the 1920s and the African and Antillean founders of the Négritude movement in the 1930s and 1940s, Paris has long served as a meeting place for African and African-American intellectuals. Similarly, Paris was marked by intense literary activity in the 1950s and the 1960s. Throughout these years, African expatriates have kept their gaze turned towards Africa.

The 1980s, however, witnessed the emergence of a new generation of African writers residing in France. Contrary to their predecessors, they provide a gaze different both in nature and direction. Theirs is a gaze no longer necessarily turned towards Africa, but rather towards themselves and their own experience, their writing taking a more personal turn. These writers, both male and female, contribute to the formation of a new literature. Often their work, only slightly preoccupied with Africa itself, addresses questions of displacement, migration, and in this regard, poses new questions about post-colonial cultures and identities, as perceived by those living in France. But they don't simply subscribe to notions of immigration literature; writing the African self, "African writings of the self," to borrow the expression and concept of Achille Mbembe, they show the possibility of writing and thinking about oneself outside the prescriptions of the West—the former colonizing power.[2]

The body of works examined here consists of approximately thirty novels from fifteen writers originally from Sub-Saharan African countries, such as Senegal, Cameroon, Guinea, Ivory Coast, ex-Zaïre (DRC), and the Republic of Congo. Because most of these writers were born after independence, that is, after 1960, this generation is *literally* post-colonial, and therefore has a relation to French language and culture different from that held by the previous generation. These writers are mostly young, talented, up and coming, such as the Cameroonian Jean-Roger Essomba, or the Congolese Daniel Biyaoula and Alain Mabanckou. Very few of them are already established writers. The Cameroonian writer Calixthe Beyala, who published ten novels between 1987 and 2000 and was the recipient of numerous literary prizes for her texts—including the *Prix de l'Académie Française* for *Les honneurs perdus* in 1996—is an exception.[3] Simon Njami, originally from Cameroon, who was born in Lausanne and today lives in Paris, and his compatriot Yodi Karone represent the early figures of these [new] avant-garde writings.

These authors have been attracting critics' attention since the early 1990s. Bernard Magnier, in "Beurs noirs à Black Babel," provides the following assessment of the situation:[4]

> Les drapeaux ont été rangés et, s'ils ne se désintéressent pas de l'avenir du monde en général et de l'Afrique en particulier, leurs élans semblent davantage dictés par une stratégie individuelle et non par une adhésion à une quelconque cause commune. Leurs héros—mais le mot paraît bien impropre—sont des solitaires qui n'assument en aucune façon le destin d'un groupe, encore bien moins d'un peuple ou d'une race. Leurs déchirures sont internes et leurs réactions relèvent plus d'une décision personnelle que d'un engagement collectif. (102)

> [The flags have been put away and, if these writers are not showing complete disinterest in the future of the world in general, and of Africa in particular, they are first driven by an individual force rather than by a belief in some collective cause. Their heroes—and the term is quite inadequate—are lonely figures who do not assume any collective responsibility, least for a people or a race. Their dilemma are personal and based on an individual decision rather than a collective commitment.]

The marked individuality as well as their visibility, the fact that they produce three quarters of what is being published in African literature, raises the question of the status of these new writings, of their definition, and of their specificities. Should we speak of a literary movement, and if so, how is it defined? Do these writers make up a new generation, a new diaspora? Or rather, should they first and foremost be considered as individual voices?

In this regard, Bennetta Jules-Rosette, in a multidisciplinary synthesis, *Black Paris: The African Writers' Landscape* (1998),[5] on the African presence in Paris from the 1940s to the early 1990s, defines a new set of authors and of works that she classifies under the term "Parisianism." Through her analyses and interviews with African writers living in Paris, Jules-Rosette brings out the principal characteristics of these writings. To her, they correspond to a generational phenomenon beginning with political engagement and moving through the rejection of any explicitly political ideology through the idea of Parisianism and an aspiration to universalism.

In fact, Jules-Rosette situates the birth of the new generation in the 1980s in what she calls a new Parisianism. She defines Parisianism as "a cosmopolitan style of Franco-African writing," starting with *Un Nègre à Paris* (1959) by Bernard Dadié, which traces Tanhoé Bertin's stay in Paris and his "naïve" observations of the habits of daily life for Parisians. The term Parisianism does not constitute, according to Jules-Rosette, a genre of its own. Rather, she remarks that "there is little critical work on the relatively new genre, but the quantity of new works and their thematic similarities warrant classification and recognition" (148). Furthermore, she asserts, "the term is particularly appropriate because the authors use it to describe their own work and to assert their cultural claim of belonging to French society" (148). In addition, her analysis links the birth of this new writing to the social and economic climate characteristic of France in the 1980s.

> The Parisianism of the 1980s would not have been possible without political pressure to liberalize legal and social attitudes toward immigration in France and to combat xenophobic sentiments. In this complex and changing environment, France saw the emergence of a new category of Black writers. (148)

While *Black Paris* intoduces and defines this new literary phenomenon, I would argue that it provides only a brief glimpse of this new generation and is mostly limited to an analysis of a few novels by Simon Njami, Yodi Karone, and Calixthe Beyala, including interviews with these writers. If all three are indeed representative of this new writing, the works by new voices in the 1990s, particularly after 1993, further broaden the dialectic. Jules-Rosette's taxinomy of their writing as Parisianist limits them to the periphery, both with regards to French literature and to Francophone literature, especially the African novel from the continent.

The writer Abdourahman Waberi, in a critical essay entitled "Les enfants de la postcolonie,"[6] where he establishes an African literary history broken down into four periods, identifies the last period—starting in the early 1990s—as that of "the children of the post-colony." Waberi remarks that these writers were born after the wave of Independence; that, among the distinguishing signs to be particularly taken into consideration are: (1) The acceptance of a double identity, African and French; (2) An aspiration towards a universalism, the fact that, unlike their predecessors, they define themselves first as writers, and then as Africans, and logically following that, that they identify themselves as "international illegitimate children," thereby rejecting the burden of Third-World ideology. Finally, Waberi underscores their departure from the canonical novelistic themes, focusing instead on their arrival in France rather than on a possible return to their homeland.

Lydie Moudileno, in a special issue of *Africultures*, which deals with claims and debates over post-colonialism, challenges Waberi's categorization. In particular, she discusses the blurring of boundaries between the terms "generation" and "literary movement." She contests the idea of a generation defined by the characteristics summarized by Boniface Mongo Mboussa in his introduction to this issue: "elle estime que ces écrivains, de par leur position à 'l'intersection de plusieurs territorialités géographiques et intellectuelles' posent un défi à l'historiographie littéraire. Non seulement ces écrivains donnent à lire une diversité d'écritures, mais ils mettent en avant un brouillage d'identité nationale au profit d'une pluralité d'affiliations" (6-7) [she finds that these writers, as a result of their position at the "crossroads of several geographical and intellectual territories," pose a challenge to literary historiography. Not only do they provide a diversity of styles, but they promote a blurring of national identity in favor of a plurality of affiliations]. In this way, both articles open the debate and question the status of these new writings.

In this regard *Afrique sur Seine* fits into the line of Jules-Rosette's analysis and the hypotheses posed by Waberi and Moudileno. From a literary standpoint, we propose to examine the presence of these new writings, to consider whether they are indicative of a new generation of the African diaspora, and to define the characteristics of this literary presence in its development from the 1980s to the late 1990s. Taking Jules-Rosette's definition of a "Parisianist" genre, we raise the question whether such a categorization is wholly applicable to these newer narratives, and consider the risks of classification and of ghettoization in this literature. We then explore the other paths of possible reading when dealing with a narrative fabric that treats questions linked to the migration/immigration of Africans. Indeed, the presence of new voices has implications for both a literary analysis and its critical discourse. How might we avoid the risk of confining these writers into a restraining categorization? Thinking about the existing terminology also brings up implications for both French literature and for Francophone literature. With respect to the Francophone African novel, how do these writers differentiate themselves from the previous generation in the diaspora? How do they differentiate themselves from their colleagues writing on the continent? How do they distinguish themselves, if such is the case, from those writing from a non-Parisian setting within France?

The notion of individualism comes back in each analysis, from Magnier to Jules-Rosette, Waberi, and Moudileno. In the attempt to achieve individualism, however, we witness a convergence towards a systematic decentering of the themes and of the narrative fabric. This decentering of the writing renews the perspective on questions of identities and of post-colonial cultures, and in fact forces us to rethink the notion of post-colonial voice and to consider the phenomena of multiculturalism and integration from a new angle that challenges the dominant paradigms, both French and African. Starting with some parallels with other types of literature—literature of exile, literature of immigration, the *Beur* novel (generated by the descendants of Maghrebi immigrants born in France), and the Antillean novel, as well as the novel from the African diaspora in London—I propose to examine how these writers contribute to a decentering of both the African novel and French literature, and to the development of a distinct type of literature.

In this context, the terminology of "literature of immigration" must be re-examined in greater detail, with regard to the references it makes and to the implications that the usage of such a term, and thus the attribution of a new label, has for the writers. The notion of immigration literature allows us to challenge today's nomenclature. When we think of immigration literature, we think of it in relation to what in the 1980s was called the *Beur* novel, in other words, a novel that deals with the generational identity gap between parents and their children when faced with the dilemma of choosing assimilation or integration.[7]

The themes par excellence—difference, otherness, foreignness, racial and cultural mixing, the "Orient" and the West, exoticism, incarceration, delinquency—always go back to questions of identity.[8] Some of these same issues appear in the new writings of *Afrique sur Seine*. The themes of incarceration and of delinquency are not, however, at the heart of the works studied. When they do appear, it is merely in the background.

From the start, the *Beur* novel highlights a difficulty in accessing the original culture, which is represented by the parental figure (alternately depicted as an authoritative or a fragile character). The young protagonists' reactions range from an obsession with memory (as when the father figure is missing in *Shérazade* [1982] by Leïla Sebbar, for example[9]) to the rejection of all moorings, the refusal to understand and speak the Arabic language being one of the most typical manifestations (as in *Le thé au harem d'Archi Ahmed* [1983] by Mehdi Charef). The characters define themselves largely by a feeling of lack, which leads to a total de-identification. Theirs is the rejection of a bilingual and bicultural life, which does not necessarily mean their adherence to a monoculture. Consequently, as it appears in the novel, the *Beur* discourse is primarily characterized by its reclaiming the "right to be different," and the desire to find "une identité collective externe à l'identité nationale" (Laronde 22) [a collective identity outside of national identity]. The approach of *Beur* discourse is to pluralize the national discourse through a language of inversion and shattering: "nous les *Beurs*, notre Différence est ce qui fait notre similarité" (22) [For us Beurs, our Difference is what makes us similar]. Laronde notes the importance of the singularity of the Other in the identification of the self in this process. But the very feeling of singularity implies the need to feel part of a whole. Out of this flows the need to blend into the group, which in turn offers the following two alternatives for the Outsider: either blend into collective homogeneity unknown to him/her (thereby accepting assimilation), or to stand apart as different and opt for Alterity/Otherness, by deciding to exclude him or herself.

The same type of equation is posed in the texts studied in this work, with regard to the mother culture (Africa) and the society one belongs to (France). It must nonetheless be pointed out that the mother societies in these cases are more culturally diverse, with the main common point among all of them being simply that they were all former French colonies. It remains to be seen within which society the relationship bonds are stronger, and whether, as in the case of the so-called *Beur* generation's slogan image of non-identification, "neither French, nor Arab," the writers of the new diaspora reject one of the two affiliations, if not labels: "neither African, nor French."[10]

The problem of a fragmented and virtual collective identity (the French and the African) is at the heart of most of the novels selected here. We will examine in chapter 1 how the mechanisms of rejection and of central power control, symbolized by the police force—but also, more subtly, by the teacher or the social worker—play a role in new writings by the African diaspora; finally, we'll see how and to what extent the modification of the Parisian urban land-scape, with a move from central Paris to the suburbs to the ghettoization of these suburbs—characteristic of the *Beur* novel—operates in the novels considered in this text.

The novel by Maghrebi or Franco-Maghrebi writers incontestably puts an emphasis on the marginality of not only the characters, but of an entire commu-nity demanding the right to be different. But like the demands of the young *Beurs*, the writers very rapidly displayed a resistance to this naming in fear of becoming confined and marginalized, because of the implicit distinction made between French literature and literature of immigration. The latter indeed meant running the risk of being relegated to the fields of sociology or peri-literature.[11] This new output has thus facilitated the shattering of traditional labels. We have gone from the notion of a Franco-French literature, including Arab-French and Afro-French works, to reclaiming the terminology proposed by Michel Laronde in "Les littératures des immigrations en France. Questions de nomenclature et directions de recherche" (1997).

Our own body of texts would of course belong to the last sub-category, with the only difference being that the term Afro-French refers to specific geographi-cal, cultural, and national norms, with which the writer does not necessarily as-sociate him or herself. A novelist may feel Parisian and be attracted to the city's cosmopolitan and multicultural universe without necessarily claiming a French identity. Inversely, his or her writing may not necessarily limit itself to the framework outlined by the Parisianism Jules-Rosette defines. Furthermore, con-trary to the *Beur* novel, this writing relies on an actual national experience and is written by first-generation African emigrants, for whom memories and links with Africa are, for the most part, still fresh in their minds. For those born in France (or in Switzerland or Belgium), like Simon Njami and Sandrine Bessora, for example, the dialectic is evidently thicker.

The case of a literature of immigration, generated by the African diaspora, is not restricted to the Francophone African world.[12] The phenomenon is in fact much more visible and recognized as such in the Anglophone, Caribbean, and of course, African-American novel, as well as in the Anglo-Indian or American-Indian novel. The Nigerian author Ben Okri declares that he can only write and speak about Africa, about his country, when he is outside of Africa, that this geographic *distanciation* facilitates the *distanciation* necessary for more sea-soned writing. His gaze and writings will thus differ in perspective from those of others in the same generation. Buchi Emecheta, on the other hand, even though she does not belong to the same generation age-wise, joins the other post-colonial writers in that she displays a literary journey which progressively distances itself from the African continent to anchor itself more specifically in the African or Caribbean immigrant community of London. In so doing, she in turn contributes to what we could call the Afro-Londonian novel if we adhere to a nomenclature parallel to that of Jules-Rosette.

If indeed the parallels between the literature of the diaspora in Paris and in London seem obvious, if the arrival of new generations in either city facilitates a renewal of literary expression, it may be necessary to go a step further and think about the breadth of these phenomena, no longer limited to one country in particular, be it France or the UK, but rather looking at the whole of Europe. The configuration of Europe itself has indeed undergone important changes in recent years, as much in its geographical profile with the fall of the Berlin Wall and the unification of Germany or the fall of the Soviet Union, as in the arrival and re-distribution of new populations—including non-European migrant populations—throughout its territory. New entities, and later, new literatures, corre-spond to these new geographical and cultural contours: German-language Turkish, Syrian, or Lebanese literatures, Italophone literature in Italy (primarily of Maghrebi origins, but also originating from Sub-Saharan Africa), Black British literature, post-Soviet literature, Yugoslavian literature, etc.[13] Gisela Brinker-Gabler and Sidonie Smith shed valuable light on this issue in *Writing Identities: Gender, Nation and Immigration in Contemporary Europe* (1997). Placing the emergence of these new writings in a European context, they analyze it as a global phenomenon of writing new identities, thereby showing evidence of a process of identity renegotiation which is no longer simply individual or collec-tive, but national, showing a process of integration, of assimilation, and of the rejection of immigrants in each respective society (Germany, France, and Italy in particular), and finally, showing evidence of the subsequent reconfiguration of the respective "central" literatures (German, Italian, French, British, Swedish, etc.). An analysis of these new African writings within this framework allows us not only to understand the generational changes and the changes in the writings in post-colonial terms, but also to go beyond the French perspective and to insert a missing piece in the puzzle of world literature as active participants in a global phenomenon on the European and world scale.

Pascale Casanova, in *La République Mondiale des Lettres* (1999), shows how political and literary histories have coincided in the case of France, making Paris the universal capital of literature: Paris, fascinating city, cosmopolitan city, city of liberty, incarnation of both political liberties and of literary values, Paris, literary city, at all times attracting writers from all over the world. Paris, "deve-nu littéraire au point d'entrer dans la littérature elle-même, à travers les évoca-tions romanesques ou poétiques, se métamorphosant en quasi-personnage de roman, en lieu romanesque par excellence" (Casanova 43) [becoming literary to the point of entering literature itself, through romantic or poetic evocations, transforming itself into a quasi-fictional character, into the fictional space par excellence].

In this context, it is appropriate to revisit on one hand the representations of Paris as material for these new diasporic writings, and on the other, Francophone literature written within France. All of these representations are part of an effort towards recognition and participation in world literature as identified by Casanova in a completely innovative manner. Indeed, her analysis shows that the phenomenon of universalization in literary subjects derives its very meaning from the opposite of what is generally meant by that term, defining it as follows: "le phénomène par lequel on croit possible de penser la totalité comme la généralisation d'un même modèle applicable partout: dans l'univers littéraire, c'est la concurrence qui définit et unifie le jeu tout en désignant les limites mêmes de l'espace. Tous ne font pas la même chose, mais tous luttent pour entrer dans la même course et, avec des armes inégales, tenter d'atteindre le même but: la légitimité littéraire" (63) [the phenomenon by which it is thought possible to conceptualize the totality as the generalization of one model applicable everywhere: in the realm of literature, it is competition that defines and unifies the game, as it marks the very limits of this space. Not every writer is necessarily doing the same thing, but all are struggling to enter into the same race and, with unequal tools, attempting to reach the same goal: literary legitimacy]. Consciousness of hierarchy and of hierarchization, both very much part of the dynamic in the field of literature, are central to this definition.[14]

Still in this framework, questions of the differentiation between Francophone literature/Afro-Parisian literature (or Franco-African) and French literature come up in addition to questions of interaction and differentiation between immigration literature/German-language foreign literature (*Migranten Literatur/Gastarbeiter Literatur/Gast-Literatur/Ausländischer Literatur*) and German literature or Italophone literature and Italian literature. The notion and the need for compartmentalization/labeling require closer study, particularly with respect to their implications within French society, in Europe, and later, in the world arena.

To speak of new writings requires an examination of early Francophone African literatures. For decades, Francophone novels written by African expatriates living in France dealt with Africa, Africans, and questions of identity. Some writers wrote outside the continent, not by choice, but as a result of political exile or of trouble in the writer's country of origin.[15] Such was notably the case of Mongo Beti, who settled in France after 1958 and was banned from Cameroon until the end of the 1980s, his books being severely censored at the time. It was not until 1991 that he saw his country again and settled there soon thereafter with his wife. During his thirty-two years of exile, his novels remained focused on Africa and Africans. Ambroise Kom points out that "assez paradoxalement, l'écriture de Mongo Beti se ressent à peine de son exil. Tout est focalisé sur l'univers africain où se déroule l'action et auquel appartiennent ses personnages" (2) [paradoxically enough, Mongo Beti's writing isn't really affected by his exile. Everything is focused on Africa, the world in which the plot unfolds and his characters belong]. But, as Kom remarks, the writings between 1974 and today do not show any break in continuity, which is quite surprising, considering the fifteen-year silence between *Le roi miraculé* (1958) and *Remember Ruben* (1974). Conceived in France, these texts are as much an illustration of an open critique of the neo-colonial regime and the African elite in power as of the stronghold of France on the internal and foreign politics and the economic decisions of Francophone African countries that were former French colonies. Despite long years of personal experience in France, Mongo Beti opted to not speak of Africans or their negative experiences when thrown into the Western experience.[16] He also made the choice to not speak of the self, but associated himself instead with a tradition of "littérature engagée" and activism through writing.

One of the prevalent themes of Francophone African novels from the 1960s and 1970s was that of identity for young Africans transplanted into the West. In fact, the African student in Paris, as seen in texts such as *Kocoumbo, L'étudiant Noir* (1960) by Aké Loba, and *L'aventure ambiguë* (1961) by Cheikh Hamidou Kane, is central to the collective African imagination. These Africans, ordinary students, struggle to maintain a balance between their African roots and the Western ways of thinking they absorbed through their schooling. The novels are representative of the *malaise* of a character who is confronted with a decentering of his identity.[17] In the 1980s, the focus is now on the *Revenants* (the *Been-to's* in Anglophone world), that is to say, this generation gone abroad to study and now back home struggling to re-adapt and choose a mode of education for their own children.[18]

But the 1990s present a new reality: we are no longer dealing with a limited stay for studies in France, but rather with a departure motivated by economic reasons and a stay of undetermined length for someone in search of a new life, whether alone or in a family. In five of her latest novels in particular,[19] the Cameroonian writer Calixthe Beyala offers a new perspective on African immigrants in France, highlighting not only a decentering of identity, but also a decentering of her own writing and, more broadly speaking, of the African novel. To the decentering of identity corresponds a decentering of writing.[20] This perspective is echoed in the texts of a number of her younger colleagues, living like her in Paris. *Afrique sur Seine* touches on the essential components of the writing of this new African diaspora in its recording of the (African) self in Paris and within French society, and in its complex exploration of the here-and-there thematic (or maybe of the "neither-here-nor-there"), making readers more familiar with the talented writers who are challenging the norm.

The following novels will serve as the central texts of this study: *Cercueil et Cie* (1985) and *African Gigolo* (1989) by Simon Njami, *Discopolis* (1993) by Philippe Camara, Calixthe Beyala's six "Parisian" novels,[21] *Le petit prince de Belleville* (1992), *Maman a un amant* (1993), *Assèze l'Africaine* (1994), *Les honneurs perdus* (1996), *Amours sauvages* (1999) and *Comment cuisiner son mari à l'Africaine (2000), Le paradis du nord* (1996) by Jean-Roger Essomba, *L'impasse* (1996) and *Agonies* (1998) by Daniel Biyaoula, *Agence Black Bafoussa* (1996) and *Sorcellerie à bout portant* (1998) by Achille Ngoye, *La Poly-*

andre (1998) by Bolya Baenga, *Bleu-Blanc-Rouge* (1998) by Alain Mabanckou, *Un amour sans papiers* (1999) by Nathalie Etoké, *53 cm* (1999) and *Les taches d'encre* (2000) by Sandrine Bessora, as well as *Un regard Noir* (1984) and *Le Nègre Potemkine* (1988) by Blaise N'djehoya, which will serve as reference points.[22] This body of work does not claim to be exhaustive, but illustrates either a thematics or an approach and style of writing characteristic of this generation of authors. To complement these texts, we will also examine works by novelists who do not necessarily focus on the French or African community in Paris, and who do not use the Parisian or French landscape as their canvas. These include texts by Marie Ndiaye,[23] as well as Bolya Baenga with *Cannibale* (1986), Catherine Ndiaye with *Gens de sable* (1984), Thomas Mpoyi-Buatu with *La reproduction* (1986), Yodi Karone with *Nègres de paille* (1982) and *Les beaux gosses* (1988), *Kin-La Joie, Kin-la folie* (1993) by Achille Ngoye, Gaston-Paul Effa with *Tout ce bleu* (1996), *Ma* (1998), *Le cri que tu pousses ne réveillera personne* (2000), Kossi Efoui with *La polka* (1998) and Abdourahman Waberi especially with *Cahiers nomades* (1996), *Balbala* (1997), and *Moisson de crânes* (2000), Jean-Roger Essomba with *Les lanceurs de foudre* (1995) and *Le dernier gardien de l'arbre* (1998), or Calixthe Beyala's first three novels, *C'est le soleil qui m'a brûlée* (1987), *Tu t'appelleras Tanga* (1988), and *Seul le diable le savait* (1990), as well as *La petite fille du réverbère* (1998) and most recently, *Les arbres en parlent encore* (2002). These works are centered on the African continent and the writer's location remains secondary.[24]

This essay is organized around three queries: (1) to examine how the innovations on a thematic, narrative, and aesthetic level not only raise questions of critical terminology, but also force us to consider the relation between perception taxinomy and literature in the context of immigration; (2) to think in this sense about discourse and about the interaction between the living space (and thus writing space) of the author, identity, and creation, and to look at how the construction of this discourse and these subjectivities as they appear in some novels contribute to re-drawing the boundaries between French, Francophone, and African literature; (3) to analyze along the same line the impact of the place of publication, the readership, and the critical reception of these writings and the terminology, and to rethink the critical categories of analysis in function of the variables for post-colonial literature.

Division of Chapters and Sections

Afrique sur Seine consists of the following four chapters: "Literary Explorations: Negotiations of Identity Gaps," "Language and Identities: When 'I' ceases to be 'the Other,'" "Questions of the Addressee: Africa or the Seine?" and "Specificities of the New Writings of Self."

"Literary Explorations: Negotiations of Identity Gaps" examines the main directions initially taken by authors in this literature. While I begin with the idea of the gaze and the quality of this gaze, as Jules-Rosette defines each, I attempt to determine the thematic and narrative axes that will permit a deeper reading of these texts, be it what I would call literature of detachment or literature of displacement or literature of immigration. Whatever their orientation, these new writings essentially gravitate around the individual exploration of the protagonists' futures, evolving in the Parisian, or more broadly speaking, the French environment. As a result of its commitment to individualism, the novel ceases to be political, in the old sense of the word, since writing does not imply a political engagement on the part of these authors. The idea of mission has disappeared. Nonetheless, in their individual quest, these writers meet on common ground, allowing the critic to determine certain characteristic similarities. The male or female protagonists who are initially incapable of finding a specific goal for themselves start to lose their cultural anchor and their mastery of traditional space, and eventually they find themselves tied in one way or another to the African community living in this new environment. We will see, for those born in France, whether a difference in place of birth and childhood influences their work. Common to all these novels is the fact that, in spite of different social, religious, or cultural origins, the process of the protagonists' socialization depends largely on their integration into the new community.

Beyond their individual approach which precludes a common thematic even if many of the protagonists display similar characteristics, three main categories can be identified:

(1) Literature of detachment: disinvestment and rejection of the African community

This section contains the novels that a priori reject all ties to Africa, every trace of collective engagement. They display a definite, not to say total, disinterest towards all questions relating to Africa or Africans. Through these narratives, the writer indicates a refusal to see African authors almost forcibly assigned to a so-called engaged literature, moving towards socio-realism. Works by Simon Njami, Philippe Camara, Blaise N'djehoya, and Marie Ndiaye are part of this section.

(2) Literature of displacement: from testimony to political and sociocultural engagement

The notion of displacement deals with traumatic connotations that suggest a tearing away, a dislocation in space and identity. This literature therefore brings up questions of identity in its relationship with space and with the African community in France. Contrary to those in the previous section, the novels selected here display an interest in the future of Africa, which, by itself, is unoriginal. What makes the difference with the African novel from the continent is the way in which this interest is translated by a bitter critique about the ways of life of Africans in France and their mutual relationship with their countrymen in Africa rather than the question of Africa's future. *L'impasse* by Daniel Biyaoula and *Ici, s'achève le voyage* by Luc Léandre-Baker will serve as the focus of this section.

(3) Literature of immigration: gazes onto the African community in France

This literature examines the process of im/migration and what kind of dynamics it implies for men and women when they are placed in a new setting susceptible to globalization.

Characteristically, the account describes a spatial displacement from Africa to France during which the gaze changes and turns to African immigrants in France as a community. What matters here, more than spatial displacement, which is also found in the early African novel, is the direction of the gaze now turned to Africans living in France. This is notably the case of Calixthe Beyala, Jean-Roger Essomba, Alain Mabanckou, and Nathalie Etoké.

This first chapter will allow us to rethink the questions of terminology used in France with respect to the African novel, to the Francophone novel, to the perception of literature as a whole, and of what guides the determination of its limits. In particular, we will attempt to reconsider within this framework the notion of immigration literature and what it implies regarding the perception of the non-European immigrant and immigration.

Chapter 2, "Language and Identities: When 'I' ceases to be 'the Other,'" examines how the textual construction of discourse and subjectivities recorded in the texts participates in a new definition of the contours of literature. Using the critical analyses of Azouz Begag, Abdellatif Chaouite, and Michel Laronde on the novel of Maghrebi immigration as a departing point,[25] as well as the works on multiculturalism and integration in France by Eric Taieb, Michèle Tribat, Patrick Simon,[26] and on racism—notably by Michel Wieviorka and Philippe Bataille[27]—I study the process of inversion of the discourse through which the African becomes an insider-outsider observer of both the Westerner and his/her African counterparts, looking at how the terms "familiar" and "foreign" take on new meanings. I thus examine the discourses enclosed within these narratives: the discourse of the African on the European, of the European on Africans, but also, and more unusually, the discourse of Africans in France on Africa, and of Africans living in Africa and vice versa, the discourse of Africans in Africa on France and on the Africans residing there. All of these highlight cultural assumptions about the perception of the non-European immigrant and of immigration as a phenomenon, and how the decentering of identity and subjectivity of the discourse on immigration and the ideology hides behind these cultural constructions. *Le petit prince de Belleville* and *Maman a un amant* by Calixthe Beyala, *Le paradis du Nord* by Jean-Roger Essomba, and *L'impasse* by Daniel Biyaoula will be the starting point of this study.

The second half of the chapter, inspired by Mireille Rosello's *Declining the Stereotype, Ethnicity and Representation in French Cultures* (1998) and by Françoise Lionnet's *Post-colonial Representations. Woman, Literature, Identity* (1995)[28] and their work on the myth of return and authenticity, treats the question of cultural fragmentation and the answers that Afro-Parisian authors provide for it. Lionnet starts from the hypothesis that the presence of other communities amid the dominant groups creates mixing, so that the term "assimilation" no longer occurs in a single direction, but rather implies a cultural mélange and fusion where the dominant discourse and culture must absorb some of the marginal: how it has evolved, how it has absorbed some of the dominant discourse. In this regard, Beyala's texts are an excellent illustration of the multi-directional absorption of language and culture and an example of "transculturation," as used by Lionnet in her analysis of post-colonial representations. This section aims to analyze the manner in which Beyala deconstructs "the myth of stability surrounding the dominant culture, its myth of sameness" and to show "a positive valuation of the diversity and heterogeneity of the other" (Lionnet 177). The deconstruction of another myth, that of the stability and homogeneity of the African community in France as well as the notion of cultural mixing and the phenomenon of transculturation, is also analyzed in *Assèze, l'Africaine* and *Les honneurs perdus*. I would like in this way to show how—to take Lionnet's words with regards to Leïla Sebbar—Beyala "invents a new France, tailored to the migrants, working their way across it" (177). Beyond questions of thematics and new narrative structures, beyond the fundamental linguistic and cultural mixing these address, these narratives send us back to the fundamental question of the ideology that underlies the cultural representations of immigration in France. Following the theoretical analyses of Homi Bhabha in *The Location of Culture* (1994), Uma Narayan in *Dislocating Cultures* (1997), and of Gayatri Spivaks on the way that ideologies seep into the construction of literary and cultural works, particularly what is called immigration literature, I discuss the novel by the African diaspora in Paris in its cultural/literary representations of the self, as well as the discourse associated with it through its affiliations, inclusions, and exclusions.

Chapter 3, "Questions of the Addressee: Africa or the Seine?" addresses the issue of readership and its impact on these new writings. Starting with specific examples, notably Beyala's novels, I examine the phenomenon of post-colonial voices that express themselves from France and are mostly read in France by the French (also, the gendered identity of the reader may be a significant parameter). In so doing, we will also look at the paradox of readership, the fact that an author, although controversial in the African community, may still play a representative role for Africa and Africans in the eyes of French readers. In this regard, the very phenomenon of Beyala's mediatization, and her popularity despite accusations of plagiarism, as well as the evolution of her writing, from African novels to "Parisian" novels, are worth a closer study. In contrast to Beyala, the example of Marie Ndiaye, whose novels are first and foremost considered French and are read by an almost exclusively French readership—causing her label as "African" to disappear in the process—requires analysis. Beyond these examples, I reflect further on the definition of a given literature and its limits. The hybridity of the texts and of their readership facilitates the formulation of the question and poses it in terms of power and of the ideology of language, as Michel Foucault and Homi Bhabha analyze it. Through these examples, I examine the interaction between post-colonial voices and the reception of their message and its implications with regard to the very evolution and creation of post-colonial African literature.

Chapter 4 is a concluding chapter. It explores the definition of a new literature and a new generation of works. The writing of post-colonial identities
within France has further implications for terminology: Francophone/French
literature, French literature/French-language African literature, even African
literature/Afro-Parisian literature. This nomenclature obviously refers to a larger
cultural concept, which guides us in our perception of the literature in question,
its definition, and the delineation of its limits. This concept is derived from an
ideological construct of power in the definition of the French citizen, French
society and, by extension, its culture and literature.[29] These new writings force a
re-framing of questions by introducing post-colonial parameters. The new terms
to take into consideration are: ideology, dominant hegemonic discourse, risks
posed by peripheral discourse, relationship of the immigrant with his fellow
metropolitan city-dwellers, and decentering of the center and the periphery. In
this regard, the theoretical analyses on the concept of identity by Tzvetan Todorov in *Nous et les Autres: La réflexion française sur la diversité humaine*, by
Paul Ricoeur in *Soi-même comme un autre* (1990), and by Alec Hargreaves in
Post-colonial Cultures in France (1997) allow us to better evaluate the different
variables.

The conclusion offers a summary of how these "Black Parigots,"[30] these
"*Beurs noirs à Black Babel*"[31] bring in their distinctive ways a new dimension to
the Francophone African novel. The decentering of identity and writing in turn
influences French literature and allows for the determination of new contours for
French society today and tomorrow. Our analysis demonstrates that these authors are creating a new wave of African literature where linguistic and cultural
'métissage' becomes a privileged vehicle; that the exploration of questions of
identities, cultures, and integration on a philosophical but also textual level renews the definition of post-colonial African voices and the contours of literature
as a whole.

Notes

1. Michel Fabre's analysis, *La rive noire* (1985), and more recently, *Paris
Noir: African Americans in the City of Light* (1996), by Tyler Stovall, are evidence of the American literary and artistic dynamism which bloomed in Paris in
the 1920s and which lasted until the 60s.
2. See Achille Mbembe,"A propos des écritures africaines de soi," *Politique
Africaine* 77 (March 2000): 16-43.
3. Such a level of output in so brief period of time is indeed impressive. Two
essays must also be added to these ten novels, *Lettre d'une Africaine à ses
soeurs occidentales* (1995) and *Lettre d'une Afro-française à ses compatriotes*
(2000). Three of her novels have been translated into English (*C'est le soleil qui*

m'a brûlée, Tu t'appelleras Tanga, and *Le petit prince de Belleville*), and most have been reissued in paperback.

4. See Bernard Magnier, "Beurs noirs à Black Babel," *Notre Librairie. Dix ans de Littératures* I, 103 (1990): 103-107.

5. This synthesis bridges the fields of literary criticism and cultural studies, and incorporates literary analyses and interviews with other African writers settled in Paris. It focuses on two periods, from 1947 to 1968, and 1969 to 1993; in particular, she examines, through a sociological approach, three generations of African writers and what they represent: the movement of intellectuals associated with the creation of the publication *Présence Africaine* and with the movement of Négritude, revolutionary writings, and the new generation.

6. Abdourahman Waberi, "Les enfants de la postcolonie. Esquisse d'une nouvelle génération d'écrivains francophones d'Afrique noire," *Notre Librairie* 135 (September-December 1995): 8-15.

7. In *Hospitalité Française [French Hospitality]*, Tahar Ben Jelloun characterizes this new generation as follows: "C'est une génération certes, mais elle est orpheline, vivant en suspens, devant inventer avec les moyens du bord une identité visible, valorisée, c'est-à-dire qui les distingue positivement. Ce n'est pas toujours le cas; les moyens sont de l'ordre de la derive délinquante, ou de la violence désespérée, aveugle, sans but précis, sans sens, où l'on dépense le corps dans le risque, le danger—les rodéos de voiture, la drogue, la prostitution—c'est très rarement qu'ils s'ouvrent sur une volonté de faire, d'agir, de créer quelque chose pour transformer des données de misère" (102-103) [They certainly are a generation, but they are orphans, hanging in between, forced to invent with the available resources a visible and valued identity, meaning one which positively distinguishes them. This is not always the case; the strategies revolve around delinquency, desperate, blind, aimless, senseless violence where they put themselves at risk and in danger—through car races, drugs, prostitution—it is only rarely that they are they willing to act, to create something to transform their misery].

8. For a detailed study of the *Beur* novel, see the analysis by Michel Laronde, *Autour du roman Beur* (Paris: L'Harmattan, 1993) and Alec Hargreaves, *Voices from the North African Immigrant Community in France: Immigration and Identity in Beur Fiction* (Providence, RI: Berg Publishers, 1991).

9. Leïla Sebbar is Algerian and came to France towards the end of her teenage years. She is therefore not a *Beur* writer per se, but her novels are interesting in that they deal, through her protagonists' journeys, with questions of identity and the future of the generation born on French soil to immigrant Maghrebi parents.

10. My reversal of the two terms, African/French versus French/African, is deliberate; since these authors were in most cases born in Africa and then came to settle in France at some later point in time, we may assume that their first affiliation would be the strongest, the one they claim, which is not necessarily true of Africans born in France.

11. See Michel Laronde, "Les littératures des immigrations en France. Questions de nomenclature et directions de recherche," *Le Maghreb Littéraire* I, no. 2 (1997): 25-44.

12. In the Francophone world, the notion of immigration literature generally refers to Maghrebi literature and more specifically to *Beur* literature.

13. For a detailed study of the writings of these new identities and on the encoding of Europe's reconfiguration, see Gisela Brinker-Gabler and Sidonie Smith, eds, *Writing New Identities: Gender, Nation and Immigration in Contemporary Europe* (1997), particularly the introduction "Gender, Nation, and Immigration in the New Europe," 1-27.

14. Furthermore, the author introduces an extremely important idea for our analysis, that of heritage, to be interpreted according along two lines: that of national writers' literary heritage and its positioning in world literature; and then, the legacy of Paris as a literary representation. We will return to these two points in chapter 3, with respect to Africa and the Seine as the addressees.

15. The equivalent is of course true for Anglophone African literature. For instance, the Somali Nuruddin Farrah who today lives in South Africa after a long stay in Nigeria has spent the past twenty years writing far from home.

16. *La Revanche de Guillaume Ismael Dzewatama* (1984) is, however, an exception. Guillaume's stay in France is deemed temporary, with Marie-Pierre struggling with the government and various organizations in France to try to free her husband and return home. The novel ends with the announcement of Guillaume's return as a soccer player in return for his father's liberation.

17. By decentering, I mean a geographic displacement that corresponds with a change in interest and the move from Africa to France and the community of African immigrants in France.

18. See *L'Appel des Arènes* (1982) by Aminata Sow Fall; *Le Baobab Fou* (1983) by Ken Bugul.

19. *Le petit prince de Belleville* (1992), *Maman a un amant* (1993), *Assèze l'Africaine* (1994), *Les honneurs perdus* (1996), and *Amours sauvages* (1999).

20. See Odile Cazenave, *Femmes Rebelles: Naissance d'un Nouveau Roman Africain au Féminin* (Paris: L'Harmattan, 1996); "Calixthe Beyala: l'exemple d'une écriture décentrée dans le roman africain au féminin, " in *L'écriture décentrée,* ed. Michel Laronde (Paris : L'Harmattan, 1996), 123-148.

21. We will also refer to *Comment cuisiner son mari à l'africaine* (Paris: Albin Michel, 2000).

22. Because of his age, N'Djehoya does not belong to this postcolonial generation strictly speaking, but his texts are the result of postcolonial ideas and go back to the question of writing about the self when placed in a space other than the one's original space.

23. *Quant au riche avenir* (1985), *Comédie classique* (1986), *La femme changée en bûche* (1989), *En famille* (1990), and *Un temps de saison* (1994).

24. We will examine briefly how their works may or may not differ from novels written on the continent, particularly in their representations of Africa.

25. Azouz Begag and Abdellatif Chaouite, eds. *Ecarts d'identité* (Paris: Seuil, 1990); Michel Laronde, *Autour du roman Beur* (Paris: L'Harmattan, 1993); Alec G. Hargreaves, *Immigration, 'Race' and Ethnicity in Contemporary France* (London: Routledge, 1995).

26. See Eric Taieb, *Immigrés: l'effet générations: rejet, assimilation*, intégration, d'hier à aujourd'hui (Paris, Editions de l'atelier, 1998); Michèle Tribat, *De l'immigration à l'assimilation: enquête sur les populations d'origine étrangère en France* (Paris, Editions de la découverte, INED, 1996); Michel Wieviorka, ed., *Une société fragmentée?: le multiculturalisme en débat* (Paris: Editions La découverte, 1996). Also see *Mon dieu, que vous êtes français* by Paulin Brune (Paris: Editions France-Empire, 1996).

27. Michel Wieviorka, *Violence en France* (Paris, Seuil, 1999); Philippe Bataille, *Le racisme en France* (Paris: Seuil, 1993). Also see Philippe Bataille, *Le racisme au travail*, (Paris: Seuil, 1997).

28. Both are on the post-colonial representations of ethnicity within the framework of immigration. See also, Mireille Rosello, "Caribbean Insularization of Identities in Maryse Condé's Work: from *En Attendant le bonheur* to *Les derniers rois mages*," *Callaloo* 18.3 (Summer 1995): 565-578; *Post-colonial Representations. Woman, Literature, Identity* (Ithaca: Cornell University Press, 1995).

29. The concept of citizenship must obviously be considered in light of the distinctions between right and (on a sociological level) the factual.

30. The term is borrowed from Achille Ngoye's *Agence Black Bafoussa*.

31. This is the term given them by Bernard Magnier and the title of his article on the new African writings written in France; already cited on page 1.

Chapter 1

Literary Explorations: Negotiation of Identity Gaps

> La migration est un risque. Elle est angoissante. Entre un
> arrachement douloureux et un réancrage conflictuel s'installe
> le temps d'une crise. C'est celle d'une expérience traumatique
> marquée par la peur de perdre définitivement les objets quittés
> et d'affronter l'inquiétante étrangeté . . . Elle ne se mesure pas
> en mètres mais en indices de changement. Il s'agit d'une
> rupture dans une continuité vivante et une greffe sur une autre
> continuité vivante.
> Azouz Begag et Abdellatif Chaouite, *Ecarts d'identité.*

> [Migration is a risk. It is worrisome. Between a painful
> displacement and a conflictual re-anchoring, the time for a crisis settles. This is
> the crisis resulting from a traumatic experience marked by the fear of losing for
> good the objects left behind and that of facing the worrisome strangeness . . . It
> is not measured in meters but rather in indices of change. It is the rupture in one
> living continuity and the grafting onto another.]

> L'errance, c'est cela même qui nous permet de nous fixer,
> de quitter ces leçons de choses que nous sommes si enclins à
> semoncer, d'abdiquer ce ton de sentence où nous compassons nos doutes.
> Edouard Glissant, *Traité du Tout-monde, Poétique 4.*

> [Wandering is the very thing that allows us to affix ourselves,
> to leave behind these life lessons which we have such
> a tendency to scold, to cut short this tone of sentencing where we orient our
> doubts.]

The notion of identity linked to bilingualism and biculturalism is at the core of
the French-language African novel from the time of Independence to the end of

the 1980s. It corresponds to a search for a difficult balance between the African value and thought systems on one hand, and the Western on the other. In novels such as *L'aventure ambigüe* (1961) by Cheikh Hamidou Kane or *Le baobab fou* (1983) by Ken Bugul, this preoccupation is manifested by alternate feelings of nostalgia for a lost or abandoned space and time and the desire to melt into the new Western mold.

In *Black Paris: the African Writer's Landscape*, Bennetta Jules-Rosette outlines the contours of a similar recurring motif, a narrative of longing and belonging. Compared to the African novel from the continent the notion of nostalgia for a distant Africa and past loses out to the notion of belonging.[1] In the case of new African writings in France, the question now relates to representations of Africa and of Africans on the continent as insiders/outsiders' representations, linked to a time that no longer necessarily coincides with any real time, whether in France or in Africa. Rather, this representation is the confrontation of two spaces and two times, the notion of modern wandering, of a post-colonial form of nomadism.

> The authors who write in the Parisianism genre represent a more nuanced and finely tuned view of life as Africans in France, with an emphasis on subjective reactions to specific circumstances. The writers advance a philosophy of inclusion, but also emphasize the psychological suffering that results from assimilation. Narratives of longing and belonging motivate the writers' characters as they cope with alienation of daily life in France and dream of Africa. (Jules-Rosette 157)

In light of this interpretation, I would like to start this chapter by examining the main study lines for diasporic novels. It is not a matter of classifying these pieces and assigning them labels in what would prove to be a somewhat restrictive framework, but rather of capturing what may be some distinctive traits when compared with novels from the continent.[2] Contrary to Jules-Rosette, the possibility of capturing the incidence of questions of identity with Africa on one hand, and with Paris on the other hand, seems wider in this framework. Questions of identity are at the heart of these novels and are visible from two main angles. First, they are addressed through the characters' rejection of their cultural identity and their unwillingness to search for their roots, and even the choice to run away from them. To the extreme, the characters refuse to take any stand whatsoever in both the Parisian/French and the African landscape. Second, questions of identity are also evidently at the core of these new writings because this body of works constitutes a literature of displacement, containing occasionally bitter social criticism of some aspects of Africans and/or Africa, starting with a difference in the gaze—an African gaze from the outside, a confrontation between an internal Africa, carried within the individual, and the image of a distant Africa. Finally, this literature is a continuous back-and-forth between Africans in Africa and those settled in France, where characters are constructed as part of the immigrant African community.

Novel of Detachment and Rejection of the African Community

Reverse Rejection: Simon Njami's *Cercueil et Cie*

Simon Njami, who is originally from Cameroon, is one of the few writers who were born outside of Africa—in his case, Switzerland—and who settled in Paris. He was one of the first writers from the young generation to contribute to the different orientation of the African novel. Indeed, the back cover of the novel posed the question: "le premier roman d'une 'Black' Generation?" [the first novel of a "Black" Generation?] At the time, the author stood apart because of his young age: he was twenty-three years old when his first novel was published.[3] Each of his texts also broke from the canonical African novel because of their versatile writing style.

Immediately, the cover page sets the tone for the novel: in front, two Black police officers with felt hats and long raincoats, cigarette at their lips, in colors and a style characteristic of police novels; in the back, a typewritten page that constitutes a real index of characters and places, a memory aid or a page of notes for a police officer or a journalist. It shows the variety of characters (two Black American police officers from Harlem [Dubois and Smith], an African-American writer [Chester Himes], an African journalist born in Cameroon and living in France [Yegba], a White American woman living in France [Fate], a mixed-race woman [Myriam], etc.) and of places (New York City, Paris, Cameroon, and other African countries) mentioned. The order in which the characters and the various geographical spaces enter the story is surprising: first, Americans enter against the backdrop of New York's Harlem; only after them does the protagonist Yegba appear. Another immediately striking detail is the characterization assigned to Paris: "*Paris*, Black Babel." The novel also displays a mix of fictional and actual characters (Chester Himes, for example) set in a fictional context. Through these simple facts, as well as through the title, the author instantly stands apart from his fellow writers and entices the readers by making them anticipate something out of the ordinary. Only the two epigrams (one, by Chester Himes, the other by Vernon Sullivan in *Les morts . . .*)[4] suggest an unusual context and indicate that we are not dealing with an ordinary police novel, but rather with a text dealing with racial and cultural issues. Inspired by Chester Himes, this text was actually born after Njami wrote a necrology of the author that was so original that he was encouraged to derive a novel from it.

Cercueil et Cie opens up on Dubois and Smith, two individuals inspired by Himes' characters. The two Harlem police officers live off the legend of their adventures, immortalized by Chester Himes in his novels. But trouble erupts when they learn that the writer makes them die in his last novel, thereby proving that their adventures were all fictive. Now illegitimate in their own eyes, and even worse, constantly running the risk of being illegitimate in Harlem as a whole, they decide to travel to Paris to meet Chester Himes and convince him not to translate this novel, and thereby avoid losing face. From this point on they encounter the narrator, Amos Yegba, a journalist. A police mystery adds itself to this situation, and the news/police investigation begins. Indeed, a Senegalese man who had left a message on Yegba's answering machine regarding revelations he had to make disappears before their planned meeting; Yegba, tracing the clues, finds out that the man's sister has disappeared and that she worked for a certain N'Diaye character in charge of a business which takes care of young African women arriving in Paris, a cover in reality for all sorts of trafficking, including that of African art pieces stolen from museums and galleries.

By describing an investigation on one hand—which not only validates the narrator's existence, but also allows him, alone and later with his two companions, to travel from place to place, ask questions, and draw up a summary—and the experiences of African-American characters in Paris on the other, the author is able to broach questions of color, acceptance, integration, and exile, not only for Africans in France, but also for African Americans through Dubois and Smith's observations on how France compares to the US for these issues, and through their opinions on Africa. We thereby arrive at a comparative global depiction of the relationship between Whites and Blacks in France and the US, of Black identity in three geographic reference points (the US, France, and Africa as a single entity), and of the importance of cultural roots. Through several tactics, ranging from the use of African-American characters to their conversations with African characters on White-Black relations in France as compared to the US, and through the inclusion of a great name of African-American literature (Chester Himes) as a fictional character, the author decenters his novel and gives a glimpse of African-American influences and thereby attempts to recreate the transatlantic link between Africa and the US, this time in the US-Africa direction.[5]

The awakening of the characters is staggered. The two Americans immediately undergo a culture shock as a result of their first experience in France: their reactions quickly follow.

> Tous ces Blancs et ces Blanches qui bécotaient des Nègres et des Négresses lui occasionnaient un malaise qu'il ne parvenait pas à surmonter. Malcolm X avait dit un jour: "lorsqu'on met une goutte de lait dans son café, le café devient moins fort . . . " Les nègres de Paris lui faisaient penser à ce café passé! Des aveugles qui ne voyaient pas qu'ils étaient perdants à essayer de blouser les Blancs en leur faisant du gringue. (139)

> [All these White men and women that were kissing Negroes made him feel an unease he could not shake. Malcolm X once said: "When you add one drop of milk to your coffee, the coffee becomes weaker . . . " The Paris Negroes reminded him of this past coffee! Blind people unable to see that they were losing out by trying to kiss up to Whites.]

Their remarks are two-fold: first, they compare the behavior and relationship between Whites and Blacks in France and the US, as well as the behavioral differences between African-Americans and Africans. In both cases, the two

Americans highlight a difference in mentality, betraying a critical tone towards Africans. Even though they have African roots, their evolution is specific to them as a result of the way things happened.

> Nous sommes américains. Que tu le veuilles ou non, les pères de nos pères ont été vendus, il y a des siècles par les pères de tes pères si ça se trouve. Depuis on a dû se battre chaque putain de jour que Dieu nous a fait parvenir au rang d'homme. Maintenant, on arrive presque au bout du tunnel. On a des maires dans les grosses villes. On paie nos impôts, mais on ne l'a jamais léché le cul du Blanc, mon petit père. On a gagné le droit d'aller se faire buter à la guerre comme n'importe quel couillon et c'est bien comme ça. L'Afrique nous a laissé tomber, petit père. N'oublie jamais ça. Jamais . . . (142-143)

> [We are American. Whether or not you like it, our fathers' fathers were sold, centuries ago, by your fathers' fathers perhaps. Since then, we have had to fight every fucking day that God has given to bring us to the status of man. Now we're almost at the end of the tunnel. We have mayors in big cities. We pay our taxes, but we have never kissed a White man's ass, pops. We have earned the right to go get shot down at war just like any other fool and we like it like that. Africa let us down, pops. Never forget that. Never . . .]

If the two American characters display instant reactions, Yegba on the other hand goes through a long maturation process modulated by the narration. The time taken for the narration corresponds to his awakening to the realization of a lack, of a void he must face, which leads to his breakdown into an identity crisis where he completely questions all that he is and the way that he lives. This is the realization of his "otherness" in a foreign city and of his need to write (a novel) as a way of coping with the pain and the unease of displacement.

The story of Yegba's investigation allows him rub elbows with the "Black" milieu of Paris, which, without being completely hidden, had until then lain at the backdrop of his life.[6] Consequently, his thoughts convey a desire to distance himself from others, to show his own success, which he judges by the fact that he is not mistaken for the "other Blacks" in urban transportation, for instance. His need to differentiate himself from his countrymen translates in a devaluation of post-colonial minorities in France (immigrants from the Maghreb and from Sub-Saharan Africa).[7] He thus attempts to distinguish himself in his behavior, his dress, and the company he keeps, from "des stigmates de l'immigré collectivement dévalorisé" (Abdelkadber Belbahri 162) [all stigmas of the collectively devalued immigrant].

At the same time as he auto-marginalizes himself, Yegba becomes aware of the void in his life, of the fact that he has "perdu le fil " (91) [lost the link]. His growing closeness to Myriam, a mixed-race woman, reflects his hope of finding in her what he is missing.

> La vérité, c'est que je suis paumé, avoua-t-il d'une voix brisée. Je piétine, . . .
> Ils attendent que je me plante pour me montrer à quel point je suis nul . . . Et
> peut-être qu'ils ont raison. Peut-être que je devrais tout planter là, ma voiture,

le journal, ma femme blanche, tout laisser et rentrer au pays. Peut-être que je n'ai pas compris les règles de leur monde. Je suis perdu, Myriam. J'ai besoin qu'on m'aide . . . Aide-moi. (176)

[The truth is that I'm lost, he admitted in a broken voice. I'm going around in circles. They're waiting for me to mess up to show me just how bad I am . . . And maybe they're right. Maybe I should dump everything here, my life, the paper, my White woman, leave everything, and go back to my country. Maybe I didn't understand the rules of their world. I'm lost, Myriam. I need someone to help me . . . Help me.]

A subtle shift occurs through the change in the use of pronouns: they/them (used to refer to other Africans) shifts to refer to Whites. Yegba therefore redraws the mental map of frontiers he had drawn for himself.

In the scene following the previous excerpt, the two characters make love. Yegba returns to Myriam's place several times, in need of comfort and communication (both verbal and nonverbal). Conversely, he distances himself more and more from Fate,[8] his White girlfriend, and ultimately breaks up with her. Initially, even though he did not mention his White girlfriend to his family, Yegba felt very good about his interracial relationship. Rejecting and altogether averting the possibility of being a part of the clichéd image of an African man with a White woman, he instead draws satisfaction from his ability to self-marginalize this way. He textually imitates the usual cliché descriptions of interracial couples, highlighting their distinctive generic traits in order to subvert them.[9]

Qui aurait pu prétendre qu'une harmonie parfaite ne s'était pas installée entre des lèvres épaisses et des lèvres minces, des cheveux raides et une toison crépue, de longues jambes et des jambes musclées ? A deux, il faisaient mentir Aristote : non l'être originel ne s'était pas divisé de moitié. Ou alors, il l'avait composé en noir et en blanc. Et si Yegba lisait parfois dans l'œil des autres de l'étonnement, voire une complicité égrillarde, prompte à se muer en haine, il en faisait son affaire. C'était aux yeux des autres que leur couple pouvait avoir l'air d'un cliché. Pas aux leurs. (54)

[Who could claim that perfect harmony had not settled between thick lips and thin lips, straight hair and a nappy mop of hair, long legs and muscular legs? Between the two of them, they made a liar of Aristotle. The original being had not divided himself into two halves. Or if he had, he had been both black and white. And if Yegba sometimes read surprise and even a kind of complicity quick to turn into hatred in the eyes of others, that was his business. Their couple could only look cliché in the eyes of others. Not in their own.]

This theme of identity crisis linked to the subsequent breakup with a White woman reappears in other texts such as *African Gigolo* (in a slightly modified form which we will see hereafter) and *L'impasse* for example.[10] In each case, the breakup is portrayed as a result of the need to reconnect with one's own culture, incarnated by the African woman (maybe even Antillean or mixed), after the culture has somehow been betrayed or simply ignored or refuted through the African man's relationship with a White woman. This is the usual discourse offered in French-language African literature on the conflicts of interracial couples. It is notably found in *Un Chant écarlate* (1981) by Mariama Bâ, through Ousmane who asserts that he has detached himself from Mireille and grown closer to his African sister because he needed to "return to his roots" ["retour aux sources"], since his wife could not understand some of his most fundamental needs.[11] The complaints Fate has with regards to Yegba are very similar to those Mireille had for Ousmane. Even if their priorities are different (friends, late-night outings among men), Yegba's subsequent reactions to Fate's complaints mirror those of Ousmane, as he progressively distances himself from Fate and looks for communion and comfort in Myriam.

Beyond the detective story which becomes a mere backdrop, the novel opens up on the protagonist's identity crisis regarding the way of life he had until then chosen for himself. In other words, he has enjoyed his professional success without worrying about issues of Africa or Africans, whether in Africa or France, and, despite his being a journalist, he never used this position to facilitate attention towards Africa. *Cercueil et cie* describes the process of the protagonist's awakening, which goes from an awareness of these issues and the desire to ignore them, to confrontation and the decision to make a new start. This decision implies life, but also suffering. Indeed, because from now on he agrees to face the void he felt as an African in Paris; he can no longer be contented with his comfortable life.

The novel, beyond the fact that it introduces a new trajectory towards the US and the African-American influence—which also appears in *A la recherche du cannibale amour* (1988) by Yodi Karone—inaugurates the African mystery novel, a genre which has grown over the past few years, most often in the new diaspora's writing. We can notably cite *Black Bafoussa* (1996), *Sorcellerie à bout portant* (1998), and *Château Rouge* (2001) by Achille Ngoye, and *La Polyandre* (1998) by Bolya Baenga.[12]

This issue of an emotional, national, and racial disinvestment, of the desire to exist without a thought for Africa, or one's origins, appears even more clearly in Simon Njami's second novel, *African Gigolo*.

Don't Tell Me about Africa!

The title, *African Gigolo*, in itself is striking. What meaning should we see there on the part of the author? What are the implications for the readers? Does this not mean engaging them, not to say encouraging them to a certain reading? But we must remember Simon Njami's interest in African-American literature and culture. Beyond his novel *Cercueil et Cie*, a translation of a "Chesterhimean" universe, one need only think of his biography of the African-American writer James Baldwin, which notably dealt with his time in Paris.

African Gigolo is without a doubt the best example of a rejection of political or collective engagement through its implicit commitment to individualism. The narrator, Moïse, makes a special effort to display complete disinterest in the cause of Africa and Africans. The use of the third person plural pronoun "they" clearly marks his distancing and his desire to exclude himself from the group and the community.

> Si je souffrais d'un complexe, disait-il, alors, assurément, ce serait celui de la supériorité. Je suis une espèce d'intouchable. Je n'ai ni combat ni credo. Je suis libre totalement. Il ne militait pour personne d'autre que lui-même. (17)

> [If I had a complex, he would say, then surely, it would be one of superiority. I am an untouchable. I have neither struggle nor motto. I am completely free. He struggled for no one other than himself.]

To go along with his beliefs, he criticizes his compatriots settled in France who think that they are making a difference through their presence in France rather than in their country, and who persist in dreaming about a utopic, homogeneous, and monolithic Africa. The only exception to this rule is his friend Etienne, also Cameroonian, older than him, and, contrary to him, engaged in a constant ideological debate (even if—and even more so than Moïse—he lives in a Bohemian fashion).

As the title suggests, Moïse uses his charms, if not as a sort of currency, as a means of integrating himself into French society. Paradoxically, he exploits to his advantage all the sexual fantasies that French men and women have about African men and women.[13]

> Les femmes occidentales, (. . .), étaient pour la plupart des victimes consentantes du fantasme du mâle nègre. (66)
> Dans les yeux des jeunes filles, des femmes, la lueur de curiosité ne s'adressait pas à lui seul, mais au fantasme sur pied qu'il représentait. (99)

> [Western women, (. . .), were for the most part consenting victims of the fantasy of the male Negro.
> In the eyes of young girls, of women, the light of curiosity was not directed towards him alone, but rather towards the physical representation of the fantasy that he was.]

Undeniably, the word "hero" appears in his case completely inadequate, with his way of moving through society nonchalantly, detached from all problems and living an easy and idle life. The same type of situation and feelings can be found in *Ici, s'achève le voyage* (1989) by Luc Léandre-Baker:

> En somme, Jean Diko et moi vivions aux crochets de cette pauvre caissière de super-marché qui par amour, coupait son salaire en deux. La Ginette n'avait jamais connu l'irruption volcanique de l'amour avant d'être séduite par les beaux muscles de mon cher cousin, et ce sont ces muscles-là qui nous assuraient en partie la bouffe, le loyer et le téléphone. (41)

[Essentially, Jean Diko and I lived off of this poor supermarket cashier who split her salary in two out of love. The woman had never known the volcanic irruption of love before she had been seduced by my dear cousin's nice muscles, and those were the very muscles that partly ensured grub, rent and phone expenses for us.]

There again, the protagonist's life consists of "killing time" while he is unemployed and has nothing to do. Contrary to *African Gigolo*, a certain anguish linked to the precarious nature of his situation grows as the plot evolves, even though it may seem that the character does not really intend to find work.[14] His only motivation comes from the fact that his friend Sally shows him that unemployment is hard for any woman to deal with, and so if he intends to maintain a relationship with Anna, he should do something about the situation. Through his attempts to find a job and his wandering through Paris, from the *banlieue* to Belleville, then in the center of the city, he becomes aware of the artificial and illusory image of France, that of easy success which prompted him to leave his country. Through his wandering, he also subverts the usual representations of Paris. The graffiti on the walls and his discovery of a poor and gray Paris make him realize the racist current existing around him:

"VERROUILLONS NOS FRONTIÈRES!" tonnaient certains extrémistes. Déjà les murs de France étaient barbouillés de propos incongrus à l'endroit des ex-colonisés. "NÈGRES, BOUGNOULES ET JUIFS HORS DE FRANCE!" "LA FRANCE N'EST PAS LE GRENIER DU TIERS-MONDE!" "LA FRANCE AUX FRANÇAIS." La France craignait d'être colonisée à son tour. (. . .) Merde à la fin! Qu'étais-je venu foutre dans cette galère! Moi qui croyais que le chemin du paradis passait forcément par ici . . . (38)

["LET'S CLOSE OUR BORDERS!" roared some extremists. France's walls were already smeared with incongruous statements aimed towards formerly colonized people. "NIGGERS, BOUGNOULES, AND JEWS OUT OF FRANCE!" "FRANCE IS NOT THE THIRD WORLD'S ATTIC!" "FRANCE FOR THE FRENCH." France was afraid of being next in line to be colonized. (. . .) Shit, man! What had I come to do in this hell hole! And I thought the path to paradise inevitably passed through here . . .]

In *African Gigolo*, however, Moïse—at least apparently—does not show any particular interest in issues of race, identity or hybridity. The question of racism is not on his mind. Nonetheless, he is perfectly aware of what he represents: a Black man in a world of White people; that's how he defines himself. This reality jumps at him through his White acquaintances (notably Durand), who take him to African music concerts or to so-called "Black" clubs: "Moïse se sentait alors complice du voyeurisme le plus abject. Il jouait un rôle de Blanc, incompatible avec l'idée qu'il se faisait de lui-même" (98) [Moïse then felt like an accessory in the most abject form of voyeurism. He played the role of a White man incompatible with the idea he had of himself]. The experience also gives

him the opportunity to realize how little he knows about the "Black" milieu in
Paris, which has happened because he has avoided other Africans and Antil-
leans.

The Africa which has apparently been erased from his background resurges
brutally through a letter from his mother telling him that his father is ill and that
he should consider paying them a visit. The possibility of a return to Cameroon
after several years' absence forces him to confront the web of lies surrounding
his life.[15] Indeed, a barely perceptible anguish subtly takes over the narration,
thereby forcing the reader to think about the consequences of Moïse's actions.
The narration thereby becomes an attempt to procrastinate, a strategy that should
allow the protagonist to delay any confrontation with himself. In this framework, love and sexuality lose all intrinsic value and have no other use but to
serve the one objective of avoiding all "disturbing" issues. Friendship is also
excluded, as Moïse tries to avoid all relationships that would require any obliga-
tions on his part. There again, Etienne is the only exception. Paradoxically, a
constant discourse on Africa and Africans occurs, just as Moïse claims a complete disinterest in anything touching on the continent.

For some time, he was able to calm his anxiety as he spent time with
Mathilde, a wealthy widow who asked and expected nothing of him. Their tacit
agreement on impersonal conversation detached from feelings of possessiveness
allows us to explore—almost without the protagonist's knowledge—his feelings
and opinions with regards to Africa and African-ness. That is precisely the point
where the distinction between "them" and "him" bursts, where he identifies
himself as other, both with regards to his people and with regards to Mathilde,
thereby asserting—against his will—his African-ness even as he denies it.

> -Vous avez déjà fait l'amour avec un Africain? . . .
> - Il me semble que je ne pourrais jamais avoir un rapport normal de femme à
> homme avec l'un d'entre eux.
> - Vous parlez d' "eux" comme si je n'en faisais pas partie.
> - Mais vous n'en faites pas partie, Dieu merci. Les autres étaient obséquieux,
> lâches, bêtes aussi parfois. Ils se contentaient de vous répéter ce qu'ils
> s'imaginaient que vous vouliez entendre. Aucune personnalité . . .
> S'ils pataugent aujourd'hui, c'est aussi leurs problèmes . . . Vous ne croyez
> pas ? . . .
> - Je ne sais pas. Ce que je pense, c'est qu'il faut leur . . . nous laisser nos rêves.
> Nous ne sommes pas tous pourris. Quelques-uns travaillent à l'élévation de
> l'Afrique vers quelque chose de meilleur. J'en connais. (73-74)

> [- Have you ever made love with an African man? . . .
> - It seems that I would never be able to have a normal female-male relationship
> with one of them.
> - You speak of "them" as if I weren't one of them.
> - But you're not one of them, thank God. The others were obsequious, cow-
> ardly, even stupid at times. They insisted on continuously repeating what they
> thought you wanted to hear. No personality whatsoever . . .
> If they're struggling today, that's also their problem. . .

Don't you think? . . .
- I don't know. I think that they . . . we must be allowed to keep our dreams.
We are not all rotten. Some are working to uplift Africa towards something bet-
ter. I know some.]

As the excerpt I emphasized suggests, this is one of the only times when he
claims his African-ness, claims the fact that he belongs to the community that
Mathilde despises even though she thinks she does not warrant the label of "racist" because she counts among her friends African ministers and businessmen
and believes that she establishes distinctions based on class rather than race.
This is one of the rare moments when he clarifies and explains to someone non-
African what it means to be African in France, the risks one runs to get lost
when faced with a life which, according to him, seems too easy. Through him,
through the parties and receptions to which Mathilde invites him, Moïse is
forced to ask himself fundamental questions: the first instance occurs during an
incident with an African minister with whom he argues the question of birth-
right; he then argues with Sarah, a young Ivorian student and Mathilde's god-
daughter, about the duties of Africans towards their respective countries, which
finally leads to the million-dollar question:[16] "What must one do to be African?"
(159). He avoids this question, postpones answering it, and adopts a way of life
which belies any preoccupation he might have with this topic. Through several
stages he will come to deal with the question. His meeting with Sarah and his
trip to the Netherlands are key stages in his journey.

His affair with Sarah, which was originally meant to be a simple game of
sex, unleashes in him an indistinct *malaise*. He does not feel as if he is betraying
Mathilde, but rather experiences an intensity that he has never before known.
Moïse, however, vehemently rejects the possibility of an unconscious need on
his part to return to his roots through his choice of a Black partner.[17] Similarly,
he rejects all talk of love. His stubbornness leads him to have other sexual adventures with African and Antillean prostitutes in an attempt to prove that none
of it means anything, and that he remains an entirely free man, free of emotional
ties. But his sudden sexual impotence disarms him, and seems "intolerable"
(153) to him, thereby chipping away at his self-assurance. The sexual impotence
is symptomatic of his mental impotence with regards to the questions of identity
with which he refuses to deal and accelerates a thought process which will ultimately lead to his breakdown. Consequently, during a business trip to Amster-
dam—because he is in a way placed in the official position of foreigner, whereas
in France he is only a foreigner to himself—the identity crisis which loomed
above him blows up in full force, driving him to alcoholism, drugs, and suicidal
thoughts. During his nightly meandering, he ends up in the city's red light district. Walking past a window, he is struck by the resemblance of an Antillean
prostitute with Sarah. This sexual experience ends in another failure, which
leaves the Antillean woman in disbelief: faced with her laughing at him, Moïse
loses all self-control and beats her. Her pimp runs to her rescue, beats Moïse,
takes him to a field where he subjects him to sexual humiliation, and then leaves

him for dead. Moïse gets his revenge the next day, however, emptying his gun on the man. When he sees the Antillean prostitute—who realizes what happened—he decides to try to put some order back into his life and to deal with the void within him "une souffrance pernicieuse qui condamnait à l'impossibilité de vivre" (210) [a pernicious suffering that doomed him to an impossible life].

Paradoxically, this man's death triggers in Moïse this awakening and realization of how badly off he was. It is through the act of killing, which he considers sacrificial, that, paradoxically, he is granted the chance to repent and thereby think about a possible return to Cameroon. "Oui au commencement, il y avait son père et sa mère. Et il avait accompli le pieux sacrifice qui seul l'autorisait à les rejoindre enfin" (211) [Yes, at the beginning there had been his father and his mother. And he had accomplished the pious sacrifice that alone allowed him to join them at last]. At this point, Africa reappears: for the first time, his country is brought up through familiar scenes, such as the memory of a talk with his father. He has finally come to a point where he can mentally link back with his roots and consider going back to his country. The textual motif of nostalgia, coupled with that of a need to belong and to integrate himself, takes shape in a roundabout way. The narration consists of describing the process he undergoes to ultimately recognize the nostalgia he had denied and consciously erased from his thoughts and to confront the inner void that inhabited him during his life in France.

Behind the mask of cordial racial relationship, of insensibility, and of hybridity, which he had manufactured for himself, his true pain springs up in full force. From that point on, at the end of the denouement, the central issue can finally be dealt with: that of his de-culturation and his own perception of a lack of authenticity. Furthermore, he ultimately has a turnaround in conscience and finds himself responsible for a mission: that of writing about his pain/suffering, thereby relating that of all his brothers.

> Il écrirait pour eux un livre. Non, il l'écrirait pour tous les Africains de la terre, tous les apatrides, tous les gigolos et les terroristes du cœur, les maîtres chanteurs de la conscience qui n'avaient pour seul trésor que leur solitude. Il avait toujours été, il serait toujours des leurs, de leur côté, par fatalité. (211)

> [He would write a book for them. No, he would write it for all the Africans on earth, all those without a nation, all the gigolos and terrorists of the heart, the blackmailers of consciousness whose only treasure was their loneliness. He had always been, and would always be one of them, by their side, by fate.]

What he had therefore denied and run away from, some sort of racial solidarity, suddenly becomes his reality. Moïse's journey shows a constant back-and-forth between fierce clear-sightedness and a total rejection of reality as it presents itself. The theme of concern for authenticity, while taking unusual turns, such as the use of a marginal character on the periphery of society, a gigolo, appears throughout the text. We will come back to this aspect in a comparative study with *L'impasse*, where the protagonist's approach, which may a priori be opposite, nonetheless culminates in the same results.

What Njami or Léandre-Baker's novels show is also the desire of the protagonists to dissociate themselves from the image of the African immigrant who came to France for economic reasons. If the African novel from the 1960s to the 1980s brought up issues of the alienation of the exiled African who is transplanted in Paris/France in the world of Whites, it is essentially on a temporary level, in the capacity of a student.[18] But African immigration in reality is the result of economic forces linked to a (colonial) history and to special ties maintained after independence between Francophone African countries and France.[19] If the gaze in African cinema—whether with *La Noire de* . . . (1966) by Ousmane Sembène, *Concerto pour un exil* (1967) by Désiré Ecaré, or *Soleil O* (1970) by the Mauritanian Med Hondo—turned very early on towards immigrants in France, it was not until the late 1980s and the 1990s that this topic was evoked in a central fashion in the African novel.[20]

That implies on one hand that the notion of immigration in a sense remains static, that the profile of the non-European immigrant is reduced to a mix of various stereotypes, anchored in the collective French imagination. In literature, the author also indicates the desire to dissociate him or herself from both the label of African novelist—through the rejection of politically engaged writing—and from the label of immigration literature, which would revert him or her to a new marginalization. We will return to this point at the end of the chapter.

Only Music Matters

Philippe Camara was born in Paris. He is a journalist specializing in the art world, and as a singer himself, he has been part of the music world. This is the universe established as a canvas for *Discopolis* (1993). Camara introduces a world that was never broached in African literature—that of music, showbiz, and all that comes with it: drugs, money, artificial realities. Borrowing from the auto-fiction and police mystery genres, the writing is striking in the constant alternation among several registers, a mix of dialogues, colloquial language, slang, as well as changes in the narrator's wandering "I," who is alternately "I" and "him."

> Pressentant une suite plutôt houleuse, l'auteur de cet—hum!—ouvrage électrique allume nerveusement une cigarette, (. . .), pousse un long soupir de désolation, et se décide à passer au chapitre suivant . . . (24)

> [Foreseeing a rather tumultuous continuation, the author of this—hum!—electrifying text nervously lights a cigarette, (. . .), lets out a long sigh of desolation, and decides to move on to the next chapter . . .]

If Africa seems to be somewhat absent in *African Gigolo*, it completely disappears in this novel, as does any sort of Black consciousness. It is impossible to determine the origins of the narrator/protagonist, except for one or two indirect references, which may lead the reader in the direction of his African origins, and finally, an explicit sentence that mentions it, but as a secondary point.

> Pro-black et résolument mal élevé (il a lu tout Marcus Garvey et "putain, ce mec avait des couilles!"), Laurent G. est un photographe talentueux et redouté de ses modèles. (25)
> Je m'appelle Philippe Black, je suis noir, chanteur, anxieux, sourd et muet. (93)
>
> [Pro-Black and resolutely rude (he read all of Marcus Garvey and "goddamn, that guy had balls!"), Laurent G. is a talented photographer, feared by his models.
> My name is Philippe Black, I am Black, a singer, anxious, deaf-mute.]

The narration barely gives a glimpse of any preoccupation with regards to relationships (racial or otherwise) between people. Only the example of the protagonist's encounter with a young Beur in trouble, which inspires a song ("Dirty People") from his second album, is a brief glimpse of it. Apart from these scarce remarks, the novel remains centered on the protagonist's detoxification after entering a clinic, his suffering during times of withdrawal, his need for alcohol, and his crises, which all lead to the ultimate explosion of a violent crisis which results in unconsciousness. When he awakens, he has also lost some of his physical abilities: he is deaf-mute, the ultimate nightmare for a singer. From that point on, the story becomes fantastic: regaining his senses, the singer learns from the author himself that he only has a few months left to live; he discovers that his agent is a crook. Finally, his girlfriend, Alexandra, shoots him on the very day that had been predicted by . . . the story and the author.

At this point, the story loses its meaning and importance. The interest of the text, however, lies in the game of narration, where "game" must be taken literally. What spices up the narration is the interaction, the constant interference, we should say, between the author and his character, and finally, between the author and his own text.

Parts of the selected linguistic elements are meant to provoke the reader. The shock may come from the use of colloquial language or of daring, even vulgar, images, which provoke a decentering of the usual stylistic tools. Despite the would-be "cool" Anglo-French vocabulary where slang, drugs, and music jargon meet, where the use of quotation marks indicates neologisms, lexical borrowing and foreign terms, the narration differentiates itself above all else through its humorous side. The narrator, as a storyteller (but a futuristic storyteller), plays off of his audience, guides it through his tale, slows it down, and makes it lose track of the action.

This rapprochement between author and character is visible elsewhere, this time in a scene taken to the extreme—when the character undergoes a violent sentimental breakdown, breaking everything within reach. The author appears by his side and gives him a magazine to peruse. The magazine is dated 1984, when the given year for the story is 1980. In this anticipated magazine, he reads the mention of the fourth anniversary of his death: he thereby learns (as does the reader) that he is dead/will die/will die any minute now. The surprise makes him lose consciousness. When waking up, the protagonist is back in the normal time-frame of the story, yet breaking the rules of the game, since the character "knows" ahead of time what will happen. The author has become an active, visible character. Indeed, in the following chapter, we find him at the radio station and at the newspaper office. The given year is now 1990, in other words a ten-year jump from the written story. There he looks through newspaper releases on Philippe Black, learning from the employee the precise date of the character's death. We therefore witness a confusion between spatial-geographic and time borders, between the limits of reality and fiction, documentary and novel, where the author is not only able to travel through time—which is his privilege par excellence—but also between walls and through space, which is not unusual for an omniscient narrator, but which does break away from the norm as soon as the author takes on the form of a character. The author seems to enjoy himself, to play with the narration for the reader's benefit.

Discopolis is certainly the most probing example of a total lack of engagement on the part of the author, as it is generally found in the work of African novelists. Neutral writing, neutral audience. Such neutrality in turn brings up the question of the status of such writing. The novel has done away with the "African" label. Does it necessarily foresee the replacement of the old label with the new one of "French literature"? The writing's neutrality is annulled by the name of the publishing house (L'Harmattan, Collection Encres Noires [Black Inks Collection]), which thereby re-establishes the category to which the writings (should?) belong. The issue of naming and of qualification (African literature, French literature) brings up a crucial question for the Afro-Parisian novel, in terms of its belonging and of the extent to which it is related to African or French literature. Must we still speak of African literature? Do the writers—on one hand—and the readers—on the other hand—necessarily accept the "French literature" denomination? Here we introduce a critical question which will be dealt with in greater detail in chapter 3.

Le Nègre Potemkine by Blaise N'djehoya, like *Discopolis*, opts for a story with a double meaning, laden with humor and irony. Blaise N'djehoya, who produced two documentaries with Jacques Goldstein, *Voyage Au Bout De La Quinine* (1991) and *Un Sang D'encre* (1996), and has worked with many publications on jazz and African music, is firstly known as a writer and even as *the* extravagant Cameroonian writer, a "delirious realist" ["réaliste délirant"], as he is described in the *Guide actuel du Paris mondial* (1992).

In 1984, he published *Un regard noir* in the *Collection Autrement* and the novel sold two hundred fifty thousand copies. It described the gaze of an African anthropologist attempting to examine French society through its paradoxes and indigenous habits. Inverting the usual perspective of the gaze, which masks a hierarchical order, N'djehoya creates a character, Makossa, who came to France to study the indigenous Frenchman and his habits. The fields of anthropology and ethnological and ethnographic studies are evidently questioned. The text is laden with color and humor, from very visual descriptions of anything from vacation-time highway traffic to the love of the French for dogs. The second part, an anthropological study applied to the case of *marabouts* and *maraboutage* describes—still with the same mix of comical and serious tones—this phenomenon's influence and the meaning of the presence of *marabouts* for French society and for the immigrant African community.

Le Nègre Potemkine by N'djehoya directly follows up on *Un regard noir*, continuing the alliance between linguistic color and the search for aesthetics through the narrator's perspective (where the object of discourse becomes subject and the other way around). The story opens in Africa, on an African veteran, a former *tirailleur* (West African soldiers employed by French authorities to fight against Ally enemies during World War I), summoned to the French embassy where he learns that he must take part in a military parade in Paris for the celebration of yet another military anniversary. The following chapter is situated in Paris, in an apartment where many gathered Africans watch the parade in question. From that point on, the story switches to instead focus on young African students all in the process of writing a thesis with a historic theme, one on the origins of so-called *petit-nègre* speak, the others on the language of *tirailleurs*, etc. The following chapter brings us back to Africa, to Côte d'Ivoire, where Boris Nivakine and Ki-Yi have gone to conduct research during summer vacation. The story therefore oscillates between Africa and France (Paris) but without the story itself ever warranting much attention.

From the start, a sort of tacit agreement seems to be made between readers and the author, notably that the story will draw its meaning from the narration process, from the very content of the dialogues, and not from the interaction between the author/narrator and his characters. Unlike in *Discopolis*, Africa and the "Parisian" life of African characters exist in the background under the cover of humorous verve and are just an excuse for underhanded critiques of sociopolitical aspects of today's Africa.

Indeed in both novels, the aesthetic efforts made on the language move to the forefront, in turn generating a meta-text, a discourse of deconstruction of the so-called central and peripheral discourse.

Un regard noir, for example, plays off of the deconstruction of stereotypical images and expressions remarkably well. In a dense writing, a complex assembly of cliché images, reworded or broken idiomatic expressions, N'djehoya explores, almost in passing, French people's habits, their ways of thinking, their innumerable preconceived ideas. For instance, he uses expressions such as "la tempête de sable aux yeux" [the sandstorm in their eyes]. Here the author has attached two expressions each having a semantic meaning built around sand in French: "une tempête de sable" [a sandstorm] and "jeter de la poudre aux yeux" [to throw powder in their eyes] (an idiom evoking blinding by the subject). The surprise effect is immediate, causing the reader to stop and go over the sentence.

The author also resorts to zeugmas as in the following example: "Passioné de numismatique, collectionneurs de nairas et de naïades, d'ivoire et d'Ivoiriennes, de zaires et de Congolaises" (100) [Fascinated by numismatics, a collector of nairas and naiads, of ivory and Ivorian women, of zaires and of Congolese women"]. N'djehoya performs a double semantic shift around the use of the conjunction "and." While "numismatic" validates a network of terms like "nairas," "zaires"—currency of Nigeria and Congo (ex-Zaïre) respectively—or "collector," the second term of each conjunction relates to animated beings, notably women (Ivorian women, Congolese women). The humor comes from this unexpected association where the proximity in phonetics—ivory/Ivorian women—or meaning—currency associated with country name—is deceiving. Under the cover of humor, the narration unmasks certain aspects of Western mentality with regards to Africa and Africans. In this case in particular, the issue at hand is the fact that the African woman remains relegated to the level of a collector's item in Western fantasies, in the same capacity as a coin or even precious matter such as ivory (also a forbidden item since its import is illegal).

The author also makes several allusions and references to cultural or political events. For example, in the following phrase, "Ceux qui avaient traversé le pays Mossi en s'arrêtant juste *pour balancer une bouteille de coca-cola sur la tête des dieux*" (106) [Those who had crossed the Mossi country, stopping just long enough *to balance a Coke bottle on the Gods' heads*], the italicized expression (my emphasis) refers to a key scene from the Australian movie, *The Gods Must Be Crazy* (1980), in which a Coke bottle is seemingly thrown through the clouds, into a ditch, and lands on an aborigine's head. To take another example, "Tintin retournait au Congo après le Nouvel An" [Tintin was headed back to Congo after New Year's] obviously refers to the Tintin comic book series and the "Tintin in the Congo" issue whose racist content has been addressed by several critics. By exposing stereotypes, N'djehoya succeeds in highlighting some truths about the relationship of French people with Africa and Africans. For example, through their intrinsic ways of being and functioning on clogged highways during vacation time (with all that this implies since France attempted in the 1980s to modernize its transportation system and equal that of Germany and Scandinavia). Other examples include renting apartments in Paris and the dictatorship of the concierge; French habits of stocking up or eating out; or finally, the French fascination for the Paris-Dakar race.

Fifteen years later, the novel *53cm* (1999) by Bessora obviously echoes this first text, as much through its verve as through the narrative process—during which she subverts the norms and justly questions the authority of the discourse that determines what constitutes central and peripheral discourse. Through the trials and tribulations of a young woman trying to register as a student who is forced to confront the massive and elaborate bureaucracy to obtain a residency permit and to register at the university, the reader discovers a world of crossroads: French society, students, and immigrants. Difficulties around her child soon arise for the protagonist, when the mother is granted a residency permit but her child is not; from that point on, the narration explores (and travels) with the reader through the hallways of this or that office, as the protagonist is sent back and forth like a ping-pong ball. As a "gaulologue," Bessora observes French society with a humorous, caustic, and occasionally ferocious gaze. She continues this same pointed observation in *Les taches d'encre* (2000), this time extending her part-anthropology, part-police investigation to a more in-depth exploration of the meaning of French society through its components, attitudes, racism, and modes of thinking towards Africa in particular. Through her protagonist, Muriel, an astrologer-therapist from Rwanda who has lost all anchorage since the 1994 genocide, and the characters in her periphery, we discover the French profile in its slightest nuances—whether or not he or she is first-generation. For instance, Bessora presents a bored couple, who like to think that they are open-minded but who, in fact, believe in the worth of conservative values, thereby masking a certain xenophobia and homophobia behind the façade of a volunteer association they created. Further, the wife, a descendant of colonizers,' illustrates French perceptions of Africa and the Caribbean. The interruption of the film episodes by advertisements (for losing weight, achieving whiter laundry, etc.) and close-ups on people's anomalies further breaks down and uncovers mechanisms of French attitude toward immigration.

A Literature of Displacement: Constructions of Identity

L'impasse (1996) or, What is a True African?

L'impasse by Daniel Biyaoula critically addresses the issue of identity as well as the concept of authenticity. From the start, the tone is dark and critical; the questions with which Joseph, the protagonist, will be confronted, are posed: issues of color, class, and social status as well as the challenges of interracial relationships and integration into French society and his own community. There isn't anything really new in that. Indeed, these are the themes par excellence of the "romans de formation" of the 1960s, which portrayed an African coming into contact with the Western world. What differs here is the surprise of the narrator—not in response to the way of life in France, but rather to that of his fellow Africans during a trip back home. The first page opens up quite naturally with a departure scene, but contrary to the "romans de formation," the departure is from France (at Roissy Charles de Gaulle airport) in the direction of the African continent. While Joseph waits to board a flight for Brazzaville, he makes observations about the "strange" things surrounding him, more precisely, on the behavior of the "Other" whom he deems disconcerting. His observations are particularly unusual in that the category of "Other" corresponds to the Africans surrounding him, rather than to the French or White people. Indeed, in the company of his friend Sabine, Joseph is struck by the display of luxury and brand names exhibited by the Africans about to leave:

> Et je perçois chez tout ce monde comme quelque chose de faux, d'apprêté. Je ne parviens pas à le définir, mais ça provoque en moi un haut-le-cœur, une sorte de pitié et de honte. Mais pourquoi ces gens attachent-ils autant d'importance aux habits? (13)

[And I sense something fake about all these people, something fabricated. I am unable to define it, but it makes me nauseous, makes me feel pity and shame. Why do these people attach so much importance to clothes?]

The author thereby introduces the novel's main theme: criticism of the excessive importance granted to outward appearance (both physical and in terms of dress) in modern African society. Through his depiction of the *"Sape"* phenomenon, Joseph questions the criteria of success for Africans in their community's eyes. The novel sheds light on a phenomenon which had until then been little addressed in African literature.[21]

The author additionally attaches two other points to this topic in the same introduction scene: the current perception of interracial relationships and the issue of skin bleaching creams for people who deem their natural skin too dark. These three points—*Sape*, artificial skin bleaching, and interracial relationships—become the protagonist's quasi-obsession as the story progresses. His marginality will only increase during his airplane journey and at his arrival in Brazzaville. From that point on, the narration describes Joseph's growing alienation. The process occurs in three phases.

The first phase revolves around the culture shock he experiences when he returns to the Congo after an eleven-year absence. What his Congolese compatriots call a modern lifestyle, the signs of professional success in France, upsets and revolts him. Indeed, from the moment of his arrival at the airport, Joseph perceives a distinct disapproval from his family due to his modest outfit. The pressure about appearance will increase during his stay.

Il [son frère aîné] s'éclaircit la gorge puis il me dit qu'il y a des règles à respecter, que je ne les aime peut-être pas les costumes, mais que je suis un Parisien, que le Parisien a une image à défendre, que pour eux, les gens de ma famille, ce sera la honte insoluble qu'il y ait parmi eux un Parisien qui ne ressemble pas à un Parisien, qu'il faut que je pense aux miens . . . (39)

[He [his older brother] cleared his throat and told me that there are rules to observe, that maybe I don't like suits, but that I am a Parisian, that the Parisian has an image to uphold, that for them, my family members, to have among them a Parisian who does not look like a Parisian would mean permanent shame, that I have to think about my family . . .]

From then on, his three-week visit becomes an unending succession of frustrations for Joseph who finds himself forced to act against his will and to abide by a set of chores forced on him by his family, wearing a suit, going to church, fulfilling his manly duties with women, slipping a bill here and there, etc.

Once again propelled regardless of his opinion into the mold of what, to him, represents tradition, Joseph becomes a sort of "cultural infiltrator"[22] because of his status as both an insider and an outsider. He almost automatically prompts a number of discussions which offer a set of implicit comparisons of rules of life in African communities in Africa and in France. These comparisons introduce the first decentering of the character through his distancing from his family and his friends as well as life in Africa. His stay in Congo shatters a set of images that Joseph had on friendship, hospitality, and the conviviality of the African community. What he also realizes is the persistence of biases on Africans living in France. For his family and his friends, for everyone in the street, France remains a myth of easy success and financial comfort. They cannot imagine that he is a mere factory worker, that he does not have a driver's license and does not own a car; it is even less believable to them that he does not wear a suit and does not dress "like a Parisian." What he also perceives is the impasse in which all his compatriots find themselves. Their primary objective remains to seem to belong, and even for the one who has almost nothing, to nonetheless play the role of the generous one; that is, by buying drinks for people and forgetting the unbearable details of everyday life with every sip. At the end of his trip, Joseph's initial impression of a separation between his world and that of his compatriots back home has proved much more severe: what he had imagined to be a mere wall has proved instead to be a precipice.

The second phase corresponds to his return and his inability to readapt to his way of life in France. Besides his anxiety due to the risk of unemployment, he feels internal tensions towards the African community in France, particularly towards women, whom he violently critiques for their use of skin-bleaching products, which he interprets as a desire to look like White women. The issues of skin-bleaching products and of straightened hair styles become an obsession for Joseph, who systematically opposes them through reactions ranging from silence to aggressiveness. These issues have been addressed by a number of novels from the 1980s, particularly in *La voix du Salut* (1984) by Aminata Maïga Ka and *G'amaràkano, au carrefour* (1983) by Angèle Rawiri. The first novel mentions the illegal nature of these creams and the dangers that they pose for the skin. The second develops this aspect in greater detail, showing through the transformations of Toula, the protagonist, the importance that body and appearance have for the African woman. Daniel Biyaoula addresses some of the same points as Rawiri, though he provides the male perspective on the question. In the framework of this novel, the question acts as a catalyst and triggers horrible migraines in him at the sight of his female "made-up" compatriots.[23]

Through his description of women's "captive" bodies, Joseph actually accounts for his own constriction and for what Françoise Lionnet calls geographies of pain. Nonetheless, the protagonist avoids the question of his own captivity and alienation and projects it onto women, whom he considers to be "alienated" bodies. Here, as in *Le petit prince de Belleville* by Calixthe Beyala, we once again encounter the same type of blame by men in their criticism of women's behavior or appearance and their responsibility for the transformations of the entire community. Once more women are considered to have the duty of guarding moral and traditional values. We will refer to this point in more detail in our analysis of Beyala's "Parisian" novels.

The female body here is used as a literary reference to the (post-colonial) violence inflicted on women and, through them, on Africans. Here, violence is equated with the cultural pressure which forces women to espouse a certain ideal of beauty based on Western standards. As highlighted by Lionnet in *Post-colonial Representations: Women, Literature, Identity* (1995), "the [female] body remains a privileged code for a range of messages which, in the end, serve only to enslave this body to the ambiguous images that the cultural code carries, translates or creates" (98).

Joseph rejects skin bleaching as a sign of alienation. Through his rejection of fashion and its dictates, he nonetheless submits his own body to other types of mortification meant to ultimately bring him to higher ground.[24] In so doing, to follow Lionnet's analysis of the use of the female body as a literary representation of suffering, Joseph revisits the motif of reformation and rebirth, which however, ends in failure, since he is born again as an artificial being who is none other than the negation of his own principles. Paradoxically, his visit back home, where he felt different, made him conscious of the diffracted reality of France. A second decentering occurs at that point with the appearance of a growing *malaise* surrounding his life in France, which leads to his inability to combine the various cultural codes and to construct a self other than that expected by society, both African and French.

His transformation in the third phase depicts the logical outcome of his inability to combine the cultural codes, or in other words, the identity crisis that leads him to treatment in a psychiatric unit. The refusal to face his alienation actually drives him later to place the blame on the other community, that of White people. The initial mask of cordiality disappears. Joseph's growing bitterness towards others is soon directed towards his girlfriend Sabine, whom he now views as the representative of her race; their relationship consequently deteriorates and ultimately ends. We are reminded here of Frantz Fanon's discourse on issues of color and interracial-ness, of his discourse on the ensuing lack and anger. Indeed we come across the usual components (in terms of tensions and difficulties) of the literary portrayal of interracial couples. *L'impasse* is also a novel about love, but about a love that succumbs from a lack of real discussion between the two parties. We could draw parallels with *Un chant écarlate* by Mariama Bâ. However, two differences are noteworthy: first, the spatial change which brings the element of migration into consideration and to the forefront; second, the fact that in this case it is an African male character who, unrooted and displaced from his original cultural milieu, suffers from the alienation that leads to his institutionalization in a psychiatric unit.

The final phase of the novel describes his so-called therapy, and finally, the new alienation of Joseph now that he is poured into the very mold that he initially despised—that of the *"Sapeurs."* The notable aspect is that the therapy is carried out by a French psychiatrist, Dr. Malfoi—whose name leaves no doubt on his position—and who is renowned for his "knowledge" of Africa and Africans, having spent a number of years on the continent. It is thus he, a Westerner, who teaches Joseph the essence of what it means to be a "real African." This is obviously an ironic glance by the author towards those who have "covered" Africa, "know" it—such as journalists, psychiatrists, and anthropologists—and who even think that they have the right to give Africans directions on how to live, as in this particular case.[25]

Following his therapy, Joseph also becomes a slave to fashion trends and the dictates of African modernity, to the point of even trying skin-lightening creams (which he has to renounce because of burns and an allergic reaction). He gains weight (seen as an indication of success), never leaves the house without a suit, and of course plays the role of the generous one, in the company of African "friends," the same people whom he avoided earlier and despised for what appeared to be self-interest and snobbery on their part. Through a final event, he realizes the fragility of his current balance and of his need for more 'therapy,' whatever that may mean.[26] We could extrapolate onto Homi Bhabha's analysis of the act of mimicking in *The Location of Culture* (1994). The imitation here is also double and denounced: the author denounces African women's imitation of their White counterparts through cosmetic and dress transformations (and through that, their ways of life). The two modes of imitation highlight their ambiguity in that they not only reinstate but also transpose the usual terms of the forbidden desire for power and subjection in a post-colonial framework.[27] The fetishing of what used to be colonial culture continues to exert its attraction on today's context, to the point of attempting to give—through an artificial similarity of body and mind—an illusion of semblance between Parisian and urban African space.

In fact, once the denouement has occurred, despite a different—not to say opposite—itinerary, we notice possible parallels with Moïse's trajectory, such as the continuous risk of alienation and the precariousness of his situation as an African in France. Both characters have lost their original geographic and cultural anchor. For Joseph, the space of Africa (space A) stops being a pole of attraction. In fact, this space disgusts him and, progressively, France (space B) also loses its magnetism. For Moïse, the original anchor (entirely in space B, or Paris) changes and he orients himself once again towards the original pole, Cameroon (space A), which "saves" him *in extremis* from the crisis looming above him. Because Joseph's energy is not captured and channeled towards a single point, he suffers from dispersion, which leads him to a loss of balance, of which he becomes unaware once engaged in what he takes to be his therapy. In both cases, the loss of attraction to one pole or the other is at the root of the imbalance, acting as a catalyst and leading to the character's identity crisis.

In this regard, Ambroise Kom highlights the precarious nature of the characters created by the authors in his analysis "Une littérature plurivoque; pays, exil et précarité chez Mongo Beti, Calixthe Beyala et Daniel Biyaoula."[28] Joseph is one such character who relies on others, particularly on his psychiatrist, to throw him a lifeline that would help him out of the maze that is his identity crisis. Kom regrets on this topic that "au terme de son exil intérieur, la métamorphose de Joseph Gakatouka ne se traduise pas par une victoire sur l'aliénation et sur les invariants qui l'objectivent" [at the end of his internal exile, Joseph Gakatouka's metamorphosis does not manifest itself in the form of victory over the alienation and the emblems of his objectification]. He notes that the character, prisoner of his impasse, then becomes a "synonym of procrastination" on the part of the author who prefers to simply speak of impasse without dealing with the reasons and motivations for the phenomenon.

The text however takes on an immediately socioculturally engaged dimension in the reach of the problems that are broached. *L'impasse* is an intense thought exercise on Africans in France and in Africa, on the perpetual myth of France as a welcoming land, as the land of success. Through the narrator's severe attacks on the need of his compatriots to imitate and adopt an appearance that seems to represent success, the author raises the question of the fetishing of French culture and of the subordination in which his compatriots place themselves. He thereby shows how the overvaluation of appearance in Africa fits directly into the myth of Paris's aesthetic and cultural superiority as a world capital. It is in this perspective that *L'impasse* poses the question of identity and authenticity for emigrating Africans who live in France, the main question remaining: what does the characterization of "true" African mean in the current world? The protagonist in *Ici, s'achève le voyage* poses the same question with regards to Maléka:

Maléka n'avait rien d'une africaine, tout en elle était occidental, depuis les murs glacés de son appartement, la décoration, les meubles, jusqu'à sa façon de respirer entre deux phrases. Naturellement, il ne lui restait que son physique racé. Et même, pour peu que je m'attarde à regarder le noir luisant de sa peau, il y avait comme une couverture épaisse de culture occidentale, elle en était pétrie jusqu'à la moëlle des os et se donnait tout le mal du monde pour avoir l'air d'une petite Française. (75)

[Maléka had nothing of an African woman, all in her was Western, from the frosted walls of her apartment to the decoration, the furniture, to her way of taking a breath between two sentences. Naturally, all she had left was her raced physique. And still, by fear that I linger on the glowing blackness of her skin, it was as if it were covered by a thick blanket of Western culture; she was made of it, down to the marrow of her bones, and she took all the trouble in the world to look like a little French girl.]

In both novels, the individual's behavior is deconstructed beyond the feature of race. But even if Joseph seems to have an obsession with his color, his behavior—just like Moïse's—in fact points to a lack of Black consciousness, or at least of a Black consciousness that would serve as an organizing principle.[29]

As in *African Gigolo*, the novel describes an inverted quest that leads to alienation and to thoughts of death. Nonetheless, to refer to Lionnet's analysis of female Antillean writers and the search for authenticity for their female characters,[30] the male characters do not embark on a quest for their origins that looks back on the past. Quite to the contrary, they engage—sometimes unwillingly—in a random quest, retaining the feeling of a void within them, which is explained by their feeling of unfulfillment with regards to what modern Africa has to offer them and to what they perceive to be a life devoid of meaning in France.

In this case, Joseph is therefore rejecting all feelings of nostalgia towards the past and his native land, but he is also rejecting any desire of belonging to this new land. Furthermore, through the glance he directs towards his compatriots in France, Joseph—like Moïse—questions the existence of a "community" and consequently, of the interaction between place and identity.[31] His initial rejection of this community and his isolation are the causes of his decentering and identity crisis and create the need for an artificial community living off the very principles that he abhorred. In this manner, the author poses the question of interaction between place and identity, as well as that of the decentering of the African community in France from the perspective of the African continent (and inversely, he deals with the decentering of the African community in Africa by looking at France as a model). The novel's title appropriately summarizes the resolution of the dilemma between choosing a "substitute" artificial community and resigning oneself to isolation and solitude, or in other words, impasse.

The topic of the importance of one's dress, of appearance as a trait of social success, of what makes a "real" African, takes new dimensions in *Bleu-Blanc-Rouge* (1998) by Alain Mabanckou, as we will see in the following section.

Both *Ici, s'achève le voyage* and *L'impasse* participate in the writing and the uncovering of new identities, as functions of their new space (contemporary Europe), as well as of their gender, status, and class.[32] For both protagonists, the question of choice and balance with regards to the interaction of at least two modes of thought and life is difficult to resolve individually. In both cases, their experience is characterized by the precariousness of their situation with regards to the West, which absorbs them, and Africa, which they do not—or no longer—understand and which, in extreme cases, they reject. In this context, the presence (or absence) of an African community remains secondary when it does not have a negative impact on the individual's future. What distinguishes *L'impasse* from a novel such as *African Gigolo*, in other words, a novel of displacement from a novel of detachment, is the perspective of the protagonist who either continues to situate himself with regards to Africa and Africans, or instead refuses to do so. Each type of novel therefore displays a different pole of attraction for the protagonist. Both recognize what goes into this polarization—or complete lack thereof—in their future as Africans living in Paris/France.

Gazes into the Immigrant African Community in France

Even though *L'impasse* and *Ici, s'achève le voyage* describe the life of Africans living in France compared to life in Africa and each group's assumptions about the other, the novel remains centered on a character who is marginal as a result of his alienation and attempt to exclude French society and African society—whether in Africa or in France—at the same time. We never come across the feeling that a real community (in a form other than a small group, and which has rules of functioning particular to the group) exists. The novels we examine in the following section instead direct their gaze towards Africans settled in France as a community and raise questions on the existence of a group animated by a social and collective life. The difference with traditional African novels relating the departure of an African man or woman for France or another European nation is that this departure is no longer considered in the framework of a temporary stay corresponding to the individual's time in university, but rather to the departure of one or several people in the hope of finding in this new place an improvement of their financial and social situation. The return home, which is envisioned because the departure is not a result of exile, nonetheless proves to be difficult and less likely as time passes. Due to this perspective, the framework here is entirely different.

The issue of a return that is not envisioned or that *cannot* be envisioned recurrently appears in Calixthe Beyala's texts. Immigration and the immigrant African community in Paris, essentially in Belleville, consequently take on a primary place in her texts.

Calixthe Beyala: from Africa to the "Parisian" Novels

Over the past fifteen years or so, Calixthe Beyala has written thirteen novels and two essays. Her first three novels, *C'est le Soleil qui m'a brûlée* (1987), *Tu t'appelleras Tanga* (1988), and *Seul le diable le savait* (1990) represent a first stage in her writing in that they draw from what one of the protagonists, Ateba—later followed by Megri—denotes as a program: TO FIND THE WOMAN AGAIN (Ateba) and TO BECOME (Megri). Consequently, these three novels appear as the search for a new sexual ethic and for different bases in the relationships between individuals, between men and women, between women, and this in order to build a new Africa that is no longer equated simply with despair and lies. In this framework, each novel corresponds to a stage in the aforementioned program.[33] *C'est le soleil qui m'a brûlée* displays the need to kill the man, *Tu t'appelleras Tanga*, the need to (figuratively) kill the mother, and finally *Seul le diable le savait*, to kill the fake woman and fake dreams that hide reality. From then on, there is a possibility of building true relationships based on values other than mercantilism. *Le petit prince de Belleville* is thus a milestone in Beyala's work in that it opens a new phase in two ways. On one hand, it is the first novel to grant a glimpse of the possibility of a new sexual ethic between men and women and the man's search for a dialogue with the woman. On the other hand—on the topic most relevant to the framework of this project—this novel displays a geographic displacement and a new angle of vision which moves from Africa to France and to the community of Africans implanted in France. Contrary to other authors, Beyala not only looks at the protagonist in his or her individual undertakings, but rather in his/her belonging to a new community, that of the immigrants of Belleville. In fact, the Traorés give off the image of an immigrant family in the midst of a community of immigrants. The novels *Maman a un amant*, *Assèze l'Africaine*, and *Les honneurs perdus*, which are often characterized as Parisian novels, thereby remain essentially implanted in France (with the first part of the novel retracing the character's trajectory from the village to a city within Africa, and then from Africa to

France).[34] *Le petit prince de Belleville* and *Maman a un amant* (which came
after *Le petit prince*) introduce the Malian community of Belleville. Through the
alternation of the voices of a seven-year-old boy, Loukoum, and of his father,
Abdou Traoré, the author recounts the multiple disillusionments the newly unemployed Abdou faces, such as problems of adaptation and the transformations
of his wives and of Loukoum, which all followed their discovery of a new way
of life and thought.

Beyala examines, in a fresh way for African writing, the meaning of the verb
"to leave," the reasons for the departure, thereby denouncing the mythic image
of France as a land of success.[35] The father's voice offers a synthetic view of the
Malian immigrant community in Belleville: "La fortune a ouvert ses ailes, l'exil
a commencé. Je suis venu dans ce pays tenu par le gain, explusé du mien par le
besoin" (22) [Fortune has opened its wings, exile has begun. I came to this country in the grip of material gain, expelled from my own land by need]. These
words of introduction elaborate on the disillusionment which results from the
status of immigrant and on the role of women in their adaptation to life in this
country that is not theirs. Through each of his actions, the man betrays the depth
of his wound, of his vulnerability as a non-being that has now become transparent, a nonentity. In his evocation of exile, of the reasons that prompted his departure, Abdou reminds us of the language used to represent France as the place
of success and luck. Abdou highlights a number of facts for his interlocutor,
who can be identified as White and French. Notably, he expresses the immediate
contempt that the status of immigrant confers upon him:

> A la police des frontières, tu as immatriculé mon corps et tu l'as enrobé de mé-
> pris, de haine. Dans tes yeux grands ouverts, j'étais déjà suspecté de viol ou de
> meurtre. Un obsédé sexuel. Un amas de boue chargé d'obstruer les mémoires et
> de propager le sida. (37)

> [At the border patrol, you registered my body and wrapped it in contempt, in
> hatred. In your wide-open eyes, I was already suspected of rape or of murder.
> Obsessed with sex. A pile of mud charged with obstructing memories and
> propagating AIDS.] (*Loukoum* 20)

In my analysis of the novel in *Femmes Rebelles* (1996), [*Rebellious Women*
(2000)], I have shown how these interjections directed at the interlocutor
"désignent une certaine responsabilité dans la dénigration de soi, dans son mal-
heur, rappelant le temps de la colonization, de ce que les aïeux de cet interlo-
cuteur ont fait à son pays" (292) [assign a certain responsibility in his self-
denigration and misfortune, reminding us of the time of colonization, of what
the interlocutor's ancestors have done to his country]. Beyala depicts men as
extremely vulnerable and fragile as a result of this immigrant status, which gives
women the role of savior, that of the only anchorage point allowing the men to
survive, and through which "exile moves away" (118).

This reference is also a way for the author to account for a shift between men
and women with regards to their situation of exile. As a matter of fact, Beyala

considers the distortions in way of life between men and women and parents and children.[36] The woman searches for a new freedom, discovers other ways of being and of acting as a woman and as a wife (hence the physical transformations that the man neither understands nor accepts). To the contrary, the man shows nostalgia. Lost in this world, he turns his gaze to the past, no longer able to communicate his pain to his wives since they no longer listen to him.[37]

The same goes for the children's generation. The generation gap blows up between immigrants and their children who integrate themselves more deeply into the other culture. The author re-addresses the issue of generational conflict. The summary of Abdou's experience culminates in the loss of all his bearings: his thoughts thereby betray a preoccupation with parenting and fathering. The question of his African children's future, of the education that African parents should choose for their children, takes on a breadth which is only now so explicit and manifest in Beyala's novels.

In her "Parisian" novels, Beyala focuses on highlighting the identity gaps (to use the title of Begag and Chaouite's analysis) between parents and their children, between men and women, which are manifested in the details of day-to-day life. For example, Loukoum, as I said, "devient dans le nouveau cadre d'un regard sur la communauté africaine immigrée, représentation hyperbolique de la jeune génération. Le danger d'acculturation apparaît plus sérieux dans ce contexte, dans la mesure où l'Afrique n'existe que dans son évocation; que le fils, l'enfant cesse de l'écouter et l'Afrique disparaît de la maison, et avec elle, une identité stable pour l'enfant, et par suite pour la famille" (Cazenave 1996, 254-255) [becomes a hyperbolic representation of the young generation in the new framework of a gaze directed towards the African immigrant community. The danger of acculturation seems to be more serious in this context since Africa only exists through its evocation; since the son, the child, stops listening to it and Africa disappears from the house, along with a stable identity for the child and subsequently, for the family]. We once again come across some parameters that play a role in the dilemma faced by Joseph, but which differentiate themselves through their symptoms: a physical manifestation of insanity shows a man made fragile, resigned, and subject to extreme fatigue and reduced to (mental) impotence.

While *Assèze l'Africaine* and *Les honneurs perdus* adopt the structure of the first novels in that—as in *Tu t'appelleras Tanga*—they are centered on interacting female characters that are at once antithetic and complementary, they fit into the direct continuation of *Maman a un amant*, dealing more specifically with the African woman. They differ from this model, however, in that they look at the issue of singledom and the consequences for a woman coming to France by herself in the hope of becoming someone else.

This is the concretization of what Megri announced in *Seul le diable le savait*: becoming. Indeed, *Seul le diable le savait* was essentially an extended flashback of Megri recounting her life in Africa, explaining her journey from Africa to France. *Assèze l'Africaine* and *Les honneurs perdus* show two parts, the first in Cameroon (the country is identified), and the second—more extensive—showing the evolution of the protagonist in Paris, in this new milieu. Each novel finds a second female character (Sorraya, Ngaremba) joining the first, with the narration thereby reproducing the respective evolution and journey of the two characters (Assèze and Sorraya, Saïda and Ngaremba). One depends on the other and shows that despite an initially completely opposite trajectory, the two characters' itineraries eventually converge to the same point, an impasse, defined by the confrontation of the void in their meaningless lives in France, when they come to the point of returning to Africa. If Assèze—and Saïda in a greater capacity—illustrates the possibility of becoming, Sorraya and Ngaremba are reminders of the difficulties of such an enterprise and of the risks of failure.

In both novels, the two female characters are in conflict and complement each other through their individual approaches to life, developing a complex relationship of love and jealousy, not to say hatred, which is all the more significant since one takes charge of the other and "educates" her.

In *Les honneurs perdus*, we come across the same self-denigration by Saïda, which reaches its heights, as in Assèze's case, during her youth and which corresponds geographically to her time in Africa. It must be emphasized that this self-denigration operates geographically in the reverse direction for Beyala's male and female characters. Indeed, Abdou feels stifled, non-existent, and transparent in France, while Assèze and Sorraya, Saïda and Ngaremba instead experience these feelings in Africa. In each novel, the departure for France is represented for both women as the promise of improvement and the hope to be free and thus to be. In both cases, the departure for France and the ensuing renegotiation of identity are not only expected, but also desired.

Once in Paris, the self-denigration that Saïda felt will be doubled by a fascination with Ngaremba, and will progressively dissipate and leave room for a feeling of trust coupled with a critique of Ngaremba's character, mainly her weaknesses and all the artificiality surrounding her.

In fact, a comparison of Assèze and Saïda on one hand and Sorraya and Ngaremba on the other hand brings out various parallels in behavior, maybe because the women all correspond to typical characters: the (young) naïve and slightly ignorant village girl who is initially incapable and is always struck by a calamity of some sort; the well-off urbanite who follows the latest trends, displays a certain cultural flair, is ambitious, and apparently succeeds in all her undertakings. The two characters develop intense feelings of love and hate for each other and compete for respective authority through their relationships with third parties (Frédéric, Sorraya's husband and Loulouze, Ngaremba's daughter), with the third party becoming closer to the other person. But in both cases, the evolution of these two types of characters is similar in that the calamitous woman (Assèze, Saïda) wins over the lucky one (Sorraya, Ngaremba) to the extent that she indirectly causes the fall of the "lucky woman" since the latter kills herself in both cases (Sorraya takes an overdose of pills and Ngaremba throws herself out a window). In both instances, one woman blossoms at the expense of the other, who stands in the shadow of her companion's success and happiness and resents her for it.[38]

Ngaremba verbally attacks Saïda in public, thereby trying to reinforce the woman's image as a loser and a fool. A similar scene appears in *Assèze l'Africaine* where Sorraya cruelly mocks Assèze. Gradually, Sorraya and Ngaremba show signs of depression, of becoming more fragile, signs to which the other women are more or less sensitive. The reasons for this depression, for their loss of balance and the frustration of their identity are reminiscent of questions of hybridism as they appear in Ken Bugul's *Le baobab fou* (1983).

> Vous pensiez que je me sentais supérieure à vous parce que je ne me sentais nullement inférieure aux hommes. J'aurais tellement voulu être des vôtres. Vous ne me considériez pas comme une des vôtres. (. . .) En France, j'appartiens encore à une minorité. Jamais je ne serai considérée comme une Blanche. Je n'appartiens à rien. Une hybride! Un non-sens! *(Assèze* 339)

> [You thought that I felt superior to you because I did not feel inferior to men. I would have so loved to be one of you. You did not consider me to be one of you. (. . .) In France, I am still part of a minority. I will never be looked at like a White woman. I belong to nothing. A hybrid! A nonsense!] [Sorraya speaking]

Despite Assèze's efforts to keep Sorraya alive, and the efforts of Saïda to give Ngaremba a new will to live, Sorraya and Ngaremba prefer death. A difference nonetheless occurs between the two women left behind, in that Saïda, contrarily to Assèze, shows an inner strength that allows her to face the loss of Ngaremba and to immediately think of what will become of Loulouze (even if in so doing she feels that she in a sense takes over Ngaremba's soul since she naturally and immediately substitutes herself as a mother to the little girl). Assèze—even though she substitutes herself for Sorraya by becoming Sorraya's husband's wife—is haunted from the moment of the other woman's death by the same problem as her, and now "absent from reality," will take her *mal de vivre* with her from one place to the other, to Africa and to Paris.

The two novels, in the direct continuation of *Maman a un amant*, explore the possible outcomes for an African woman who left her home to make a new start in France, in a new environment. In the continuation of Beyala's previous novels, *Assèze l'Africaine* shows the limits of the dialogue between men and women and women's impossibility to define themselves differently, outside of men, and their responsibility in the perpetuation of this situation. *Les honneurs perdus*, on the other hand, leaves the door open for a better situation for women: Saïda's journey displays a deep growth of the character, who moves from naïveté and defeatism, from the feeling of being a useless burden, one that nobody cares for, to self-assertion and a feeling of well-being. Some marking stages contribute to this progression, notably the beneficial effects of dialogue with another woman (outside of the questions of jealousy and the tensions broached earlier), of education (learning how to read and write), of love for a child, Loulouze, as well as of romantic experiences (including the disillusionment and lies that they may bring about, as with Ibrahim). Ultimately, Saïda's well-being seems to result from her relationship with Marcel, a formerly homeless man, and is therefore still linked to a man. Nonetheless, there is some hope in that this love seems sincere and grants her the freedom to be. For Saïda, the experience of immigration is synonymous with a transformative dynamic process.

These two novels evidently constitute a gaze towards African women and their future, but also evidence a set of questions posed by the author on Africa and on the African community in France. Through Beyala's words, questions of identity, of the female self, take on breadth and an immediately political turn; they are linked to the future of Africa, to the future of the African community in France:

> Où est l'Afrique dans ces déchaînements d'ambitions et de corruption ? Où es-tu ? Où suis-je? (. . .) Je n'ai pas réussi ma vie. J'ai raté ma vie en tant que jeune fille et aujourd'hui en tant que femme, tu comprends? (*Assèze* 341)

> [Where does Africa fit in this unleashing of ambitions and corruption? Where do you fit? Where do I fit? (. . .) I didn't have a successful life. I messed up my life as a young girl, and today as a woman, you understand?]

Assèze otherwise remains strongly anchored in Africa, at least in the desire to "speak of" Africa. In this sense, the novel exhibits the same desire to initiate a program visible in Beyala's first novels, the primary function of the narrator/protagonist becoming that of speaking of Africa and of talking about life, all the while confronting the interlocutor, the reader, to an unembellished Africa.

> Aujourd'hui, je n'écris pas pour vous parler de nos misères, mais de quelques moyens pour y échapper. (. . .) Je ne parle pas de désespoir. Je parle vie. J'écris ce livre pour une Afrique qu'on oublie, pour l'Afrique au long sommeil. (*Assèze* 20)

> [Today I am not writing to tell you about our misery, but to tell you about some ways to escape it. (. . .) I am not speaking of despair. I'm talking life. I am writing this book for an Africa that is forgotten, for the long sleeping Africa.]

> Je représente un continent dont la survie est bien compromise. Je suis née en voie de développement. Je vis en voie de disparition. Je n'ai aucune névrose. Ma torture hurle ailleurs, vers l'Afrique qui vit un blues dégueulasse et qui ne se voit qu'à l'ombre de ses propres ruines. Je ne noircis pas la réalité. Je la verdis, à la façon de l'Afrique qui faisande. (*Assèze* 348)

> [I represent a continent whose survival is quite compromised. I was born as a developing species. I live as an endangered species. I have no neurosis. My torture screams elsewhere, towards Africa who lives a disgusting blues and who now only sees herself in the shadow of her own ruins. I am not darkening reality. I am this reality, like a rotting Africa.]

The issue of decentering for the African immigrant, introduced in *Le petit prince de Belleville* and *Maman a un amant*, is of course also present in *Assèze*

The issue of decentering for the African immigrant, introduced in *Le petit prince de Belleville* and *Maman a un amant*, is of course also present in *Assèze l'Africaine*. The novel actually summarizes a journey—depicted as almost inevitable—of alienation undergone by the protagonist: from a fascination for the other culture to the White complex and the desire to bleach oneself, to cultural mixing and finally to doubt and the erection of a wall. The following excerpts highlight the main points.

> Tous ces gadgets français nous faisaient glisser vers une griserie de modernisme, un progrès qui nous laissait babas. (16)

> [All these French gadgets made us slip towards an intoxication with modernism, a progress that left us gaga.]

> Nous ne voulions plus subir l'exil intérieur qui nous mettait à l'écart de la race humaine. Nous voulions devenir des anges, prêts à nous envoler sans le savoir. L'influence blanche. Le complexe blanc. L'anticomplexe blanc. Des enculables en puissance. On croyait que l'homme pouvait se blanchir. (37)

> [We no longer wanted to submit to the internal exile that left us on the margins of the human race. We wanted to become angels, ready to fly away without knowing it. The white influence. The white complex. The white anti-complex. Fuckers in power. We thought that man could bleach himself.]

Textually, this journey is indicated on one hand by the move from "they" to "I" and "we" and inversely from "we" to "I," and on the other hand by the accumulation of passive tenses, which indicate that "I" and "we" have undergone a sort of forced intoxication which empowered them to act and think as they did. The alternation between the "I" and the "we" also signals the close link between individual and collective discourse, between the individual and collective experience. This journey also goes along with a geographic journey from the village to the city, from Cameroon to Paris, from childhood to adolescence to adulthood, from single life to that of a married woman. Each displacement was a factor/a vehicle for an additional phase in the decentering of Assèze, which results in the immeasurable fear of emptiness, of loneliness. In the summary she draws up, Assèze not only admits her fear of loneliness but also the extent of her alienation, of the way in which she suffers her non-belonging. Even though she is aware of her troubles, and of the fact that they do not simply affect her as an individual, but rather plague an entire collective, she does not display a degree of no return and her inability to get out of the situation any less.[39] What comes out of both novels is the fragility of the protagonists as immigrants. As Ambroise Kom says on this topic: "Mal préparés à appréhender la complexité de leur milieu d'accueil, ils ne peuvent pas se présenter comme les apôtres d'un nouveau dialogue interculturel, ni encore moins proposer une nouvelle approche de l'identité africaine. Ils s'inscrivent irrémédiablement dans les marges et vivent une pitoyable précarité tant au niveau personnel qu'à celui des relations personnelles et familiales" (6) [Ill-prepared to confront the complexity of their place of arrival, they can neither present themselves as apostles of a new inter-cultural dialogue, nor propose a new approach to African identity. They irreme-diably place themselves in the margins and live a pitiful precariousness as much on the personal level as on that of personal and family relationships].[40]

In this context, while *Assèze l'Africaine* first refers to Africa through its dark depictions of misery, *Les honneurs perdus* displays a more marked decentering from this initial objective, and instead focuses on the immigrant African com-munity in France, even though it continues general interrogations on Africans in general.[41] The novel certainly directs a gaze towards Africa, on the marginal life of the New-Bell neighborhood of Douala. But it appears as a sort of refrain reit-erating the motifs of previous novels, including the first ones, through depictions of poverty, of resignation, and of the impossibility of becoming other than what is prescribed by the initial geographic and social situation. The Africa presented here in fact seems to hold the space of a cardboard décor, a simple paper-mâché façade, like the street sets in Westerns, like the "recycling of things," as an-nounced in a sort of epigraph to *La petite fille du réverbère* (1998). However, the novel appears more garnished textually in its parts on the African commu-nity in France. As in *Le petit prince de Belleville*, *Les honneurs perdus* repeats certain motifs of the life of African immigrants in France, with regards to issues of integration, of what keeps the character from having a complete identity in light of the constant decentering that occurs in Saïda and in Ngaremba and the Africans surrounding them.

> Pour vivre en France, un immigré doit être fort, comme elle, ou simple d'esprit de manière à organiser sa vie sans se poser de questions. Il me fallait pour vivre ce qui est indispensable à la vie d'une femme en Afrique: les claques d'un époux, les colères des parents, les critiques, des cousins, les jalousies des tan-tes, les caprices de petits-enfants, et tout le tralala qui accompagne ces états pour que mon univers ne soit pas désaxé. (*Honneurs perdus* 357)

> [To live in France, an immigrant must be very strong, like her, or simple-minded in order to organize his or her life without asking him or herself any questions. In order to live, I needed what is indispensable to the life of any Af-rican woman: the slaps of a husband, the anger of parents, the criticisms, the cousins, the jealousies of aunts, the capriciousness of grandchildren, and all the madness that goes along with these states of mind so that my universe does not lose its orientation.]

We find echoes to the didactic explanations of Loukoum on the Other, on their language and customs, for his novice reader. Beyala deals with the question of trans-culturation in the sense that Françoise Lionnet uses it in her analysis of post-cultural representations, thereby thinking about the mandatory phenomena of osmosis and cultural absorption in both directions, from the margins to the center, and from the center to the margin, as well as the destitution of the very categories of center and periphery.

In this regard, Beyala operates a decentering through language and the humorous manipulation of stereotypes and idiomatic expressions that are an integral part of the French language. Part of the humorous effect comes from the shattering of some expressions that are considered idiomatic because they are an integral part of the language, but which, when analyzed in the detailed context of language, reveal a stereotypical component. To this effect, Mireille Rosello shows in *Declining the Stereotypes. Ethnicity and Representation in French Cultures* (1998) how Calixthe Beyala was able to subvert stereotypes by "cheating" on them in *Le petit prince de Belleville*, thereby creating a surprise effect where one would have expected repetition due to the nature of the stereotype.[42]

The shattering of stereotypes and the creation of neologisms draw from this same approach: to create a certain internal relationship between these texts, while differentiating themselves from the two initial literatures—African and French.[43] Rosello notably shows the uselessness of believing in the defusion of stereotypes simply because the stereotypes do not necessarily appear in daily language. Nonetheless, even if they are not used, they remain acquired and digested, buried in the collective subconscious. She cites the example of the comic book, *Les aventures de Tintin au Congo*, which—even if its original title was changed, even if this particular episode was denounced for its racist commentary—still maintains its initial message. Stereotypes, summarizes Mireille Rosello, are in this sense like cats, benefiting from nine lives.

Rosello contextualizes the study of stereotypes by drawing the profile of the evolution and transformation of the French scene and social fabric in her introduction.

> France is [therefore] implicitly asked to give a schizoid self-portrait of its current fears and anxieties, as well as its hopes and optimism. It is no secret that the social fabric of late-twentieth-century France is a patchwork of faces and ethnic groups that does not unanimously celebrate diversity. If French suburbs are, on paper, a wonderfully multiracial melting pot, a theoretical celebration of hybridity, the reality of the encounter between different races, religions and cultures is far from peaceful and harmonious. Even if the sensationalist apocalyptic predictions favored by certain factions of the mass media are greatly exaggerated, it is just as silly to pretend that the banlieues are prosperous cradles of diversity, bilingualism, biculturalism, mutual respect, and tolerance among different waves of more or less well settled immigrants. Racist stereotypes cannot wish multiracial cohabitations away, but conversely multiracial cohabitation has little effect on the practice of stereotyping. (2)

Rosello thereby reminds us that economic and social conditions have changed and that even stereotypes have evolved in the representation of the Other. While representations revolved around "phantasmagoric images of bloody sheep slaughtered in bathtubs" (3) and around crowds of men praying with their faces to the ground, which were then replaced by photographs of young veiled girls after the "*affaire du foulard*" in 1989, in the nineties, the displacement of stereotypical representations moved towards the image of the Arab terrorist involved with international terrorist organizations. The same remark applies to this immigrant population from sub-Saharan Africa. Even if the pictures of the Senegalese *tirailleur* have disappeared from the boxes of Banania cocoa powder, the world of advertising and fashion continues to use an exotic—even erotic—representation of the African man and woman. The nature of the stereotype has thus evolved in terms of its discourse, but the initial message's content persists.

Stereotypes being difficult to break down, Rosello proposes that they must be challenged by subverting them through the substitution of a surprise effect for the usual repetition on which the stereotype rests, for example. Because the surprise results from the additions/transformation of the end of the sentence, it forces the reader to stop on the precise point of the sentence and to consider the exact value of the words not only in their combination, but also individually. She therefore proposes to fight the enemy "on its own turf" (129).

In her study, she thereby devotes a chapter to Emile Ajar, Calixthe Beyala, and Didier Van Cauwelaert on the way to cheat on stereotypes. The first observation Rosello makes on *Le petit prince de Belleville* is that the style gives the reader the impression of a false simplicity. Hence, the surprise effect when the reader comes across a word or an expression "in the wrong place at the wrong time": ". . . the texts often leave us frustrated and confused by the absence of a predictable word or, to the contrary, by the addition of an astonishing supplement to a set phrase expression. Generally speaking, the cheating consists of a constant shuttling between the banal and the extraordinary, the totally known and the totally unknown" (131). As an example in her article on the use of stereotypes in the works of Ajar and Beyala, Rosello uses the expression "broyer du noir," which was replaced by "broyer du nègre" by Beyala. She shows that the substitution forces the reader not only to stop on the sentence, but also to think about the meaning of such a juxtaposition and then to challenge the stereotype as well as all that it implies (the treatment of immigrants, the attitude towards them, etc.).

In this regard, the choice of a child's voice for the narration, which does therefore not have an extensive political consciousness, allows Beyala to play more freely with the subversion of codes and stereotypical representations, whether they refer to the *banlieue* of Belleville or to the implantation of immigrants and their daily life. The act of evolving in a multiethnic *banlieue* grants Loukoum a constant mobility between "perfect adaptation and complete alienation" (133). The use of a type of discourse which is all at once anchored in French society—through its borrowing of stereotypes and ready-made expressions—and outside of the central discourse—by the displacement of expressions and the surprise effect caused by the irruption of an unexpected word—shatters the stereotype. Loukoum, who is himself in the process of learning the French language, makes mistakes that subvert the stability of language.

> [he] apparently believes in preserving a complete (and perhaps) ignorant independence from the rules of grammar and semantic coherence. [His] humor

seems almost involuntary, as its source is primarily a series of apparently hap-
hazard errors of vocabulary, approximate uses of idioms, and faulty syntax.
(132)

It is through the child's discourse that Beyala shatters the language, even re-
peating certain stereotypes in a new context, which uncovers their preposterous
character and sheds light on their racist component.

At times, what is fixed and immobile is manipulated in an apparently apolitical
moment of humorous transgression; at other times, the most basic level of
originality is abandoned and replaced by sentences that even the most conventional author would refuse to take credit for. Throughout the texts, stereotypes
stand out as though framed and displayed in a gallery, but they are never discussed, criticized, or denied. Whether the stereotype is flattering or insulting
the texts treat it in a similar manner. (134)

Choosing to shatter idiomatic expressions and stereotypes is neither a new
phenomenon nor one particular to the work of Beyala. In fact, this trait is notice-
able as the mark of a new writing in the first novels by authors from the young
African diaspora, a new writing striving to decenter both African and French
literature through the language it manipulates.

Beyala's work is different from other new diasporic writings in that she on
one hand maintains a gaze turned towards Africa (even if, as we have seen, this
gaze is somewhat superficial—even artificial), and on the other hand, she opposes men and women in their conception of immigration: she offers images of
nostalgia, a gaze towards the past, and attempts to retain a set of traditions
through the formation of a surrogate African community for the men, and the
potential for change, aspirations towards a better situation, as well as the dynamism of immigration and a gaze towards the future for the women. As in the
case of the other diasporic authors, Beyala's protagonists display a lack of direction, difficulties in finding a goal in life, and especially, more crucially, the inability to integrate themselves into French society.[44]

Daniel Biyaoula's second novel, *Agonies* (1998), joins *Les honneurs perdus*
in addressing the issue of the existence of an African "community" in France, as
well as the representation of the interrelation between place and identity and the
transformations subsequent to displacement.

Agonies (1998): From Parisian Urban Space to the *Banlieue*

After *L'impasse*, Daniel Biyaoula poses with new vigor the question of the interrelation between identity and space. This second text, which was written before
L'impasse, no longer poses the question in singular terms, but rather on collective terms. From the first pages, the tone is set and appears even more somber
than in *L'impasse*, with a depiction of life in urban Parisian zones. The narration
conveys an immediate feeling of stifling for those called to settle there, a feeling
to which desperation and the deep-seated belief that nothing will ever change in

the situation add themselves, leading to determined attempts by the immigrants to escape this environment.

Through parallel stories and the fate of characters who come across each other, the novel offers an account of the daily life of Congolese immigrants, of financial difficulties, but also of an overall gray and psychologically sordid life.

The focus is essentially placed on two couples: a couple of adolescents—the African Maud and Guy, a White French boy—and the couple including Maud's aunt, Ghislaine—who figures as the rebel of the family because she lives outside of close familial ties and dates Camille, a Ntchiyafua, or member of an opposing ethnic group. Ghislaine had previously been courted by Nsamu (who incidentally introduced her to Camille one night in a club). Ghislaine initiated contact with Camille, persevered, and eventually managed to set aside the reservations he had with regards to Nsamu.

From that point on, Nsamu's anger, resentment, and quest for revenge (not to mention the fact that he still "wants" Ghislaine) are the dynamic springs for the progression of the story. As an illustration of the old saying which claims that revenge is a dish best eaten cold, the story describes in parallel the progression of the romantic relationship between Ghislaine and Camille and the plotting by Nsamu and his friend.

As things turned out, Camille has been involved with an older White woman, a wealthy widow who supports him financially, bought him numerous gifts, and notably brought up the possibility of getting him a larger and more comfortable apartment of his own. Camille therefore simultaneously maintains the two relationships until his secret is uncovered and his relationship with Ghislaine ends. Once again, Nsamu courts Ghislaine until she finally gives in to him. Camille, on his end, discovers who is responsible for the revelations that have been made to Florence (his White girlfriend) about his second relationship. The denouement is inevitable: mad with pain and drunkenness, Camille awaits Nsamu and Ghislaine at the woman's door one night; both die from his stabs.

The story shows characters who have reached a state of mental agony and creates a gray and depressing context on top of which a set of sordid considerations inscribe themselves: indeed, the narration depicts the tensions between ethnic groups from the same country, which lead to jealousy, notably when it comes to romantic relationships and friendships. The example of Bernard, who reveals Camille's past (such as the fact that the latter had momentarily been homeless and that it was Bernard who had helped him out of the bad situation), is more than striking. As a result of conversations with a compatriot of the same ethnic group, Patrice, who scolds Bernard for associating with such an individual (meaning a member of the other group), the friendship between Bernard and Camille ends.[45] In addition, Bernard participates in Camille's misfortune by making the revelations to Florence. Indeed, the narration shows the terrible implications of such rumors in the community when it is governed by the principles of exclusion along ethnic lines.

Gabriel's excessive reaction when he finds out that his daughter Maud is dating a White boy is another example of the weight that popular rumors carry. He beats his daughter several times, forbids her from going out, and finally sends her back to his home country on a one-way ticket, even though she has not finished school and will thus remain without educational or professional formation, all because he does not want to be the laughing stock of the community in which he lives.

Through this story, Daniel Biyaoula comes back to issues he had already broached in his first novel, *L'impasse*, that is, issues of the importance of the gaze and of perception, and thus of appearance and way of dress for both men and women. Differently from *L'impasse*, he no longer limits himself to the protagonist as an individual, but rather depicts an entire community in interaction: the Congolese community in the Parisian *banlieue*. Through an extremely dark story and the actions of Nsamu and Bisso, the author denounces the little frauds ("*les affaires*") from which they make their living, and also the issues of rivalry between ethnic groups in the immigrant African community in Paris, and the notion of exclusion. This novel returns—albeit from a new angle—to the myth of the homogeneity of the African immigrant community in Paris denounced by Moïse (*African Gigolo*) and Joseph (*L'impasse*). Because the novel was also written some years before its publication—and thus a few years before the Congo-Brazzaville events—it takes on a visionary dimension, triggering an alarm as to what can happen when ethnic tensions on the continent increase to the point where they have repercussions among the immigrant community in Paris. The myth of homogeneity collapses. Furthermore, Biyaoula poses the issue under a new angle, as to whether in the framework of migration and of the process of defining new contours of identity within French society, the existing African community provides a support network or instead acts as a destabilizing element, implying additional tensions resulting from those that agitate the country of origin.[46]

Denouncing the Myth: *Le paradis du Nord* and *Bleu-Blanc-Rouge*

By dealing with the difficulties and dangers of illegal immigration, Jean-Roger Essomba introduces a new angle of vision on the issue of being African in France.

Through the unfortunate experiences of the protagonists Jojo and Charlie, the author denounces the utopic image of France as the promised land for Africans. The story describes an escalation of fraudulent and criminal acts for these two men. First off, at the time of their departure from Africa, their desperate need to find the money necessary for their journey pushes them to conduct an armed robbery of a factory (which results in the death of one of the security guards). And then they encounter several problems during their boat trip to the coast of Spain, then crossing Spain, hidden under a truck, before finally arriving in Toulouse, France. Expected there by compatriots, they are drugged and find themselves at the wee hours of the morning, abandoned and penniless in a parking lot. When they ask a woman who comes into the parking lot for directions, she is frightened and shouts rape.

From that point on, events escalate. The two men are soon running from the police. They are victims of lies and empty promises. Their experience appears as a long chain of unfortunate events that end tragically, since one of them dies and the other ends up in court charged with murder, rape, and drug trafficking. Under the cover of a police mystery, this text not only highlights the illusory nature of their dreams and of the myth of success, but also the manner in which these Africans are exploited by the system—including their compatriots living in France or French people themselves, all trying to take advantage of their illegal status. Furthermore, the text brings out the impact of racial prejudice, which locks these people into a certain status and position that almost immediately makes them slip into a certain predicament.

Le paradis du Nord is one of the first novels to direct its gaze onto the world of clandestine immigration. For this purpose, the author uses a mix of humor and biting irony directed towards Africans and French people. Another example to cite would be Baker's novel, *Ici, s'achève le voyage* (1989), which shows a protagonist whose story begins somewhere in a French prison. Narration, in the form of a journal by the prisoner, is a long flashback, helping the readers to understand how he landed in that cell. Like Jojo and Charlie, he came to Paris with his mind full of images of success. Even though he is always able to figure things out—finding a place to stay here and there, with a friend or a cousin, and eventually finding his own place—his journey describes the vicious circle in which he finds himself closed: running after a residency permit, looking for little jobs, finding temporary work, scarce unemployment compensation, etc. In turn, his lack of financial autonomy holds women back, frightens them. Because he stays with Anne for three weeks and does not respond to a registered letter asking him to take steps that might allow him to stay in France, he abruptly slips into illegality. Following an altercation with Anne's ex-boyfriend that disintegrates into a bloody fight, he is charged with murder, arrested, and incarcerated. The novel highlights the thin line between legality and illegality, and the fact that the status of immigrant is precarious and in need of revision.

In the same frame of mind, we must also cite *Un rêve utile* (1991) by Tierno Monénembo. The novel is no longer situated in Paris, but rather in Lyon, in the neighborhood of Roquebrune, the immigrant neighborhood. As in many of Monénembo's earlier texts, the novel is striking in its lack of a plot. It is instead the picturing of a certain atmosphere, of the immobility and loneliness of immigrants in the grayness of the ghettoized area. The novel does not really have main characters, but rather a myriad of characters who evolve side by side in a sort of silence or dialogue of deaf people.[47]

Bleu-Blanc-Rouge (1998)—the first novel by Mabanckou,[48] a Congolese poet settled in France and recently relocated in the US—is at the intersection of the novel of un-rooting and the immigration novel in that it focuses on the presence of African immigrants in Paris. Because of its focus on the illegality of the characters and their exploitation by an exploitative network, this novel seems to be a direct continuation of Jean-Roger Essomba's *Le paradis du Nord*. It also inscribes itself in the trend marked by Biyaoula's *L'impasse* in its evocation of the difficulties of being a so-called "Parisian" African (according to people in his country), and simply an African in France, but also in the evocation of the importance of appearance and of external image as associated with social success.

Bleu Blanc Rouge, however, provides a new angle in its specific focus on the *Sape* phenomenon, on "*Sapeurs*" and "*aventuriers*," young Congolese men who invest all their money on clothing, somehow find a plane ticket that will allow them to leave for Paris, and finally become "Parisians," the ultimate title both in their eyes and in those of their family and friends in Africa.

Justin-Daniel Gandoulou explores this phenomenon—which started in the 1960s and reached its peak in the 1980s—from a sociological perspective in *Entre Paris et Bacongo* (1984). He notably defines "*la Sape*" as follows:

> La Sape est un mot d'origine argotique qui signifie vêtement, avec une connotation d'élégance prestigieuse et de dernière mode. Ce mot veut aussi dire "Société des ambianceurs et personnes élégantes" (SAPE).
> Se saper est une des principales activités de la fraction très minoritaire de la jeunesse congolaise que constituent les sapeurs, fraction essentiellement urbaine et populaire. La Sape, c'est pour ces jeunes, le symbole de l'Occident véhiculé par une certaine société congolaise, celle des gens qui ont réussi, et la façade de tout un système de valeurs. Tout se situe au niveau des apparences. Il s'agit de capter les signes extérieurs de la réussite, de les répercuter pour sa propre satisfaction et pour l'approbation et le renforcement du groupe de référence. (18)

> [*Sape* is a slang term which means clothing, with the connotation of prestigious elegance and of latest fashion trends. This words also means "Society of Elegant People and *Ambianceurs*" (SAPE).
> To "*saper*" oneself is one of the main activities of the small minority fraction of Congolese youth made up of *Sapeurs*, a popular and essentially urban fraction. *Sape* for these young people is the symbol of the West that has been propagated by a segment of Congolese society, that of people who have succeeded, and the façade of an entire value system. Everything occurs on the level of appearances. The goal is to capture outer signs of success and to reproduce them for one's own satisfaction and for the approval and reinforcement of the reference group.]

In this framework, the "*aventuriers*" are those who, sacrificing all financial means at their disposal, insist on following fashion at all costs in order to acquire suits, ties, and shoes in line with the latest trends, and for this purpose emigrate to Paris. Gandoulou tells us that "the '*aventurier*' is an emigrated *sapeur*, and the emigration is called the *aventure*; hence the following schematic itinerary: *Sapeur—aventure* (journey to Paris)—*aventurier*" (19). Once they have gathered the necessary money for the price of the ticket and arrive in Paris, their life is characterized by periods of squatting here and there and using a thousand and one strategies to acquire their dream accessories and clothes. Those who stayed behind will now be able to dress decently thanks to the "*Pa-*

risiens." This aspiration to imitate and "pass for" successful people contributes to creating a contrast between "the *Sapeur* and those he imitates on one hand, and the *Sapeur*'s appearance and the reality of his existence" (Gandoulou 19).

The novel shows the flip side of the *Sape* phenomenon, the multiple risks for these young immigrants in more or less legal situations of residency through the evolution of three characters and their travels back-and-forth between Congo-Brazzaville and Paris: the narrator, Massala-Massala, Moki whose nickname is "The Parisian" and who serves as his role model, and finally the *Préfet*, who pulls the strings for all sorts of trafficking and who manages the life of the narrator in Paris. Because of their clandestine status, they are at the mercy of both French and African people taking advantage of their situation to exploit them and force them to little jobs, and even frauds.

The story is told by a first-person narrator held in prison. Alain Mabanckou evokes the downsides of immigration through the discussion of characters' intermingled fates and of the exploiters and the victims of this game. He notably denounces the "miroir aux alouettes" of France as the land of easy success. He especially details the *Sape* phenomenon in the home country on one hand, and then in Paris. In so doing, he points to the responsibility of people like Moki, who live in France and circulate images of easy success, thereby fooling their compatriots, generating false dreams and leading them to leave their country, bank everything on their appearance, and live from one day to the next, all in order to be in Paris and experience the same adventure.

In terms of his writing, Mabanckou inscribes himself into the innovative current of the new voices. With the urban landscape of Paris, the *banlieue*, but also the capital in Africa, and with characters such as Massala-Massala and Moki, Mabanckou creates a new atmosphere for the novel: much like Moïse (*African Gigolo*) and Jojo and Charlie (*Le paradis du Nord*), his characters provide a new profile for the protagonist through their marginality and illegality. This new profile is that of the non-hero, oscillating among the anti-hero, the victim, the dilettante, and the opportunist. Lydie Moudileno very pointedly notes on this topic in "Voyage au bout de L'impasse: les fictions urbaines"[49] a change in the profile of protagonists in the novels of the new generation, in particular with Daniel Biyaoula and Alain Mabanckou. While the dilettantes or unproductive marginal characters appeared as extras in the background of the "*romans de formation*" of the 1960s and 1970s, they have taken on a new importance in the 1990s, to the point of becoming the protagonists of the novels from the diaspora. What had been out of the norm, denigrated, and vilified has become the norm, not to say what is now sought and valued. These new characters evolve in the urban landscape of Paris and its *banlieue* and become emblematic of a new post-colonial context.

On the literary front, *Bleu Blanc Rouge*, *Le paradis du Nord*, *Sorcellerie à bout portant* by Achille Ngoye and *La Polyandre* by Bolya Baenga mark the emergence of a new genre. Reminiscent of Njami's *Cercueil et Cie*, they indicate a certain continuity and mark the emergence of criminal fiction, of the "polar" in African literature. Contrary to Yegba in *Cercueil et Cie*, who initially felt well-settled in French society, the characters indicate a new context made of an urban décor and new dreams of success through their dilettante, marginal—even illegal—nature. Whether they are on the continent or in Paris' 21st district, these characters also indicate through their good and bad experiences the difficulty of this context and its limits, since, as highlighted by Ambroise Kom, there is no happy return.[50] Indeed, for those who attempt to return to their home country, the experience either fails or results in tragedy. That is for example the case of Kizito in *Sorcellerie à bout portent*, who comes back to the country to attend his brother's funeral as well as to uncover the mystery surrounding his death.[51]

Beyond the verve of their narration in a truculent language, the plot of the police mystery allows Ngoye in *Agence Black Bafoussa*, Bolya in *La Polyandre* and *Les cocus posthumes*, as well as Bessora in *Les taches d'encre* to uncover the unspoken racism in relationships in French society.

The characters' unsuccessful aspiration to escape the projects and the ghettos' grayness further addresses the issue in terms of social, economic, and cultural opportunities, as presented by Pierre Bourdieu with his notion of "*habitus*" and his analysis of French society. Both novels address the issue of integration and assimilation in new terms. They do not simply deal with the formation of an identity (African, French, or mixed) and with the extent to which such a choice is conscious (as well as the levels of complexity, the difficulties, and psychological pain), but also with the conditions for success for a non-European individual arriving in French society. According to Bourdieu's analysis, the same challenges faced by a French person about whether to change his/her social *milieu*—not just economically speaking, but also culturally—in order to enhance chances of success, are magnified for a foreigner new to this system of social and cultural functioning. The themes of dreams of success, of the primordial importance of appearance and "*Sape*" highlighted by these novels, as well as the risks taken by the protagonists in order to try their luck in France thereby directly fit into this same framework.

The Humiliations of Clandestine Life: *Un amour sans papiers* (1999)

From the start, Nathalie Etoké's *Un amour sans papiers* breaks from autobiographical female writings through its sociopolitical resonances and the means used to identify and situate the author's writing through the narrative voice.

> J'appartiens à cette nouvelle génération issue de la bourgeoisie africaine postcoloniale. Mon père et ma mère, deux êtres adorables, sont les enfants de la colonisation. Nés en 1945 et 1948, leur éducation a été marquée par l'empreinte coloniale. En effet, appartenant à la classe des évolués, ils fréquentèrent les écoles françaises, chantèrent la Marseillaise et eurent pour ancêtres les Gaulois. Comme de nombreux africains, ils poursuivirent leurs études supérieures en métropole et revinrent au Cameroon les bras chargés de diplômes et la tête pleine d'espérance. (. . .) Ma jeunesse fut dorée et sans embûches. Mes parents m'éduquèrent à "l'occidentale" comme on dit chez nous. (9-10)

[I belong to this new generation that came out of the post-colonial African bourgeoisie. My father and my mother, two adorable beings, are the children of colonization. Born in 1945 and 1948, their education has been marked with the colonial influence. Indeed, belonging to the class of the evolved, they attended French schools, sang the *Marseillaise* and had the *Gaulois* for ancestors. Like many Africans, they undertook their advanced studies in France and returned to Cameroon arms adorned with diplomas and heads full of hope. (. . .) My youth was golden and trouble-free. My parents educated me "Western-style," as we say back home.]

Here Nathalie Etoké clearly defines herself, through her protagonist, as belonging to the post-colonial African generation. The differences she points out between her parents—children of colonization—and herself thus revert to those between the previous diaspora and the African generation currently settled in Paris/France. For the novice reader who might be unfamiliar with central African culture, she further explains what she means by "Western-style."

. . . c'est tout d'abord proscrire l'usage de sa langue maternelle et parler français mieux que le petit français de France, c'est s'abreuver de Chantal Goya, de Dorothée . . . tout en étant sous les tropiques. C'est également porter la nouvelle paire de Nike . . . c'est vibrer pour le PSG ou l'OM . . . C'est être initié à la gastronomie française, manger de la quiche lorraine, des coquilles Saint-Jacques, croque-monsieurs, etc. C'est aussi fêter Noël avec un sapin en plastique, c'est également fréquenter les établissements scolaires français de la place . . . sans oublier les joyeuses agapes au cours desquelles le microcosme français local et la gentry africaine rivalisent leur amitié de façade, dégoulinante de frivolité et de snobisme. C'est enfin prendre l'avion à dix-huit ans après avoir réussi son baccalauréat, débarquer à Roissy un jour de septembre 90 et commencer une nouvelle vie. (10)

[. . . first of all, it means forbidding the use of one's mother tongue and speaking French better than the little French guy from France, to live off Chantal Goya and Dorothée . . . all the while being in the tropics. It also means wearing the latest pair of Nikes . . . cheering for the PSG or the OM . . . It means being familiar with French cuisine, eating *quiche lorraine*, Saint-Jacques shells, *croquet-monsieurs*, etc. It also means celebrating Christmas with a plastic Christmas tree, it also means attending the French schools in the area . . . without forgetting the joyous events during which the local French microcosm and the African gentry rival artificial friendships dripping with frivolity and snobbism. It finally means getting on a plane when you turn eighteen, after having passed the *baccalauréat*, showing up at Roissy one day of September 1990 and starting a new life.]

Even if certain aspects such as the use of the French language, culinary habits, participation in the French milieu as a whole—and attendance at schools in particular—are reminiscent of the post-independence atmosphere and reveal a set of habits and criteria stuck in time, certain details of dress and of the world of entertainment and sports revert to the present and concisely highlight the constant nature of a situation, which is the domination of a cultural model and of the fetishing of all that is French. The narrative voice's critical verve immediately places us back in a post-colonial space.

Furthermore, *Un amour sans papiers* breaks away through its rare combination—in the works of the young African diaspora—of representations of the student world, the work world, and the world of illegal immigrants, all in interaction, or at least in contact with one another.

Malaïka's first-person narrative shows us her journey as a young Cameroonian student who came to Lille to study, and through her, that of the Africans with whom she comes into contact. In addition to the usual first impressions reminiscent of other stories about people's coldness, the feeling of unfamiliarity, of a certain nostalgia for the home country, particularly with regards to the social relationships she had there, we progressively discover another world, that of clandestine immigrants. Indeed, Malaïka meets Salif, a Malian, at a student party. Their friendship develops and evolves, and Malaïka, in love, does not think about why he refuses to give her more details on his life, like showing her where he lives. By chance, one day she sees him enter a dilapidated building lined up for demolition and eventually—through conversations with her friends, some of whom disapprove of the relationship—she comes to have doubts about Salif's status, even thinking that he may be involved in drug trafficking.[52] Only after following him does she finally discover the truth: the building is an informal settlement for crowds of African men, women, and children living there.

She discovers a milieu and a situation that she had not known. Soon she attempts to mobilize the university and city to organize movements for clandestine Africans. A hunger strike is begun, in which Salif participates. After the strike fails due to an intervention by the emergency medical services, Salif moves in with Malaïka. One morning he disappears without a trace. Only months later, after suffering from this sudden disappearance, does she discover through a letter that Salif had been arrested that morning by the police, taken to Paris, expelled, and sent back to Mali on one of the "charters of shame."

The plot, a romantic relationship between two young Africans in France, is obviously a mere backdrop and rapidly takes on a much wider scope through the representation of not only the French, but also the African community which comes through. The narrative voice first highlights her rude awakening and the gaining of awareness of "une France à deux vitesses" (46) ["a two-speed France"], of the unreality of the myth of France as a rich country and a *terre d'accueil* for Africans.

Alors que j'imaginai la France comme un Eldorado où tout le monde mangeait à sa faim, je me rendis compte qu'il y avait aussi des gens qui vivaient en deçà du seuil de pauvreté. Cette image, totalement inconnue et occultée en Afrique, s'imprima dans mon cerveau. (. . .) Jamais je n'aurais pu imaginer qu'il existait dans ce pays tellement idéalisé par les Africains, des ghettos modernes portant la douce appellation de *"banlieue."* En rêvant de la France, aucun Africain ne rêve de Sarcelles, de la Seine-Saint-Denis, des quartiers nord de Marseille ou de Roubaix. Et, pourtant, c'est souvent là qu'ils échouent en provenant de leur pays natal. (46-47)

[While I had imagined France as an Eldorado where everyone ate to their fill, I realized that there were also people who lived under the poverty level. This image, completely unknown and occulted in Africa, imprinted itself on my brain. (. . .) Never would I have imagined that in this country so idealized by Africans there could exist modern ghettos carrying the sweet name of *"banlieue."* In dreaming of France, no African dreams of Sarcelles, of Seine-Saint-Denis, of the neighborhoods north of Marseille, or of Roubaix. Yet that's often where they land when they come from their native country.]

Continuing her thought process, Malaïka unveils the components of life for Africans in France today.

Drogue, alcool et violence y rythment la vie quotidienne. Rap, tag, sport et hip-hop sont l'unique porte de sortie. Lycées et collèges n'y sont plus des sanctuaires protégés, mais des zones d'expression du malaise social où couteaux et revolver réussissent à pénétrer. Mon séjour en France me permit de faire la différence entre la fiction et la réalité. Finalement, contrairement à ce que plusieurs Africains croient, la vie en France n'est pas si facile. Tout n'est pas si rose. (47)

[Drugs, alcohol, and violence set the rhythm for daily life there. Rap, tag, sports, and hip-hop are the only ways out. High schools are no longer protected sanctuaries, but rather, zones for the expression of the social *malaise* where knives and guns manage to penetrate. My time in France allowed me to see the difference between fact and fiction. In the end, contrary to what many Africans believe, life in France is not that easy. Everything is not that rosy.]

Here we find echoes of remarks made my Massala-Massala in *Bleu-Blanc-Rouge* or by Jo-Jo and Charlie in *Le paradis du Nord*, or again by the characters in *Agonies*. The contrast with these novels is, however, created through the association of the various milieus and the representation of the tensions and prejudices that exist between them in Paris's African community, in Lille, or in French urban space as a whole. The reaction of Malaïka's friend, Christian, is very enlightening in this regard.

Moi je ne fréquente pas la racaille. Je suis un étranger en règle et sans problème. En plus, crois-tu que les problèmes d'un fils de berger m'intéressent? Je ne suis pas concerné. Je ne tiens pas à m'attirer des ennuis. Et je te répète une dernière fois: quitte ce clandestin. Conseil de grand frère. (70)

[I don't associate with scum. I am a documented foreigner with no problems. Besides, do you think that I care about the problems of some shepherd's son? That's not my problem. I don't want to attract trouble for myself. And I will tell you one more time: leave that illegal immigrant. Big brother's advice.]

These remarks are reminiscent of those by Moïse (*African Gigolo*) or Yegba (*Cercueil et Cie*) in the character's refusal to associate himself with the representations made of non-European immigrants. Malaïka dwells on this point, thinks about it, and develops it, thereby confronting the issue of class and social divisions and exploring from a new angle the myth of homogeneity and the existence and solidarity of the African community in France. The hunger strike is also an opportunity to analyze the role of the media in the exploitation of sensationalism.

This text is also the expression of great despair due to the lack of public reactions in general. Indeed, back in her home country, the protagonist continues to get the feeling of fighting in vain, given the political situation, the dramatic spread of AIDS on the African continent and the daily indifference; she identifies important questions that assail the post-colonial African youth both on the continent and in France.

The final aspect of her going back home and fighting against a set of ills plaguing post-colonial Africa contrasts with the novel from the diaspora in its engagement compared to a literature of rejection where the protagonists precisely reject all activism, all association with Africa and Africans, and especially all association with representations of non-European immigrants and immigration. On the other hand, most texts display characters who do not plan on returning to their country, particularly not indefinitely.

The author's young age, twenty-three at the time her novel came out (as well as Bessora's), and the difference of her perspective as well as her engagement (when authors such as Njami characterized themselves at that age by the rejection of engagement and activism) draws our attention to a vital point: that it is impossible to speak of the young diasporic, post-colonial generation as a single homogeneous bloc. Indeed, age—and the context within which it operates— intervenes as a differentiating factor. On one hand, it is clear that a twenty-five-year-old neither thinks nor acts like a thirty-five-year-old; and on the other hand, it is clear that a twenty-year-old in the 1990s does not think like a twenty-year old at the end of the 1960s or 1970s, or the beginning of the 1980s. For each of these age groups, there was a different context and way of thinking about Africa, France, and the French language. Furthermore, the context of AIDS, of growing unemployment in European nations, and of the associated increase in racism are recent parameters specific to the 1990s, which means that a young twenty-year-old African man or woman at the end of the twentieth century cannot take on the new millennium in the same manner as somebody forty years earlier, at the eve of the Independences. The gaze is necessarily different. The writing by the new diaspora in France precisely documents these multiple nuances and aspects and consequently marks a new turning point for the so-called post-colonial novel. Through its writing space, it also poses a fundamental question on the future of Africa, to young African men and women with regards to their future and life choices: to stay on the continent or leave and try their luck in France? We will return to this point in chapter 3.

Simon Njami brings up the notion of community (in *Cercueil & Cie* he speaks of "community" in quotation marks) to highlight the paradoxes of its importance, the refusal of certain Africans to let themselves be led by this community, to let it come first, but also the need for this "community," for the bonds it creates in an entirely foreign—not to say hostile—city.[53] His first two novels develop the two options with regards to this "community": (1) Belonging to a different social milieu in terms of work, colleagues, friends, acquaintances and way of life is not powerful enough to force the protagonist to cut ties with these. Instead, (s)he decides that "this is it," that the milieu helps him/her to maintain a stable identity while faced with a foreign environment. (2) The protagonist asserts that he knows nothing of the "black" milieu, voluntarily cuts himself out of this ambiance, but finally finds himself doubly isolated both from the French and the African community. Njami analyzes what this community represents with regards to exile, not only in its immediate function as a substitute for family through the warmth and comfort it brings, but also as a national substitute, and in fact—according to Njami's analysis—as the only example of the successful functioning of pan-Africanism and of the idea of Africa as a single nation.

L'exil avait ceci de formidable qu'il fortifiait des liens qui, peut-être, sous d'autres latitudes, n'auraient eu aucune raison d'être. Le simple fait d'être noir, africain, créait des affinités qui donnaient une illusion de force aux pauvres hères largués dans la turbulence parisienne. On n'était pas seul. On recréait des structures familiales sur le modèle de celles que l'on avait laissées. Paradoxalement, l'étranger était l'endroit où les Africains formaient une véritable nation. Où Congolais, Ivoiriens, Cameroonais et Sénégalais se considéraient comme des frères issues d'un même pays. L'unité africaine ne pouvait se vivre qu'hors frontières, en réaction à l'hostilité ambiante. (98)

[Exile was wonderful in that it strengthened bonds which, perhaps, under different latitudes, would have had no reason to be. The simple fact of being Black, African, created affinities which gave an illusion of strength to the poor dumped into the Parisian turbulence. You weren't alone. You recreated family structures modeled on those you had left behind. Paradoxically, abroad was the place where Africans formed a true nation. Where Congolese, Ivorians, Cameroonian and Senegalese looked at each other as brothers from the same country. African unity could only be lived outside borders, in reaction to the surrounding hostility.]

In the same way, Beyala's *Les honneurs perdus* attempts to account for the existence of a tightly-knit African community with Belleville's rules of functioning and for the impact of interaction among various immigrant groups. Its representation nonetheless remains somewhat folklorized, not to say exoticized (which was the case for *Le petit prince de Belleville* and *Maman a un amant*). To the contrary, *L'impasse* stresses the risk of isolation and consequently of alienation for one who refuses to connect with the African community and to follow its *modus vivendi*. As for Nathalie Etoké, she highlights the class and status differences within the African community and the resulting tensions according to each perspective in *Un amour sans papiers*.

Our overview of the selected texts has enabled us to highlight some points of contrast between the African novel written in France and that written on the continent on one hand, and, on the other hand, between that written by the generation of Beti and that of the Beyalas, Biyaoulas, Bessoras, and Etokés.

Contrary to a writer like Mongo Beti, for example, for whom exile did not disrupt the continuity of work produced during his years in France, but rather highlighted the strict focalization of his writing on Africa and Africans in Africa, novelists from the new generation in Paris display a transcontinental perspective, where Africa only appears in the background. In most of the texts, particularly those which relate an experience of immigration, "Europe, as noted by Ambroise Kom, is presented as a given."[54] In the texts evolving around the issue of displacement and of migration as an individual experience, France—and even Europe—becomes the primary dimension. The question once again posed by each author is that of the quality of the experiences with regards to a phenomenon of globalization experienced on a daily basis. The authors also question the consequent pulls the protagonist experiences towards different identities because he/she is simultaneously evolving in a so-called multicultural society and an African "community" attempting to anchor itself in tradition as a mode of resistance.

Beyond this first stage, the novels marked by a certain detachment with regards to Africa, such as *Discopolis* or *Le Nègre Potempkine*, more clearly account for the authors' efforts to break out of the normative frameworks which they judge too constraining and fixed. The act of breaking with the tacit contract of an engaged writing participates predominantly in this undertaking. As novels of a certain disengagement, they challenge the stereotypical—even exoticized—image of immigration as an evident synonym of oppression and alienation, and the image of Africa as the central frame for the narrative fabric. The protagonists must negotiate the changes in their own identity as they face a bicultural environment, regardless of whether they opt for one culture at the expense of the other, or they impart an individual or a collective character to this negotiation.

Certainly, a number of the novels I have classified in the immigration literature rubric display as a common characteristic the precariousness of the protagonists' initial situation and their fragility when faced with the seemingly dichotomous context of their lives: Europe on one side and Africa on the other. We will see later how such an image affects the readership, and inversely, whether the readership influences the production of this image.

The writers can show a progression moving from the precariousness and the uncertainty linked to one's immigrant status to the possibility that migration can bring for the protagonist. In Beyala's work, for example, the female protagonists in particular show immigration as an uplifting and transforming experience.[55] Some of them also illustrate, through their failures, the possible dangers of this experience. Beyond the protagonists' precarious situation, immigration literature also denounces the myth of France as a *"terre d'accueil,"* as well as the system of double exploitation of illegal immigrants by some French people and by some emigrated compatriots, by the French government and by their own country. In parallel, the linguistic game notably used in Beyala's texts plays on the subversion of dichotomous discourse, mixing the discourse of both the Other and the self.

For the writers who place their story in the Parisian landscape, the issue is less that of a dichotomy between nostalgia for Africa and the desire to integrate into French society than that of challenging such a dichotomy for their characters. For some such as Philippe Camara, the Parisian landscape corresponds before all else to the erasing of the African component, where the "Afro" particle completely disappears without being replaced by the "Parisian" one. Inversely, in novels such as those by Biyaoula, the presence of the two components— Parisian (from the *banlieue*, to be more precise) and African—reverts to a new dimension, that of the diaspora, looking for its own individuality, and refuting certain French components, without claiming the African component. In both cases, their writing could not be classified under the rubric of the Parisianist genre. What first emerges is a voice aspiring towards liberty, singularity, and freedom from all labels, a writing primarily about the self, the African self in contrast with a multicultural universe. In the novels by Beyala, Essomba, and Mabanckou, the gaze onto African immigrants taken as an entirety and no longer as individuals but as a community forces us to rethink the definition and the contours of so-called immigration literature.

In this regard, we started off by considering three axes of analysis corresponding to thematic groupings or at least to particular perspectives, what we in other words labeled as (1) a literature of rejection and of disengagement (with Simon Njami's *African Gigolo* or Philippe Camara's *Discopolis* as typical examples); (2) a literature of displacement (illustrated by a novel such as Daniel Biyaoula's *L'impasse*); and finally, (3) a literature of immigration with *Le petit prince de Belleville* or *Assèze l'Africaine* by Calixthe Beyala, Jean-Roger Essomba's *Le paradis du Nord*, Daniel Biyaoula's *Agonies*, or Daniel Mabanckou's *Bleu-Blanc-Rouge* as examples of this last axis.

In the following table, the selected texts are grouped and classified chronologically:

Table 1: by year of publication

Title	Author	Year	Type	Country
Un Regard Noir	Blaise N'djehoya	1984	3	Cameroon
Cercueil et Cie	Simon Njami	1985	1	CH/Cameroon
Comédie classique	Marie NDiaye	1986	1	FR/Senegal
Les enfants de la cité	Simon Njami	1987	1	CH/Cameroon
Le nègre Potemkine	Blaise N'djehoya	1988	2	Cameroon
A la recherche . . .	Yodi Karone	1988	2	Cameroon
Kesso, princesse	Kesso Barry	1988	2	Guinea
African Gigolo	Simon Njami	1989	1	CH/Cameroon
En famille	Marie NDiaye	1990	1	FR/Senegal
petit prince Belleville	Calixthe Beyala	1992	3	Cameroon
Discopolis	Philippe Camara	1993	1	Cameroon
Maman a un amant	Calixthe Beyala	1993	3	Cameroon
Un temps de saison	Marie NDiaye	1994	1	FR/Senegal
Assèze l'Africaine	Calixthe Beyala	1994	3	Cameroon
L'impasse	Daniel Biyaoula	1996	2	Congo
Les honneurs perdus	Calixthe Beyala	1996	3	Cameroon
Le paradis du Nord	J. R. Essomba	1996	3	Cameroon
Bleu-Blanc-Rouge	Alain Mabanckou	1998	3	Congo
Agonies	Daniel Biyaoula	1998	3	Congo
Sorcellerie . . .	Achille Ngoye	1998	3	Rep. Congo
La Polyandre	Bolya Baenga	1998	3	Rep. Congo
Amours sauvages	Calixthe Beyala	1999	3	Cameroon
53cm	Sandrine Bessora	1999	3	FR/CH-Gabon
Amour sans papiers	Nathalie Etoke	1999	3	Cameroon
Yaba Terminus	Achille Ngoye	1999	3	Rep. Congo
Comment cuisiner	Calixthe Beyala	2000	3	Cameroon
Les taches d'encre	Sandrine Bessora	2000	3	FR/CH-Gabon
Préférence nationale	Fatou Diome	2001	3	Senegal

FR for France   CH for Switzerland

Classifying the same texts according to their writer, we get the following table:

Table 2: by writers

Title	Author	Year	Type	Country
Cercueil et Cie	Simon Njami	1985	1	CH/Cameroon
Les enfants de la cité	Simon Njami	1987	1	CH/Cameroon
African Gigolo	Simon Njami	1989	1	CH/Cameroon
Comédie classique	Marie NDiaye	1986	1	FR/Senegal
En famille	Marie NDiaye	1990	1	FR/Senegal
Un temps de saison	Marie NDiaye	1994	1	FR/Senegal
Hilda	Marie NDiaye	2000	1	FR/Senegal
Kesso . . .	Kesso Barry	1988	2	Guinea
A la recherche du cannibale amour	Yodi Karone	1988	2	Cameroon
Discopolis	Philippe Camara	1993	1	Cameroon .
Maman a un amant	Calixthe Beyala	1993	3	Cameroon
Assèze l'Africaine	Calixthe Beyala	1994	3	Cameroon
Les honneurs perdus	Calixthe Beyala	1996	3	Cameroon
Amours sauvages	Calixthe Beyala	1999	3	Cameroon
Comment cuisiner	Calixthe Beyala	2000	3	Cameroon
Le paradis du Nord	J. R. Essomba	1996	3	Cameroon
Yaba Terminus	Achille Ngoye	1999	3	Rep. Congo
Sorcellerie . . .	Achille Ngoye	1998	3	Rep. Congo
Agence Black Bafoussa	Achille Ngoye	1996	3	Rep. Congo
L'impasse	Daniel Biyaoula	1996	2	Congo
Agonies	Daniel Biyaoula	1998	3	Congo
La Polyandre	Bolya	1998	3	Rep. Congo
Bleu Blanc Rouge	Alain Mbanckou	1998	3	Congo
Un amour sans papiers	Nathalie Etoke	1999	3	Cameroon
53 cm	Bessora	1999	3	FR/CH-Gabon
Les taches d'encre	Bessora	2000	3	FR/CH-Gabon
La préférence nationale	Fatou Diome	2001	3	Senegal

Such a table immediately allows us to determine which authors have written more than one novel, which gaze they chose, and when they published. In parallel, several of these writers have published one or more other novels whose gaze remained anchored on Africa, such as Yodi Karone's *Le bal des Caïmans* (1981) and *Villa Beaux Gosses* (1988) or Essomba's *Les lanceurs de foudre* (1995) and *Le dernier gardien du temple* (1998).

A classification according to country of origin yields the following table:

Table 3: by country of origin

Title	Author	Year	Type	Country
Discopolis	Philippe Camara	1993	1	Cameroon
Le nègre Potemkine	Blaise N'djehoya	1988	2	Cameroon
A la recherche. . .	Yodi Karone	1988	2	Cameroon
Un Regard Noir	Blaise N'djehoya	1984	3	Cameroon
Comment cuisiner . . .	Calixthe Beyala	2000	3	Cameroon
Amours sauvages	Calixthe Beyala	1999	3	Cameroon
Assèze l'Africaine	Calixthe Beyala	1994	3	Cameroon
Le petit prince de Belle-ville	Calixthe Beyala	1992	3	Cameroon
Les honneurs perdus	Calixthe Beyala	1996	3	Cameroon
Maman a un amant	Calixthe Beyala	1993	3	Cameroon
Le paradis du Nord	J. R. Essomba	1996	3	Cameroon
Un amour sans papiers	Nathalie Etoke	1999	3	Cameroon
African Gigolo	Simon Njami	1989	1	Cameroon
Cercueil et Cie	Simon Njami	1985	1	Cameroon
Les clandestins	Simon Njami	1989	1	Cameroon
Les taches d'encre	Sandrine Bessora	2000	3	FR/CH-Gabon
53cm	Sandrine Bessora	1999	3	FR/CH-Gabon
Bleu-Blanc-Rouge	Alain Mabanckou	1998	3	Congo
Agonies	Daniel Biyaoula	1998	3	Congo
L'impasse	Daniel Biyaoula	1996	2	Congo
Kesso princesse peuhle	Kesso Barry	1988	2	Guinea
Un rêve utile	Monénembo	1991	3	Guinea
Yaba Terminus	Achille Ngoye	1999	3	Rep. Congo
Sorcellerie à bout portant	Achille Ngoye	1998	3	Rep. Congo
Agence Black Bafoussa	Achille Ngoye	1996	3	Rep. Congo
La Polyandre	Bolya Baenga	1998	3	Rep. Congo

Hilda	Marie NDiaye	2000	1	FR/Senegal
Un temps de saison	Marie NDiaye	1994	1	FR/Senegal
En famille	Marie NDiaye	1990	1	FR/Senegal
Comédie classique	Marie NDiaye	1986	1	FR/Senegal
Gens de sable	Catherine N'Diaye	1984	2	Senegal
La Préférence nationale	Fatou Diome	2001	3	Senegal

These first three tables point to the birth of this literature in the mid-1980s, thus at the same time as *Beur* literature (generated by writers born in France of immigrant Maghrebi parents). Table 2 shows that most authors have published two or more texts, that Calixthe Beyala has the highest level of output, and that the 1990s witnessed an increase in the number of texts and authors (contrary to *Beur* texts which were at their peak in the 1980s, but whose numbers have significantly decreased in the 1990s). Finally, Table 3 shows that these authors are primarily from central Africa: Cameroon, Congo-Brazzaville, and Congo-Kinshasa.

Returning to our three axes of analysis, a table using such a classification yields the following profile.

Table 4: by type of classification

Title	*Author*	*Year*	*Type*
Cercueil et Cie	Simon Njami	1985	1
Comédie classique	Marie NDiaye	1986	1
Les enfants de la cité	Simon Njami	1987	1
African Gigolo	Simon Njami	1989	1
Les clandestins	Simon Njami	1989	1
En famille	Marie NDiaye	1990	1
Discopolis	Philippe Camara	1993	1
Un temps de saison	Marie NDiaye	1994	1
Gens de sable	Catherine N'Diaye	1984	2
Le nègre Potemkine	Blaise N'djehoya	1988	2
Kesso princesse peuhle	Kesso Barry	1988	2
A la recherche . . .	Yodi Karone	1988	2
L'impasse	Daniel Biyaoula	1996	2
Un regard noir	Blaise N'djehoya	1984	3
Un rêve utile	Tierno Monénembo	1991	3
Le petit prince de Belleville	Calixthe Beyala	1992	3
Maman a un amant	Calixthe Beyala	1993	3
Assèze l'Africaine	Calixthe Beyala	1994	3
Les honneurs perdus	Calixthe Beyala	1996	3
Le paradis du Nord	J. R. Essomba	1996	3

Sorcellerie à bout portant	Achille Ngoye	1998	3
Bleu-Blanc-Rouge	Alain Mabanckou	1998	3
La Polyandre	Bolya	1998	3
Agonies	Daniel Biyaoula	1998	3
Yaba Terminus	Achille Ngoye	1999	3
53 cm	Sandrine Bessora	1999	3
Un amour sans papiers	Nathalie Etoke	1999	3
Amours sauvages	Calixthe Beyala	1999	3
Les taches d'encre	Sandrine Bessora	2000	3
Comment cuisiner ...	Calixthe Beyala	2000	3
La préférence nationale	Fatou Diome	2001	3

We can notice the preponderance of so-called immigration novels in the 1990s in particular, while the 1980s display a greater number of disengagement novels, with the novels of uprooting appearing in the smallest number. But a more detailed analysis of the novels shows that a text such as *Cercueil et Cie* or *African Gigolo* characterizes itself precisely with the protagonist's refusal to associate himself with the immigrant African community and thereby with the stereotypical image of the immigrant. They therefore display a dissociation coming in both instances out of a class phenomenon which leads the protagonist to dissociate himself from those like him, even if the initial context—immigration—remains. Both novels show the refusal to take into consideration the process of negotiating one's identity when faced with a bicultural life. The life for which the characters have opted is monocultural and could not in the least be—as asserted and even proudly proclaimed by the protagonists—considered problematic, nor become the receptacle for an eventual identity crisis. Evidently, the narration aims to prove the contrary.

In the second case where the focus remains on an individual and his difficulties in negotiating a new identity in his new space, the issue in question is still that of immigration. The distinction between a novel such as *L'impasse* and *African Gigolo* is that, in the first case, Joseph completely invests himself in his critique of his compatriots on the continent and in Paris, while Moïse denies the existence of a crisis and completely isolates himself (in the beginning), from the transformations and the habits of his countrymen. What especially distinguishes the novels however, is the approach towards focalization, where in the case of the novel of uprooting, the protagonist is taken in his individuality, whereas in the so-called novel of immigration, he is a member of a community, notably, the immigrant African community in Paris/France. Novels such as *Le petit prince de Belleville*, *Le paradis du Nord*, *Agonies*, or *Bleu-Blanc-Rouge* introduce the issues of clandestine immigration, delinquency, incarceration, and marginalization of the characters with regards to French society. All these novels, contrary to novels of rejection, and similarly, though to a lesser extent, to novels of uprooting, discuss a certain class consciousness. Novels of rejection mostly display characters who, as a result of their profession or sense of themselves, feel that they actively belong to French society. These different novels and axes of analysis ultimately reflect a fluctuation around the issue of identification with or dissociation from the concept of immigration.[56] The resistance of characters from *African Gigolo* and *Cercueil et Cie* against identifying with African immigrants becomes the reflection of their perception of the devalorization of non-European immigrants. Furthermore, among immigrants, immigration is first perceived as a static situation rather than a process of transformation, in terms of economic difficulties rather than opportunities for the future.[57] From this viewpoint, the refusal of authors like Njami, Beyala, or Mabanckou to reduce the idea of immigration and immigrants to a single and homogeneous entity allows them, through the diversity of their expression, to subvert the usual and stereotypical profile of the immigrant in the eyes of French society and to prove that these voices constitute something other than "immigration literature."

The analysis of these three axes leads us to reconsider the term and make it more global since novels of rejection as well as those of uprooting constitute a sub-category of this literature. Each author's way of declining immigration, his/her subversions of racial images and stereotyped linguistic expression neutralize the term and revalorize it by pluralizing it. They further proceed to a de-centering of the single concept of "a" literature of immigration, which gave a subtle post-colonial flair to the so-called French-language literature. By extension, these authors force us to think beyond the concept of immigration literatures to consider—no longer in the singular, but in the plural—the terminologies used in today's literary criticism with regards to French and Francophone literature. All at once, by being not only "not novels of immigration," but being "more than that," by going beyond this contour and in so doing, projecting a new light onto the concept of immigration, they are reflective of a new feeling of apprehension towards issues of identity and literary terminology.

In this framework, thematic variations from novel to novel are but inconclusive variants. What is most significant is the direction of the gaze turned not towards the continent, but rather towards France or, even more so, towards the self/towards one's own voice as an auto-reflexive process. The very act of writing within a given cultural space becomes central to the narration, thereby rendering the gaze, the perceptions of this gaze, and its reflections the dynamic motor of the writing. This constant tension among gaze, perception, and identity, between aspirations towards universalism and particularism, forms the very basis—to use Achille Mbembe's expression—of these new "African writings of self." We have notably highlighted the diversity in narrative approaches where the use of an often provocative language is the main strategy in the author's attempts to decenter the French-language African novel as a genre. By manifesting itself as much in the notion of belonging (to Africa) as in that of French-language expression, the decentering of the writing poses the issue of a new post-colonial spirit, specific to the new diaspora in France. This is the issue I propose to study more in depth in the following chapter.

Notes

1. At this point, it is appropriate to distinguish these new voices of the diaspora from those belonging to exile literature. Let us remember, as highlighted by Ambroise Kom, that African literature is often primarily a literature of exile. Jean-Pierre Makouta-Mboukou in his introduction to *Littératures de l'exil: des textes sacrés aux oeuvres profanes* characterizes exile as follows:

> L'exil a toujours été au coeur de la création littéraire, comme il a toujours été une des marques des sociétés humaines. Dès le premier couple humain, dès le premier groupe social, l'homme a connu l'exil. (...) comme si par essence l'homme n'était destiné qu'à être déplacé, déchu du jardin originel, chassé de son pays, de sa maison, coupé de sa culture, de sa civilisation, de sa langue; comme s'il était perpétuellement destiné à être dans les territoires et l'histoire des autres; dans les idéologies étrangères (économique, sociale, financière); dans les humanismes, c'est-à-dire dans les visions du monde des autres ; dans la foi et la spiritualité des autres; pire dans la langue des autres. Comme si en un mot, la vie de l'homme était une permanente *a-culturation*, à défaut d'être une heureuse *acculturation*. (9)

> [Exile has always been at the heart of literary creation, as it has always been a mark of human societies. From the first human couple, from the first social group, man has known exile. (...) As if man were by nature destined to be displaced, expelled from the original garden, thrown out of his country, of his house, cut off from his culture, from his civilization, from his language, as if he were perpetually destined to be in others' territory and history; in foreign ideologies (economic, social, financial; in the humanisms, meaning in the visions of others' world; in others' faith and spirituality; worse, in others' language. As if, simply put, man's life were a permanent a-culturation, for lack of being a happy acculturation.]

Regardless of the type of exile, whether or not it is deemed eternal, the literary motif of nostalgia, of missing the native country, appears to be a constant because, as highlighted by Makouta-Mboukou, "aspiration towards freedom must necessarily imply a return to the native land" (220) ["toute aspiration à la liberté doit nécessairement signifier un retour au pays natal"]. In this framework, the exile's space is in constant conflict with the desired, imagined, and sometimes mythified space, and the difficulty lies in the very evocation of this lost space. In *Literature in Exile* (1990), the Polish author Jan Vladislav notes the impossibility of going back to find the motherland as it was at the time of departure, not only because of the impact of time on the space and culture left behind, but also—and primarily—because of the impact of time on the self. The accuracy or the haziness of memories remains linked to the time factor and by extension to the effort made by the individual to remember. But the difficulty lies in this very point according to Vladislav. Indeed, the question here is not solely about individual memory, but rather about a remembrance which refers to collective memory since personal memory is shaped by the history and culture of the country of origin.

2. I am wary of using the term "canon," in that this term also invokes a certain nomenclature and process of classification. Here we speak of an African novel that essentially deals with Africa and Africans whose primary place of residence is in Africa (whether the novel is written in Africa or France).

3. Since then, and especially in the 1990s, young authors have appeared who started writing very early on: Nathalie Etoké, Bessora, Jean-Luc Raharimanana, Kossi Efoui, to name but a few.

4. The second quote touches on the issue of skin color: "I remembered what a Black friend had answered me one day at school. I was proud to be White. I told him 'How does it feel to be Black?' He looked surprised and a little embarrassed and a little hurt. He almost broke into tears and told me: 'It doesn't feel like anything, Dan, you know that.' "

5. On this topic, on the influence of African-Americans on Africa and the reception of the Black American community in Africa as seen by Africans, see Yekutiel Gerbhoni, *Africans on African-Americans: the Creation of an African-American Myth*. (London: McMillan Press, 1997). Also see Michel Fabre. *La rive noire: De Harlem à Paris*. (Paris: Seuil, 1985).

6. See the following excerpt: "La 'communauté,' cette grande famille hypothétique et abstraite de laquelle on voulait le rendre esclave devait passer et passerait toujours au second plan. Lui était un Camerounais, qui vivait et travaillait en France, avec des Blancs" (67) [The "community," this big hypothetical and abstract family to which people wanted to enslave him had to be—and would always be—second place. He was a Cameroonian who lived and worked in France, with White people]. For commentary on the quotation marks around the term community, see chapter 2 and the deconstruction of the myth of the African community's homogeneity.

7. Abdelkadber Belbahri's sociological analysis, *Immigration et situations post-coloniales. Le cas des Maghrébins en France* (1987) studies the devaluation of post-colonial minorities in detail. In particular, it points out that because of their visibility, Maghrebi immigrants are collectively mistreated and that they therefore attempt to single themselves out and to stand apart from the label applied to them.

8. Her first name is itself a commentary and a premonition of the couple's breakup. We must nevertheless note that even though Fate is a Westerner, she is—even more so than Yegba—a foreigner in Paris.

9. About interracial couple dynamics, also see *Les couples dominos* (1973) by Thérèse Kuoh-Moukouri. On White women, see Mineke Schipper de Leeuw, in *Un Blanc vu d'Afrique* (1973) as well as *Le roman Cameroonais* (1989) by Claire Dehon.

10. On the theme of interracial couples, also see *Amours sauvages* (1999) by Calixthe Beyala. We will return to it further on in this chapter.

11. For a study of interracial couples in the French-language African novel, see Odile Cazenave, *Femmes rebelles: naissance d'un nouveau roman African au feminine* (Paris: L'Harmattan, 1996), 33-63. Mariama Bâ notably shows how this discourse is the result of ratiocinations, the refusal to confront the true reasons for the misunderstandings and the tensions faced by the couple.

12. This is not exclusive to writers from the diaspora. One need only think about Mongo Beti's last two novels, *Trop de soleil tue l'amour* (1999) and *Branle-bas en noir et blanc* (2000). The police mystery genre has the advantage that because of the genre's [playful] form, it allows for the unexpected depiction of a society (French society, but also of the African community in France or on the continent).

13. This exploitation of the readers' sexual fantasies is to be extended, on a second level, to the writer, who in so doing, attracts the larger public, and no longer a restricted readership which would only be interested in Africa. This remark is also valid for other Francophone writers from the diaspora, for example the Haitian Danny Laferrière who experienced resounding success in Canada at around the same time that this novel with an equally enticing title *Comment faire l'amour avec un Nègre sans se fatiguer* (1985) (which was later converted to a screenplay). Laferrière is as a matter of fact currently experiencing similar success in France, where the French public recently discovered him.

14. See page 49, "De tout ce que j'avais fait et dit, une chose était pourtant vraie: JE NE VOULAIS PAS TRAVAILLER DANS L'IMMÉDIAT" [Of all the things I had said and done, one thing *was* true: I DID NOT WANT TO WORK RIGHT THEN].

15. Notably, his supposed studies, which he uses as a justification for his absence, when in fact he left the academic track almost as soon as he got to Paris.

16. A question that he asks Sekou, an acquaintance, during an African party in honor of Etienne's departure for Cameroon and his appointment as the minister of culture.

17. In *Ici, s'achève le voyage* by Baker, Maleka's character relates this same point, notably the need to be in touch with one's origins through a sexual relationship (even if Maleka is ironic about this aspect): "J'ai l'intention de te réclamer ma part d'Afrique. Elle disait 'Nègre,' la négresse. J'ai ouvert les yeux, elle était debout presque entre mes jambes et me tendait ses bras de négresse qui réclame sa part d'Afrique" (80) [I intend on claiming my share of Africa from you. She would say "Negro," this Negress. I opened my eyes, and she was almost standing between my legs, holding out her arms of a Negress claiming her part of Africa].

18. Ousmane Sembène's novels are evidently an exception and single themselves out in this regard in that Sembène was one of the writers (later a filmmaker) who attracted the audience's attention to the challenges faced by African immigrants.

19. It must further be acknowledged that France had a responsibility towards its former colonies, and that the country was also in need of a cheaper workforce.

20. Aminata Sow Fall's last novel, *Douceur du bercail* (1998), which deals with the "charters of shame" and the numerous bureaucratic hassles endured by immigrants both legal and illegal, as well as by Africans in transit, shows that the novel from the continent is also beginning to turn its gaze in this direction.

21. This phenomenon of the importance of dress and physical appearance (including skin bleaching) is also visible in *G'amàrakano, au carrefour* (1983) by the Gabonese novelist Angèle Rawiri.

22. On this topic, see Mireille Rosello and her analysis *Infiltrating Culture: Power and Identity in Contemporary Women's Writing* (New York: Mancester Press/St. Martin's Press, 1996).

23. The issue is broached several times during his stay at home, notably with his sister. What she offers as a justification is that men prefer women with lighter skin, which thus pushes them to these measures: "Parce qu'ils aiment que les femmes soient claires de peau et qu'elles aient des cheveux lisses, les hommes! Je ne sais pas ce que ça leur fait, mais vrai, ils nous trouvent plus belles comme ça! Il n'y a qu'à voir dans les films. Les femmes noires qu'il y a dedans, soit elles sont très claires, soit elles ont des cheveux comme les Blanches, et souvent les deux! Alors que les hommes eux, ils sont comme à leur naissance. Et dans les magazines, c'est la même chose! C'est qu'on nous dit qu'on doit être comme ça" (85) [Because they like for women to be light-skinned and have straight hair, men! I don't know what it does for them, but it's true, they find us more beautiful like that. Just look at movies. The Black women in there are either really light-skinned, or they have hair like White women, or often they have both! But the guys are as they were at birth. And in magazines, it's the same thing! The thing is that we're always told to be like that].

24. See Lionnet and her analysis of the literary tradition of suffering ("Mortification and the Myth of Reformation and Rebirth").

25. We find an equally oblique critique of this paternalistic aspect in *Sorcellerie à bout portant* (1998) by Achille Ngoye. It is the case of an Englishman living in an African country and "re-educating" the protagonist who has just returned about the general rules of conduct in the country, such as the little tricks and strings that can be pulled in the D system. The same element also reappears but from a slightly different angle in the film Clando (1996) by the Cameroonian Jean-Marie Teno. There, a young German woman in an interracial relationship pushes the lead character to action. In her capacity as a member of an international aid association, she criticizes the passivity of her friend's compatriots, exhorting him to action, even if that implies revolt and revolution. Indirectly, the filmmaker casts a partly amused, partly critical glance on this type of intervention which, although full of good intentions, nonetheless consists in "teaching" the Other on the unfounded basis of knowing better.

26. Even though the theme of insanity as a result of the inability to choose an identity appears as a frequent theme in the African novel, the madness of male characters is rarely described on a psychosomatic level where the man's body is affected and is subjected to a spectacular transformation. Mostly female characters had been the object of this type of perspective until now. We may notably think of Ken in *Le baobab fou* by Ken Bugul, of Juletane in *Juletane* by Myriam Warner-Vieyra, and of Emilienne in *Fureurs et cris de femme* by Angèle Rawiri. In the case of male characters, greater emphasis was placed on psychological transformation rather than on physical transformations, as in the case of *L'aventure ambiguë*.

27. In the chapter entitled "Of Mimicry and Man" (85-92), Bhabha notably explains the danger in attempting to look like the Other, which leads to a fetishization of colonial culture. He indeed remarks: "From such a colonial encounter between the white presence and its black semblance, there emerges the question of the ambivalence of mimicry as a problematic of colonial subjection. (...) The ambivalence of mimicry—almost but not quite—suggests that the fetishized colonial culture is potentially and strategically an insurgent counter-appeal" (90-91).

28. Paper presented during the third International Colloquium of the Association of Francophone Studies of Central-Eastern Europe (Association des Etudes Francophones d'Europe Centrale-Orientale—AEFECO), Leipzig, Germany, March 30-April 4, 1998.

29. See Ibrahim K. Sundiata's "Africanity, Identity and Culture" in *Issue: A Journal of Opinion, African [Diaspora] Studies* XXI, no. 2 (1996): 13-17.

30. In this regard, Lionnet's analysis on the phenomenon of acculturation in Warner-Vieyra's *Juletane* and in *L'Autre qui danse* by Suzanne Dracius-Pinalie proves completely pertinent. In particular she asserts: "Self-castigated by [his] 'de-culturation' and what [he] perceives to be a lack of authenticity, each [man] is in turn overwhelmed by a death wish" (90).

31. *Ici, s'achève le voyage* introduces the notion of a fictional community, one invented and created by the individual for himself: "En fréquentant quelques discothèques, j'avais réussi à me faire des amis.... Je m'étais créé une nouvelle famille. Une nouvelle tribu. Et malgré cela, je dois dire que cette ville est sans doute l'unique qui soit faite d'une multitude de solitudes" (55) [By going to a few nightclubs, I had been able to make friends... I had created a new family for myself. A new tribe. And in spite of that, I must say that this city is undoubtedly the only one made up of a multitude of solitudes].

32. We should also mention *Kesso, princesse peuhle* (1988) by Kesso Barry, which emphasized the difficulty of living between two cultures, two worlds, particularly when one of the girls, born in France, completely associates herself with this world, Africa remaining for her a tourist destination.

33. For a detailed development of this point, see *Rebellious Women: the New Generation of Female African Novelists* (Boulder, CO: Lynne Rienner Publishers, 2000).

34 *La petite fille du réverbère*, a more or less autobiographical remembrance of childhood, is a return towards Africa and the past. However, *Amours sauvages* (1999) once again deals with Paris and Belleville, as does *Comment cuisiner son mari à l'africaine* (2000).

35. This theme is developed in depth in Maghrebi immigrant writing. For a theoretical exploration of these aspects, see Azouz Begag and Abdellatif Chaouite's essay, *Ecarts d'identité* (1991).

36 Cf. Odile Cazenave, "Calixthe Beyala: l'exemple d'une écriture décentrée dans le roman africain au féminin," in *L'Ecriture décentrée*, ed. Michel Laronde, 123-147 (Paris, L'Harmattan, 1996).

37. The different attitude between men and women with regards to the experience of migration is linked to the distinctions between exile and diasporic literature. The protagonists live in Paris or elsewhere in France because they have chosen to do so. Nonetheless the feeling of displacement, of landlessness, the ideology, the culture, and the language of the other appear as a central concern in most of the studied works. The protagonist's space is one which, like the exiled individual, is marked by wandering, or at the very least by loneliness and an indefinable lack doubled by the feeling of not belonging to the new environment. Indeed nomadism and identitary wandering are also the characteristics par excellence of the postcolonial subject today. In this regard, it is important to establish a distinction between male and female characters and between male and female writing. Indeed, male characters in the works of both male and female writers express intense feelings of nostalgia, the need to turn back to the past and the place they left behind. Female characters—which are either absent or relegated to the background in the works of male writers—occupy the foreground in female writers' texts, and first of all place an emphasis on their situation of being in limbo between two cultures, as in the case of Sorraya in *Assèze l'Africaine*: "En France, j'appartiens encore à une minorité. Jamais je ne serai considérée comme une Blanche. Je n'appartiens à rien. Une hybride! Un nonsens!" (339) [In France, I still belong to a minority. I will never be looked upon as a White woman. I don't belong to anything. A hybrid! A nonsense!]. Nonetheless, this phase is only transitory. The novel by female writers, in particular through the work of Beyala, more distinctly highlights the desire of female characters to move forward, to BECOME, and to consider immigration according to the possibilities it offers them (as women) for individual accomplishment. In all of these texts—*Le petit prince de Belleville*, *Maman a un amant*, *Assèze l'Africaine*, and *Les honneurs perdus*—the emphasis is placed on the transformation of gender roles in the African community in Paris. Male writers, such as Njami or Biyaoula, place a greater emphasis on an individual *malaise* which grows until it erupts into an identity crisis, showing that stability was but a front, a conscious blindness by which the male characters attempted to eradicate all feelings of lack, any aspirations towards their native country, looking to quiet all emotional manifestations of exile. The extreme case of this undertaking consists in conceding all feelings of nostalgia—silence.

38. For an analysis of the self and the doubling in Assèze, see Kenneth Harrow's work in *Less than One and Double*, chapter 5 (Portsmouth, NH: Heinemann, 2002), 157-246.

39. The previous paragraph refers to my analysis of the novel in *Rebellious Women*.

40. Ambroise Kom, "Une littérature plurivoque."

41. See the following excerpt: "Une succession. C'est ça. Une succession de points d'interrogation. Où doit-on aller? Demain? Quoi? Comment?. . . Nous allons tous devenir schizophrènes, à force" (*Honneurs perdus* 390) [A succession. That's it. A succession of question marks. Where must we go? Tomorrow? What? How? ... It will make us all become schizophrenic].

42. Mireille Rosello, *Declining the Stereotype: Ethnicity and Representation in French Cultures* (Hannover, NH: University Press of New England, 1998). She particularly emphasizes the use of fake articulations: "the text cheats by inserting fake articulations between so-called facts and their stereotypical explanations" (136); and the substitution of the surprise effect to the usual one of repetition: "the memorability of repetition is in competition with the effect of surprise" (137). Through these various strategies, the a-grammaticality is made visible as a reference point and as a sign of the subversion of stereotypes. Also see her article, "Il faut comprendre quand on peut... l'art de désamorcer les stéréotypes chez Emile Ajar et Calixthe Beyala," where Rosello offers an excellent analysis of the phenomenon of decentering and language through the shattering and the counterfeiting of known stereotypes that are transformed to give birth to a new language.

43. Besides the shattering of idiomatic expressions and stereotypes, one should also add the use of erotic scenes and crude, vulgar language. It is not that the African novel has been completely quiet on this topic; it must however be recalled that a certain reserve with regards to sexual representations was visible in novels from the 1960s to the 1980s. The novels from the diaspora give more space to this aspect. We may notably cite Calixthe Beyala for her exploration of a new sexual ethic as the basis for new relationships between individuals and the possibility of a new society. Sexual representations are consequently an integral part of her texts. We may also cite *African Gigolo* and *Discopolis* which differentiate themselves by the directness of thoughts imparted on characters and the rawness of the language; finally, we may cite *Place des fêtes* (2001) by Sami Tchak, where sexuality moves to the forefront to play a detonating role: to disturb, point to, make one think of...

44. In this sense, *Amours sauvages* (1999) serves as a counterpoint and constitutes a step forward. Through her journey, the protagonist, Eve-Marie, delves us once again into the daily life of Belleville; the manner in which Eve-Marie provides for her needs, from being a prostitute to opening a restaurant to the relationship between neighbors; her friendship with her neighbor Flora-Flore; what comes of her ordeal with her battering husband Jean-Pierre; Eve-Marie's wedding to Pléthore, a dreamy poet who cheats on her for a while with her neighbor;

the corpse of a woman that they discover one morning on the doorstep and the rumors about the woman as well as speculations on the identity of the murderer, etc. All of this contributes to the establishment of a very colorful portrait revealing Eve-Marie's dreams of leaving the continent, the goals she had at the time of her arrival from Africa (a job and a husband "white as snow"), her disappointments, but also her way of facing reality once the myth of France as the land of candy and *foie gras* and of Paris, the city of lights is shattered. Through the evolution of the interracial couple and of the friendship between Eve-Marie and Flora-Flore, her friendship with Océan, who earns his living as a transvestite, and the writing of the community by Eve-Marie, *Amours sauvages* helps us to grasp the often difficult stages of the integration of an African woman—and African immigrants as a whole—into French society and the limits of this integration. In so doing, the author continues her ironic critique of a French society which believes in its model of integration when, as pointed out by Océan, Whites make as many grammar and syntax mistakes, "et ils veulent qu'on s'intègre comme si eux-mêmes étaient des modèles d'intégration à leur propre culture" (131) [and they want us to integrate ourselves as if they themselves were models of integration into their own culture]. Here Beyala scrutinizes the gazes and perceptions between the two groups, forcing us to think about what defines the process of identity negotiation for one who—collectively or individually—evolves in the milieu of Belleville.

45. On the importance of belonging to the same group and the consequences thereof, see *Beto na Beto, le poids de la tribu* (2001) by Aimée Gnali.

46. Furthermore, through the harshness of the critical glance it casts on the immigrant community, such a novel brings up the question of the readership and its reception of the text. We will examine these issues in greater detail in chapter 3, which is devoted to the notion of the addressee.

47. The same technique is visible in his following novel, *Pelourinho* (1995). Each of his texts adopts a certain style appropriate to the topic, which allows him to create a certain atmosphere, whether it is that of immigration or of urban life in Brazil. In fact, it is only in *Cinéma* (1997) and in *L'aîné des orphelins* (2000) that he establishes a story with a substantial narrative thread and characters with room for growth. Until then, his texts all dealt with the issue of exile, of the status of emigrant, of the loneliness of new places, without however ever dealing with his own exile.

48. Since then, he has written four more novels: *Et Dieu seul sait comment je dors* (2001), *Les petits fils-nègres de Vercingetorix* (2002), *African Psycho* (2003) and *Verre cassé* (2005).

49. Paper presented at the Congrès International des Etudes Francophones [International Congress for Francophone Studies], Sousse, Tunisie, June 2000.

50. Kom, Ambroise, "There is no happy return," (paper presented at the International Congress for Francophone Studies, Lafayette, Louisiana, May 1999).

51. See *Sorcellerie à bout portant*: "Le retour, aussi précipité que l'aller, lui laissait un arrière-goût d'échec. D'autant que les rêves formulés, les rêves de

changement, avaient fondu dans un ordre mondial truqué" (Ngoye 14) [His return, as rushed as his departure, left him an aftertaste of failure. Just as the dreams he had expressed, the dreams of change, had melted into a rigged world order].

52. Francis' brutal death a few weeks earlier gives her an example to which to refer: officially known as a student, he was in fact at the head of a drug trafficking network in the area, and was a supplier for youth in the projects and on university campuses.

53. See the character of Yegba the journalist in *Cercueil et Cie* and the character of Moïse in *African Gigolo*.

54. "In Beyala's work," Kom continues, "les Traoré sont installés à Belleville et n'envisagent nullement l'éventualité d'un retour au pays. Il en va pareillement dans *L'impasse* où l'Afrique est évoquée simplement pace que Joseph Gakatuka qui vit en France et travaille comme O.S. dans une fabrique de pneumatiques, retourne pour quelques semaines de vacances dans son Congo natal" (2) [the Traorés are settled in Belleville and do not envision the possibility of returning to their native country. Similarly, in *L'impasse*, Africa is only evoked because Joseph Gakatuka, who lives in France and works in a tire factory, returns to his native Congo for a few weeks' vacation]. Kom's remark reinforces my analysis of the issue of non-return, or at least that of the absence of nostalgia for their native land on the part of the protagonists. Their progression also marks the problematic of the future of their identity without ever falling into the dichotomy of integration or assimilation. Even though these different authors inscribe their story in the Parisian landscape, they do not therefore belong to the Parisianist genre as defined by Jules-Rosette. Inversely, their representation of Paris subverts the capital's usual literarity.

55. Inversely, *La préférence nationale* by Fatou Diome, an anthology of six autonomous yet related short stories, places the emphasis on female immigration and the negative forces and prejudices associated with immigration in the case of a young woman. "Le visage de l'emploi" demonstrates how the French employer makes certain assumptions, both in private and public situations, about a young African woman. From the exaggerated simplification of language (return to "*petit nègre*" speak) to *tutoiement*, to the lack of respect and the type of work granted or kept from the narrator, Diome details the daily manifestations of racism for the visible foreigner, whether male or female.

56. The following article is drawn from an article I wrote for a study on the literature of immigration in France. See Cazenave, "Writing New Identities: the African Diaspora in France," in *Immigrant Narratives in Contemporary France*, eds. Susan Ireland and Patrice Proulx (Westport, CT: Greenwood Press, 2001), 153-163.

57. Fatou Diome's different short stories highlight the difficulties in being accepted and considered in an equal capacity, but also in being understood. "The teacher" is thereby reminiscent of the diverse degrees of racism in its banal and

insidious aspects, including in an interracial relationship where the idea of the Black woman as an erotic object is revisited.

Chapter 2

Language and Identities: When "I" Stops Being "the Other"

Neither "we" nor "they" are as self-contained and homogeneous as we/they once appeared. All of us inhabit an interdependent late 20th century world, which is at once marked by borrowing and lending across porous cultural boundaries, and saturated with inequality, power, and domination.

(Renato Rosaldo, "Ideology, Place and People without Culture," 87)

As we saw in chapter 1, the African writers in Paris direct their gaze away from the continent, generally choosing Paris or France as a point of origin, and thus beholding the African continent and its inhabitants both in an external and a familiar manner. Their novels, consequently, diverge from the post-colonial African novel.

The issue of language and identities is central to Francophone literature as a whole and to the African novel in particular. Indeed, the writer must express—through a language other than his/her own—cultural aspects and philosophical or religious concepts, which do not necessarily exist in the French culture and language. The resulting linguistic tension and the presence of both an African and a French readership contributed to creating an "identity dilemma" in the "*romans de formation*" between the 1960s and the 1980s. This interrelation between language and identities moves to the forefront in the new writings of self.

This section will focus on the following three aspects: (1) The development of a combination of discourses, which are festered in the deconstruction of the dominant discourse: the discourse of the Other, where the Other becomes Me and Me becomes the Other; the discourse of Africans in France about those in Africa and vice-versa; the discourse of French people on Africans and the reverse. (2) The deconstruction of the myth of the African community's homogeneity and the exploration of fragmentations of identity with respect to space and time. Finally, (3) a re-conceptualization of the notion of literature where French has been seen as central and Francophone as peripheral.

Deconstructions of the Dominant Discourse

The Hybridity of Language: From Identity to Cultural Duality

A detailed analysis of language in Beyala's work reveals certain shifts occurring in all her "Parisian" novels. The multiplicity of voices, the existence of communities with multiple faces, and new environments, the redefinition of gender roles and of the notion of power, and finally the subversion of the usual Parisian landscape are all signs of the author's consciousness of a certain mix of cultures, indicative of the globalization affecting immigrant African communities. We generally speak of a globalization in terms of environments, but this notion can also be extended to characters. Indeed, in the transformations in her ways of dressing, speaking, and behaving upon her arrival in Paris, Saïda Benarafa draws more from an immigrant Maghrebi woman than a Cameroonian woman.[1] She bakes Arab pastries for Loulouze, gives her a rosewater-scented bath, and even says: "I, the Arab." During a debate on female African writers in which the author participated,[2] Beyala told the story of how *Les honneurs perdus* was inspired by real facts. Apparently, one day while she was still living in Belleville, a Maghrebi woman knocked on her door and offered her services in exchange for food and shelter. The two women reached an agreement and the newcomer shared the life of the author's family for several years, eventually becoming a good friend. A natural shift in the writing therefore occurred here, as a result of the cohesion of the character from which she drew her inspiration, a Maghrebi woman who came into contact with the original character, a Muslim Cameroonian woman.[3]

With the same freedom, Calixthe Beyala plays with the French language, Africanizing it as she pleases. In her analysis of Beyala's writing,[4] Rangira Béatrice Gallimore draws attention to several African expressions inserted into the text, as well as a number of neologisms and literal translations of African languages into French (Gallimore gives the example of the expression "to put reason into this child's head" (*Tu t'appelleras Tanga* [TTT] 143) to mean "to bring this child back to reason"). She has written on this subject:

> Dans ce monde où "on consomme au feu de bois et à la cadence du pilon » (*Assèze* 68), on parle le "poulassie" c'est-à-dire un français dont les sons sont "embrochés, pimentés et bâtonmanioqués" (*Assèze* 93) que l'auteur a "mis à la page au son du tam-tam, aux ricanements du balafon, aux cris des griots" (*Assèze* 93). (Gallimore 181)

> [In this world where "you eat by the side of a wood fire and to the beat of a pestle" (*Assèze* 68), you speak "Poulassie," or in other words, a French whose sounds were "kebabed, spiced, and *batonmanioqués*" (*Assèze* 93) and which the

author "brought into fashion to the sound of drums, the cackles of the balafon, and the cries of *griots.*"]

To her, such writing defines and classifies Beyala as a "true Francophone writer" (Gallimore 181). What defines her as such is the use she makes of the French language, indeed a tool for communication, and as such, a "tool she can—and knows how to—manipulate at her will in order to produce a violated, abused, demystified, and de-mythified language" (181). I would add that, rather than being purely Africanized, Beyala's language is culturally mixed, the reflection of daily experiences of multiculturalism. Indeed, in addition to being de-mythified, her language is also amalgamated, containing African expressions, but it also contains Gallicizations of some of these expressions, which she has decontextualized and occasionally anachronized.

By Gallicization, I mean a writing process that subverts certain French stereotypes and manipulates the French language in a certain way—which would a priori lead one to think of an "Africanization of French." Instead, it incorporates in parallel a network of terms, images, and representations given as truly African and meant to contribute to creating a convincing Cameroonian atmosphere. At least, it appears as such for a French reader, but will be recognized by the Cameroonian reader as a conglomerate of expressions and images, some of which belong to his/her cultural and linguistic network, while others suggest a different cultural and linguistic universe (African or French/Western).

La petite fille du réverbère (1998) illustrates this process of *métissage* of the images and the language. For example, the occasionally unconvincing pseudo-childish language (adult language and thoughts passing for those of a child) and the dreams of the protagonist "Tapoussière," then still a child, suggest a generic universe. The language used by the protagonist notably suggests a semantico-cultural decentering: we thereby end up with a child who dreams about the "*breuvages de Circé,*" which evokes a non-African universe. Beyala simultaneously juxtaposes what are falsely characterized as "Cameroonisms" with genuine expressions from Cameroon. While "je la *doigtai*" (84) and "une *pantaculotte* rouge" (138) are part of the daily language, "mes compatriotes *siestaient* dans leurs joies perverses" (78), "ils se *discutaillaient* la place sur le trottoir" (87), "sans *attentionner* au train" (105) are not common expressions, but rather imaginative expressions created by Beyala. Furthermore, an expression like "cela *déconfiance* la clientèle" (84) belongs to Zairian, not Cameroonian, vocabulary.

These observations are in no way attempts to question the talent of Beyala, a writer who, to the contrary, has always known how to handle the French language wittily in order to give it her own particular flair. Indeed, undeniable creativity is involved in Beyala's "*batonmanioqués*" words. She has also dared to work on the French language further than any other writer, particularly than other female writers.[5] Nonetheless, I would like to draw attention to a certain "Africanization" of the language taking place as a result of hybrid and multiple fabrications whose objective is to give the reader the impression that he/she is witnessing the depiction of a real and realistic Africa, in this case spatially and temporally identified as Cameroon/Calixthe Beyala's New-Bell.

However, the juxtaposition of fact and imagination creates a different effect depending on the readership. For a Cameroonian reader, the depicted universe and characters will have an artificial air in that he/she will not recognize him/herself (beyond issues of differences in social status and milieu). A French reader, however, will ascribe to such a representation without in any way contesting it, and without understanding the various nuances of irony, ambiguity, and decentering the representation contains and implies.

Ultimately, although the geographic displacement factor proves to be important in the transformation of female characters in the works of female African writers, the place of writing/the author's implantation is just as significant. On the level of creation, the space factor contributes to a writing which does not lean towards universalism but is instead reflective of the referents (or the haziness and *lack* of referents) of the current globalization and the forced redefinition of geographic and cultural frontiers. Subsequently, it implies the redefinition of the frontiers of African literary creation. For a writer like Beyala, the space factor reveals the influence of the readership's profile on the direction and the content of her writing. Open to daily manifestations of multiculturalism, she has created a new, literally Afro-Parisian, novel dealing with the intersection of issues of immigration with those of gender, identity, and space.[6] In her case, Bennetta Jules-Rosette's notion of Parisianism is exactly appropriate in that the integration of the Parisian—more specifically Bellevillean—landscape is an intrinsic part of her characters' integration. Furthermore, her writing displays a *métissage* of the French language occurring in both directions with an Africanization of French, but also the Gallicization of the author's writing through her use of new stereotypes or already existent ethnic or linguistic expressions.[7] Furthermore, her integration of expressions borrowed from other African languages—which do not sound right to Cameroonian readers from the continent because of their different origins—in addition to Cameroonisms allows her to work the French language in depth, leading to its Africanization and even pan-Africanization in the spirit of globalization. The paradox comes from the fact that a novice French reader may not really perceive this innovative aspect. His or her attraction to Beyala's writing may be drawn from its exotic dimension, while the author's work may have an artificial flair for Cameroonian readers because Beyala does not Cameroonize the French language (in the way that Kourouma Malinkizes it). Ultimately, Beyala's approach to writing shows that she is revolutionizing language, even though her efforts are largely not understood and in some ways even co-opted.[8] Through her undertakings, the author also points to the specificities of what is no longer simply the African novel, but rather the novel of immigration and which, to use Winnifred Woodhull's words in her analysis "Ethnicity on the French Frontier," "dislocates fixed identities not only of race, ethnicity and nationality, but also of gender, sexuality, class and language" (31).[9] The social and cultural hybridity characteristic of the author's characters extends in a cohesive manner to spoken and written language.

Neo-exoticism: Redefinition of Discourse

The following section revisits some elements from my article "Calixthe Beyala: l'exemple d'une écriture décentrée dans le roman africain au féminin."[10] I will use as a starting point for the discussion *Le petit prince de Belleville*, to which I will then add *Les honneurs perdus*. I will start with Michel Laronde's denomination and definition in *Autour du roman Beur* (1993):

> Tout comme le néo-orientalisme est une inversion moderne de l'orientalisme "classique" en ce que le discours néo-orientaliste sur l'Orient (donc, par translation, sur l'Etranger) est tenu par l'Oriental (l'Etranger) en position interne à l'Occident, le néo-exotisme est un faisceau de pratiques qui appartiennent au monde oriental (donc, étrangères au monde occidental) mais sont le fait de l'Oriental en position interne au Monde occidental.
>
> Dans les deux cas, on voit que quelque chose ne change pas: c'est la place de l'Occident comme base référentielle du discours, ce que confirme le maintien de l'Oriental dans la position d'Etranger par rapport au discours oriental. Or ce maintien est voulu par l'Etranger lui-même. En effet, pour déconstruire le discours occidental établi (le discours orientaliste), l'Etranger doit préserver sa qualité d'Etranger mais passer d'une position externe à une position interne au discours occidental, et en prendre possession par usurpation (comme on le ferait d'un pouvoir).
>
> Dans les deux cas, ce qui est *nouveau*, c'est ceci: d'une part, l'Etranger est à la fois sujet et objet du discours; d'autre part le nouveau discours (le néo-orientalisme) et les nouvelles pratiques (le néo-exotisme) sont produits à partir d'une situation géo-culturelle endogène au monde occidental dans l'intention de débouter le discours référentiel et non de s'en démarquer. (213)

> [Just as neo-orientalism is a modern inversion of "classical" orientalism in that neo-orientalist discourse on the Orient (and thus by translation, on Foreign areas) comes from the Oriental (the Foreigner) in a position internal to the West, neo-exoticism is a set of practices belonging to the Oriental world (and thus foreign to the Western world), but resulting from the Oriental individual's internal position with regards to the Western world.
>
> In both cases, we notice that one thing does not change: that is the place of the West as the reference base for discourse, confirming the continuance of the Oriental individual in the position of Foreigner with regards to Oriental discourse. But the perpetuation of this situation is wanted by the Foreigner himself. Indeed, to deconstruct the established Western discourse (the Orientalist discourse), the Foreigner must preserve his identity as a Foreigner but move from an external position to an internal one with regards to Western discourse, and take possession of it by usurpation (as one would do with power).
>
> In both cases, what is *new* is the fact that on the one hand the Foreigner is at once subject and object of the discourse as well as the creator and receiver of practices denoting this discourse, while on the other hand the new discourse (neo-orientalism) and the new practices (neo-exoticism) are created from a geo-cultural situation endogenous to a Western world and that they attempt to reinforce the referential discourse rather than distancing themselves from it.]

Laronde notes that on an aesthetic level this practice is manifested by the junction of the dialectic with the viewpoint (the gaze): ". . . c'est le discours (le Regard) de l'Autre qui commande la vision: dans une inversion de la perspective, l'Autre (l'Africain) devient le Moi énonciateur face au Moi (l'Occidental) qui devient l'Autre, récepteur du discours. Dans le domaine psychique, la démarche consiste à réaffirmer une Différence qui signifie dans le champ identitaire" (213) [. . . it is the discourse (the Gaze) of the Other that guides vision: in an inversion of perspectives, the Other (the African) becomes the enunciating Me (the Westerner) who now becomes the Other, receiver of the discourse. On the psychological front, this process leads to a reassertion of a Difference in the area of identity].

I previously showed (see cited article) that the writing of *Le petit prince* and of *Maman a un amant* is reminiscent, through certain parallels, of what was said above regarding the Beur novel. Both novels are constructed on this very tension between the doubling of both the narrator (adult voice/child voice) and the designated audience, where the distinctions between Foreigner and Other are broken up, inverted, and reinstated through the enunciation of the Me (where Me, Foreigner, loses its foreignness in the face of the receiver who becomes Other). Me, Foreigner, explains itself, defends itself, allows itself to be known and decoded.[11] Contrarily, the child-like narrative voice takes on the value of a pole of recognition in that it denotes strangeness as perceived in the midst of its community, rather than in the French milieu within which it evolves (essentially that of school and the street). The first-generation Foreigner wishes to erase the strangeness through which he/she is characterized in the eyes of the Other. For the second generation personified by Loukoum's voice, the desire is instead to once again evoke the characteristics of strangeness in his community. The narrative voice's intentions differ from those of the Beur novel, where the second generation attempts to "réaccentuer *certains* caractères pris à la société d'origine des parents qui sont atypiques de la société dominante, dans un effort de désolidarisation (désajustement) et une intention de réinscrire une différence spécifique par rapport à cette société dominante" (Laronde, 214) [re-accent *some* characteristics taken from the parents' original society and which are atypical of the dominant society in an effort of de-solidarization (de-adjustment) and an attempt to reinstate a specific difference with regards to this dominant society]. Transcriptions on the writing front are nonetheless similar, considering that the enunciation creates a series of images aimed to highlight the particularities of the African community and some of which are clichés of the African self. Western Africanist discourse is revisited, this time to find its origins in the discourse of the child Foreigner. The strangeness is dispelled, taken, and re-appropriated in the areas of marital life, of the community's traditions, of children's education, or simply of culinary habits. The cultural practices described by Loukoum as something particularly *eccentric* and *external*, are nonetheless *familiar* and *internal*. Laronde notes, still in the case of Beur literature, that this is a *fragmentary* form of neo-exoticism.[12] The expression is appropriate because the narration is inherently impacted by temporality: as a child in his phase of education in a Western environment, he experiences it all in a mode different from that of his parents. For him, the external becomes the familiar and the internal, that which appears eccentric. Nonetheless, the adoption of what he can and cannot do from the male perspective precisely suggests that this moment is temporary and that he will later adopt his father's enunciating discourse. His propensity to use a collective "us" furthermore indicates his desire to associate himself with the group: in the present case, the individual "I" is effaced behind the community "we." In the long term, his perspective is thus inverted and the *internal* must once again become *familiar*. M'am's sacrifice and her forced return to her conjugal home at the end of *Maman a un amant* backs up this interpretation: Loukoum's observation shows his adherence to the principles of African community living and consequently testifies to the completeness of his identity. Nevertheless, Loukoum has access to his roots and is able to maintain contact with traditional Africa through the reminiscences of Abdou, playing the role of an African griot, and the upholding of traditions by the Belleville community. If Abdou, M'am, and the others no longer evoked the continent, and if Loukoum stopped listening to their evocations, then the completeness of his identity would shatter and the child would then lock himself in the *familiar* and the *internal*.

This issue of the familiar, of the internal, of what needs to be decoded, of what the better informed must decode for the novice, evolves and fluctuates in the micro-text (*Le petit prince de Belleville*, *Maman a un amant*) as well as in the macro-text (Beyala's "Parisian" novels) to the point of making the borders between the familiar and the unknown hazy, since both these axes may be of concern to both the narrator and the addressee, the reader. This confusion seems more evident in *Les honneurs perdus* both in the first part, which takes place in Cameroon, and in the second part in Paris.

Even though it is defined spatially (Cameroon, Douala, New-Bell) and temporally (the 1950s-1960s), the Africa of the first part does not appear any less unreal, any less a part of a paper-mâché décor. Certain scenes and descriptions of the relationships between people appear anachronistic with regards to the time in which they are portrayed. Finally and especially, "l'Afrique-crasse" [grimy-Africa] (evoked by the publishing house Albin Michel on the book cover) comes up as the usual, almost clichéd refrain, as something already seen, the typical image expected by a reader more or less familiar with the realities of Africa.

During her experiences of Bellevillean life in *Les honneurs perdus*, Saïda sees her notions of what is familiar, internal, known, or unknown shift and become the object of constant re-evaluations. Just like Loukoum, Saïda relates to the reader all that could seem different, unfamiliar. The difference with Loukoum, however, is that she is undergoing twofold learning, not only with regards to the French way of thinking and acting, but also with regards to the African community of Belleville whose principles of life do not necessarily correspond to those she knew back home. Moreover, age intervenes as a counter-regulator. What is the norm for Loukoum, notably the act of questioning school, the behavior of the adults surrounding him, and cultural aspects of his family, comes across as unconceivable naiveté when coming from a fifty-year-old woman. She is consequently treated as a child by her countrywomen. Through Saïda's learning of what is familiar and what is not, we discover the formative, but also restrictive, role of the community. What is given as familiar is made up of a set of tacit or explicit rules established by Ngaremba for those surrounding her in Belleville. The newly arrived woman must therefore also learn the "familiar." Her integration into the group—which is much more important for her well-being than a hypothetical integration into French society—also depends on her willingness or unwillingness to follow the rules of life in the community. Such is also the case for the protagonists in Beyala's other novels, as well as those by Biyaoula, Essomba, N'Jami, N'djehoya, etc. What comes out of each text is the importance of assimilating rules for living both in French society and in the African community in France, and especially, the need for defining at every stage what is familiar, what is foreign or new, and what is of the exotic realm.

In conclusion to this first part, I want to emphasize again the essential work of the writers on the French language, which, incidentally, constitutes both a tool and a counter-tool, which allows them to distinguish themselves from both African and French literature: their narratives are distinct from African literature through their choice of a neutralized, Gallicized, or globalized language; yet, they are also distinct from French literature through their subversions of French idiomatic expressions and the shattering of stereotypical images. Both, language and idioms, are parts of the French historical heritage, even if this heritage—colonization—is one that France only claims with difficulty. Paradoxically, a certain political sense thus inscribes itself in this subversion of language and in the significance of an African writing in French, while the writer concurrently tries to differentiate him or herself from the usual mission of engagement associated with literature in Africa. Simultaneously, however, through this work on the aesthetics of writing and the innovative manipulation of language, writers from the diaspora differentiate themselves from both mother literatures—African and French—thereby claiming their legitimacy in this distancing. Through a series of decenterings and linguistic shifts, they successfully accomplish two deconstructions, of the so-called dominant or national discourse, and the discourse of the African community.

Subversion of Dichotomies and Idiosyncrasies of Dominant Discourse

Until recently, when one spoke of dominant discourse in the framework of African literature, it was as a reference to the historical situation of colonization and the Independences, and subsequently to the discourse of the colonizer/the White man in a position of authority in Africa. Responding to colonial literature and its rendering of Africa through the eyes of the White man, of the colonizer, the African novel undertook—from the time of the Independences—the task of re-exploring this same historical situation—the period of colonization in Africa—

but as seen from within, thereby at last giving a voice to those who had been colonized subjects and on whom silence had been imposed. Most of these novels also lend a voice to the colonizer and insist on re-examining his discourse and on showing the relationships between colonized and colonizer. The relationship between the two discourses, and of course between subject and object, thus not only changes but is now inverted: the Other becomes "I" and "I" becomes the Other.

Without necessarily speaking of the substitution of one dichotomy for the other, these new writings however also introduce a new twofold discourse: discourse of the African immigrant/discourse of the French person. By "dominant" discourse, one must understand discourse of French people through their reactions to and thoughts about the immigrant African community. This type of discourse, which has been a topic of exploration for the *Beur* and Antillean novel, has primarily remained in the background of the African novel. It appears in the roman de formation[13]: it is the discourse of some French people on the African student revealing racist prejudices, preconceived ideas, and all other marks of the complete ignorance of all those who talk about Africa. Examples of earlier works are: *Le docker noir* (1960) by Ousmane Sembène, *Lettre ouverte à la France nègre* (1968) by Yambo Ouloguem, *Négriers modernes* (1970) by Jean-Pierre N'Diaye, and *Exil, connais pas. . .* (1976) by Sally N'Dongo in the 1970s. Whether they are essays or personal narratives, they mark the beginnings of an analysis of the immigration of Africans and testimonies of the life of immigrant African factory workers in France. More recently, we find published testimonies of African immigrants' experiences; some are examples of integration and social and political success, for instance, Hervé Quéméné's *Kofi* (1991) and Kofi Yamgane's *Droits, devoirs et crocodile* (1992). Others illlustrate the more common experience of a difficult life, for instance in *France, Terre d'accueil, terre de rejet, l'impossible integration* (1996) by Gamé Guilao. Within the same timeframe, in addition to fiction writing, social and political analyses have been published. These include analyses of Maghrebi immigration[14] and of the second generation, the *Beurs*.[15] Also, analyses of immigration from the Indian Ocean (for example, *175.000 Réunionnais en France, Une communauté invisible* by Alain Lorraine), and from Vietnam (*Les jeunes Vietnamiens de la dernière genération* [1987] by Le Hûu Khòa) were published in the same timeframe. Although analyses of immigration generally abound,[16] many fewer texts are specifically devoted to sub-Saharan African immigration.

As they fill in the gaps—from a fictional perspective—of a certain silence, or at the very least, of a certain shift of African literature with regards to other sister literatures on this topic, the new writings from around 1985 to today deconstruct a discourse often close to discourse previously held. The difference between the two is that the current discourse deals with issues of racism and prejudice no longer directed towards a student population, but rather towards an immigrant population often considered by French society to be in an inferior position, from both economic and educational standpoints: the so-called "domi-

nant" discourse thus necessarily once more moves closer to that of the colonizer.[17]

Tahar Ben Jelloun was already testifying on the various manifestations of
French racism towards foreigners (particularly Maghrebis and the new generation of children born on French soil) in 1984 in his first edition of *Hospitalité
française*. He notably distinguishes between two types of racism: a deeply-
engrained, internalized racism and a quiet, banalized racism. In the first category, he classifies a trend of rightist political discourse whose mechanisms he
deconstructs. Ben Jelloun thus remarks that "le racisme se développe, se répand
et convainc quand il arrive à faire croire que toute une société est menacée" (38)
[racism develops, spreads, and convinces when it is able to make one believe
that an entire society is threatened]. For this purpose, anti-Arab racism, he says,
"puise dans les mécanismes de l'antisémitisme avec cependant moins de
théories et de thèses pseudo-scientifiques" (38) [draws from the mechanisms of
anti-Semitism, although with fewer pseudo-scientific theories and theses]. This
discourse is actually more grotesque and simplistic, trying for example to evoke
the risks of heightened unemployment due to immigrants who are "taking the
work of the French people." Ben Jelloun also cites the example of the Paris mu-
nicipal council (while Jacques Chirac was mayor) after the July 1983 attacks
which led to numerous deaths. The discourse there insisted on the dangers of a
high concentration of illiterate and delinquent youth in some districts.[18] Ben
Jelloun further shows the limits of the discourse by the political left wing whose
access to power in the 1980s in no way changed French attitudes towards immigrants. Next to a discourse openly opposed to immigration and its presence on
French soil appears another type of discourse, more insidious in that it is simply
inscribed in daily language, which Ben Jelloun denotes as quiet and common-
place racism. He uncovers the absolute unawareness of the presence of racism in
the speech and ways of conceiving immigrant workers and finds that this is because clichéd images and prejudices are so deeply anchored in the language that
they have almost moved to the rank of idiomatic expressions.[19] As a solution—
in the 1980s—Ben Jelloun proposed to initiate a debate that would educate
French society on the extent of the problem. Faced with this circumscribed
framework of immigration, Ben Jelloun also decried a defeatist and negative
discourse on the part of the young immigrant generation. In a somewhat didactic
manner, he held that light should be shed on the suffering and violence that
come along with immigration and which French society refuses to see, without
forgetting a positive perspective on the experience of immigration and the complex wealth it carries.[20]

Beyala's Parisian novels, notably *Le petit prince de Belleville* and *Maman a
un amant* are constructed on the very principle of the articulation of discourses,
starting on a textual level. Beyala challenges the dominant discourse, not only
by giving a voice to those who had previously been secondary, notably African
immigrants, but also through her way of creating a dialogue between this voice
and a voice representative of so-called central and dominant discourse. As we
have seen, the two novels are built on an alternation of narrative voices: (male)

voice of the child (Loukoum) and male, epistolary voice (Abdou) for the first novel, and (male) voice of the child (Loukoum) and female voice (M'am) for the second novel. Translated by Loukoum, M'am's voice is filtered, thus highlighting the differences in power and authority along the gender line. Two addressees correspond to these double narrative voices: Loukoum's and Abdou/M'am's interlocutors. Abdou's interlocutor is explicitly identified: You, the friend/You, the White man; the same goes for M'am's female Friend (the male Friend's girlfriend). The presence of an interlocutor (whether male or female) to whom voice and thoughts are lent gives access to the "dominant" discourse, a discourse that the narrators (Loukoum or Abdou/M'am) attempt to deconstruct through their questions and interpellations.

> At the border patrol you registered my body and wrapped it in contempt, in hatred. In your wide-open eyes, I was already suspected of rape and murder. Obsessed with sex. A pile of mud charged with obstructing memories and propagating AIDS. (20)

The above quote fulfills a double purpose: (1) to define the immigrant's status, an inferiorized status, one very strongly marked by the immigrant's ethnic visibility, characterized by his marginalization as a result of being "stuck" between two cultures; (2) to clearly enunciate, through the interjections towards the interlocutor, the latter's responsibility in the identity crisis faced by Abdou and many other immigrants like him: denigration and annihilation of the self to the point of transparence, to the feeling of being little more than the act of breathing. Through this statement Abdou reminds us of colonization, of the dominant discourse of this interlocutor's ancestors and what they did to his country. On the other hand, the immigrant's nostalgic evocation of the Africa he had to leave is very present. The discourse Abdou projects onto "L'Ami" succintly summarizes immigrants' position and the global attitude of French society towards them: denigration, scorn, distrust, and feelings of superiority over the Other, a potential social enemy. The colonizer's discourse on the colonized appears concurrent to the discourse in question.[21] Although the Manichean structure of Fanon's discourse on race relations unfortunately remains valid, the interaction of narrative voices in Beyala's texts, for example, manages to subvert the binary, dichotomous construction and hybridizes the terms in order to highlight the process of substituting one discourse (on the immigrant) for another (that on the colonized). Several of these novels pose the issue of the existence of such a discourse in today's society, both in Europe and on the African continent. Joseph's identity crisis in *L'impasse* partly draws from the fact that he lets himself be locked into such a thought system. The same goes for Abdou who wavers on the brink of insanity in *Le petit prince de Belleville*. It is because he created a dichotomist mode of thought (immigrant/dominant [national]) that Abdou suffers from his experience of immigration linked to an unshakable feeling of inferiority.[22]

The dialogue between narrator and receptor, between dominated and dominant discourse, however, moves to the next stage in Beyala's work, to that of the quest for a place for listening and dialogue through the intermediary of the woman as an object of conversation. In a strategy consisting in bringing its interlocutor to assess himself through his relationship with his wife, the dominated discourse lends thoughts to the dominating discourse, attempts to imagine it in other terms, to guess the "real" inner discourse behind the official, less offensive façade discourse. Through the very act of lending a voice to the dominant discourse's dialogue with the so-called dominated discourse (that of the subaltern party), Beyala creates a fluidity between the two discourses, suggesting a *rapprochement* in modes of thought. In so doing, she achieves a double deconstruction of the dominating discourse: that of the White man towards the immigrant and that of the African man with regards to the African woman. Furthermore, she subverts the traditional dichotomy between dominant/dominated discourses, thereby hybridizing the two. In both cases, the notion of power is reinterpreted. A scission occurs between the two types of dominant discourses. Indeed, in the first, the subaltern discourse takes on a voice and a shape, becomes the main discourse, while the so-called dominant discourse is merely borrowed, reported and indirect. Ultimately, a restitution of power takes place in the very use of language. But in the case of the second form of dominant discourse, even though the dominated speak through M'am's character, the fact that this speech is translated (the translator, Loukoum, is clearly given as male through his daily approach to life) renders it indirect and reported and the mere textual articulation of the macro-text—*Le petit prince de Belleville* and *Maman a un amant*—and is indicative of the prevalence of the dominant discourse, here, male discourse.[23]

In this second case of the deconstruction of dominant discourse—the male discourse—Gayatri Spivak's hypothesis, "The subaltern cannot speak," seems to hold. The woman remains forced to silence. Patriarchal authority continues to rule in the family, in the midst of a substitute African community in France. The example of Saïda's successful education, of her education facilitated by women in *Les honneurs perdus*, allows us to perceive the possibility of authority being overthrown in the African community in France. We will return to this point in the following section.

To wrap up the topic, I would like to return to *Un regard noir* (1984) by Blaise N'djehoya and Massaer Diallo, whose prime objective is precisely to deconstruct dominant discourse through humor. The text looks at France and the French by adopting a very particular gaze, that of the anthropologist, a gaze thus meant to be professional, scientific, and objective in its approach. There is therefore a reversal of the usual perspective where the West, France, turns to [rather, *looks down* onto] a particular people or a particular cultural aspect with the aim of studying its origins and internal logic. The term "to look down," which I emphasized, in itself suggests a certain inequality (between the position of the one studying and that of the man/woman/object being studied): in a sense, an implicit difference in level and a physical superiority appears, allowing one, the taller, to look down onto the other, smaller, inferior.

The preface offers the key to this reversal of situation and perspective:

. . . l'Occident n'a plus le monopole aujourd'hui de la science et de l'investigation. L'Occident peut aujourd'hui être un objet d'étude pour les observateurs venus du Sud, qu'ils soient savants ou simples travailleurs.

[. . . the West no longer has the monopoly over science and investigation today. The West can today be the object of study for observers coming from the South, whether they are intellectuals or simple workers.]

The writing project follows up on actual projects for an anthropological study[24] by subverting this study through its mocking aspect: the hero of N'djehoya's novel is a pretend-ethnologist, an "African Persian." If Diallo instead adopts the tone of a researcher as a result of his own training, their writings meet to "break down the opposition between the supposedly rational and technological North, and the supposedly savage and magical South," by highlighting for instance the fact that the majority of the clientele of *marabouts* in France is White.

N'djehoya's mini-stories/documents, of which we have seen some examples, are all humorous anecdotes. For his part, Diallo explains birth and in some sense paternity in this reverse ethnology which consists in exploring the hidden face of France, which he defines as "des cultures ethniques et régionales, des traditions paysannes, des pensées et des pratiques magiques diffuses ou non, vivaces au niveau du people" (126) [ethnic and regional cultures, peasant traditions, diffuse or non-diffuse thoughts and magical practices vivacious at the level of the people].

While Yambo Ouologuem displayed a caustic and biting irony towards France's relationship (or the apparent absence thereof) with African immigrants, N'djehoya resorts to humor. Under the cover of wit, he is able to deconstruct the dominant discourse, the official as well as the officious, in good humor without in any way compromising the accuracy of his remarks.

Bessora takes up the same approach in *53 cm* with the anthropologist becoming in this case a gaulologist. In undertaking the administrative process to register at the university, this student with a daughter discovers the unimaginable depths of the bureaucracy, learning that her daughter who was born on foreign soil cannot be granted a residency permit. The narrative voice, "gaulologist" of the 1990s, sifts through French society, drawing attention to the French administrative barriers for a foreigner, from registering at the university to obtaining a residency permit; she also looks at herself as she makes her usual "tarte tatin," her way of conforming.[25] In *Les taches d'encre*, the author undertakes a more forward deconstruction of the mechanisms of hidden racism that underlie French society's ways of speaking and acting. French habits are also carefully observed: consumerism, fashion trends from deodorants and exfoliating creams to laundry softener, sexual habits, suppressed angst, and consultations of astrologists, the Westernized version of the *marabout*.

These few examples taken from Beyala, N'djehoya, and Bessora indicate a shift—not in the writing per se, but rather in the frameworks that determine the components of the discourse and the directions it takes. The deconstruction of the so-called dominant discourse, the importance granted to it, to its representative, breaks away from the novel from the continent where French people as characters or addressees, along with the notion of dominant discourse, have completely moved to the backdrop of the story—that is, when they have not completely disappeared. Over the past ten years, how many African novels from the continent have had French characters or displayed any interest whatsoever in issues of French management or politics in Africa? How many have an addressee (internal to the narration) who can be identified as French/Western? Practically none.[26] To the contrary, the visibility of these discourses, characters, interlocutors, or addressees internal or external to the tale in the novel of the African diaspora paints new contours for the tale and testifies to an implicitly different thematic, a function of the realities of a different social framework: that of a multicultural society in the face of which France may no longer define itself as a homogeneous whole, but where it must instead consider the ethnic, cultural, and religious components that shape it. Inversely, its multiethnic components may also no longer be considered as a homogeneous whole somewhat hastily categorized as "the Foreigner," "the African," "the immigrant."

In this regard, numerous authors of the new diasporic generation have devoted much time and energy to testifying to the cultural diversity of the African community in France, starting with the deconstruction of the very notion of *an* African community, one that would be unique and homogeneous.[27]

Deconstruction of the Myth of Homogeneity in the African Community

As emphasized by Mar Fall in *Des Africains noirs en France, des tirailleurs sénégalais aux. . . Blacks* (1986), the Black quest for identity starts with "le désir de réappropriation d'une spatialité et d'une temporalité qui seraient propres aux Africains" (38) [the desire of re-appropriating a space and time belonging to Africans]. But, as he remarks, this quest "se manifeste par une adhésion acharnée à la culture maternelle: celle-ci devient en fait une culture idéalisée, mythifiée" (38) [is manifest in the fierce adherence to one's native culture: it actually becomes an idealized, mythified culture]. From that point on then, remembering the past and the native land becomes a primordial necessity for the African emigrant settled in France.

> Cette adhésion à la culture mère se manifeste dans l'exil par un attachement exagéré aux coutumes considérées comme originelles. Toutes les cérémonies religieuses, les fêtes, les traditions culinaires sont vécues et/ou présentées comme des moments où la diaspora noire reprend des forces en posant symboliquement les pieds sur la "Terre". (Mar Fall 38)

[This adherence to the mother culture manifests itself during exile by an exaggerated attachment to customs considered authentic. All religious ceremonies, parties, culinary traditions are experienced and/or presented as moments where the Black diaspora regains strength by symbolically setting its feet on "Earth."]

Here we are reminded of the dichotomy observed by Jules-Rosette in Parisianist novels, notably the feeling of nostalgia for the native land on one hand and the character's aspirations to integrate into French society on the other hand. According to the author, one of the consequences of this attachment is the risk of seeing immigrants from sub-Saharan Africa limit themselves to a static, perhaps even obsolete and anachronistic image of their country and of their culture, by respecting certain customs that may not necessarily still be practiced.[28] Fall analyzes Négritude in this context: "Cette affirmation de soi face à l'Europe débouche sur une présentation de l'Afrique comme une et indivisible, l'objectif étant de transcender les particularités nationales et ethniques . . . " (38-39) [This self-affirmation with regards to Europe leads to a presentation of Africa as united and indivisible, the objective being to transcend national and ethnic particularities . . .].

Today, several novels by the new generation settled in Paris attempt to deconstruct this united and indivisible image, in order to offer a gaze onto the multiple facets of life in the African diaspora in France. In the following section, we will reflect on certain paradigms linked to the establishment of an identity for those who, like the protagonists, have chosen to go live in France and who have made the African community in France, be it in Belleville or elsewhere, no longer a homogeneous whole, but rather a multicultural and multinational amalgam, a function of the transformation of these very paradigms. These paradigms are essentially family and the place-identity combination, where the evolution of the former depends on the latter.

Place and Identity: a Constant Interrelation

A number of articles published in the United States and in England have dealt with the issue of displacement in its traumatizing aspect of un-rooting and up-rooting.[29] In particular, in "Double Articulation: a Place in the World" (1994), Doreen Massey reflects on the relationship between location, place, and one's identity formation.[30] She poses the following questions: does place necessarily exert an influence on one's identity? Or, phrased differently, does displacement, a change in environment, in place, necessarily have an impact on one's identity? And vice-versa, how does a place adopt an identity as its population evolves? Indeed, at a time when people are moving much more, when the world is made up of hybridized communities, to what extent does this interdependence hold?

To address these questions, she starts wtih David Harvey's study in *The Condition of Postmodernity* (1989), which established an equation between the notion of place he associated with "stasis and nostalgia" and which he considered to be "the inertia of being as opposed to the (potentially progressive) dynamism of Becoming" (300). In light of Harvey's assertion that these place-identities are constructed in a particular fashion, Massey then proposes that "every identity linked to a place/space must at some time rely on the motivating power of tradition" (Massey 300).

In our particular topic of study, displacement from Africa towards France is expected, from the time of departure, to have an impact on the individual's transformations: that was already the theme par excellence in the 1960s, and then in the 1980s in the form of the re-adaptation struggle for those returning to their native country. *L'aventure ambiguë* (1961) and Aminata Sow Fall's *L'Appel des arènes* (1982) are probing examples thereof. But at the time, the sojourns in question were temporary and generally linked to an ensured return to the home country, with the idea that a diploma guaranteed employment and the prospect of a career. The current context is different. Even though migration due to economic reasons initially presents itself as temporary, in practice, it means the impossibility of returning to the home country.

In this regard, Mar Fall speaks of a process of no-return, whose intermediary stages he describes in *Des Africains noirs en France*. Originally, return to Africa is "le fondement même du projet de départ" (49) [the very foundation of the project of leaving], and permanently settling in the host country remains relatively rare.

> Pour le candidat à l'émigration, qu'il soit ouvrier, intellectuel, exilé politique ou autre, comme pour son groupe d'origine, l'émigration n'a de sens et de justification que si le retour est envisagé. Le statut d'immigré sera considéré comme provisoire. Le retour dans le pays n'a de portée que s'il s'accompagne ou se conjugue avec une certaine promotion sociale. (49)

> [For both the individual considering emigration—whether he is a factory worker, an intellectual, a political exile or other—and the group from which he originates, emigration only has meaning and offers justification if a return is envisioned. The status of immigrant will be seen as temporary. Return to the country only carries weight if it comes hand in hand with a certain social promotion.]

But this return generally proves to be impossible, depending on the initial motivations for the departure: to find work, to obtain a diploma, to wait for better conditions to replace those forced by the current African regime, etc. Time becomes a determining factor in that the emigrant settles into a certain way of life, becomes accustomed to certain levels of comfort, fears going back to a difficult economic situation, that of unemployment in his country, or becomes involved with someone in the host country. On this point, Fall notes that "le mariage mixte qui est un lien où se réunissent deux individus qui prennent des distances avec leurs groupes qui se définissent en grande partie par les critères (pays, race, religion) soulève encore plus de problèmes quant à la perspective du retour. L'appréhension chez les Africains noirs dans une situation de mariage mixte de retourner 'au pays' est bien vivace, essentiellement à cause des représentations que les sociétés africaines se font de la mixité" (50) [the mixed-race marriage, a link bringing together two individuals who distance themselves from their groups—which define themselves in large part by criteria (country, race, color, religion)—brings up even more problems in the issue of return. Apprehension about going back home for interracial couples is a fact, essentially because of African societies' representations of biracialism].[31] Fall later shows that as a result of demographic growth, an acceleration of the rate of literacy, and a level of intellectual investment more rapid than financial and economic investment over the past several years, a certain imbalance has appeared, whereby having a diploma, whether from a foreign nation or the home country, is no longer an automatic guarantee for employment. The emigrant therefore apprehends—and justly so—a return that may prove difficult and be viewed as a failure if he is unfit to help his expectant family financially.

In the case of the novel of the diaspora, of these new African writings of self, the issue at hand is to evaluate how this displacement, the permanent implantation into the Parisian milieu, often a particular milieu, a multicultural hybrid, intervenes in the evolution of the characters portrayed. Calixthe Beyala's novels are emblematic of Harvey's distinction between Being and Becoming, a distinction corresponding to a difference between men and women in the construction of her works. Indeed, both in her first novels—*C'est le soleil qui m'a brûlée* or *Seul le diable le savait*—and in her "Parisian" novels, female characters are always the ones to express a desire to change, to become someone (else) while the men are more preoccupied with maintaining what they have and what they are. In fact, in *Le petit prince de Belleville*, Abdou is the very incarnation of resistance to change, of a desire to be, to remain what he was; from which flows textually the epistolary form, a set of poetic letters, reminders of the past, where Abdou, griot of Africa, evokes for his wives, his children, and especially for us the readers, this nostalgic past that is no more. His evocation is a vain attempt to retain a life from the past that is no longer viable in their new home. Abdou, Uncle Kouam, and the other men devote themselves to preserving intact the daily rules of functioning for the African community, as these had been fixed in their native country. *Maman a un amant* marks the renewed attempt on women's part to break from traditional order and shatter this structure, now anachronistic in their new space. Indeed, the women display a desire to move forward, to change, and to live a new life conforming to this new place. The identity of the subject here is thus closely linked to his or her geographic situation. Geographic displacement brings about a shift in power in the family, a transformation of gender roles as a result of the current globalization, and consequently, a redefinition of the concept of family.

Le petit prince de Belleville, and even more so, *Maman a un amant*, emphasize the link between a nostalgic gaze towards the past, a final hold on tradition, and power. Evidently, the man maintains control, even if this control seems temporarily endangered by women's desire for change. The end of *Maman a un amant* thereby sanctions the restitution of traditional power to the man, since everything "goes back to normal" with M'am's return and her reconciliation with her husband: "Seul l'esprit de tribu compte" (298) [Only the tribal spirit matters]. Inversely, Abdou's letters, due to their quasi-elegiac evocations of the past and of legends in a language (completely) opposed to that he uses in daily life with his wives or friends, belie a disjunction, a significant gap between the tangible reality of his present situation and of his discontent and an idealized, not to say utopic, past.

Through several examples from neighborhoods/suburbs of London, Doreen Massey emphasizes that the past—preserved in a sort of void in people's minds although it is an urban milieu, prone to changes both superficial and deep—is no "purer" than this new place. Massey suggests focusing the analysis on the issue of the identity of the place itself, on the way in which a place evolves as a result of the arrival of new communities giving a new face to the area. To this effect she gives as an example a neighborhood of London which changed from a factory landscape to an entirely new landscape with the arrival of "yuppies," or of another neighborhood whose population displays a diverse heritage with Irish, Scottish, Indian, and Caribbean components. Similarly, we may think of Belleville and its evolution with the implantation of renewed layers of immigrants of diverse origins depending on the timeframe, and of the dissemination of all these immigrants throughout not only the center of Paris, but also in the *banlieues*, dormitory-cities.

In fact, the place's identity also varies according to the interaction among these different groups. Calixthe Beyala is the writer dealing with the closest thing to this particular notion of place. With *Le petit prince de Belleville* and *Maman a un amant*, Belleville remains in the background, without ever really taking shape. In *Les honneurs perdus*, Belleville takes life. Furthermore, it seems that the ways of life in Belleville are not so far from those in New-Bell, the popular neighborhood in Douala, Cameroon. The second part of the novel gives an account of the place through its composition and the impact of the interaction between the different immigrant groups. By coming across Ngaremba, Belleville's public writer, Saïda discovers a mix of people with various aspirations, all trying to carve themselves a slice of life in their new environment.[32]

The evening classes Saïda attends fit into this same process. There, Saïda meets women originating from different places, all gathered around a common goal: to change (let us emphasize that we are revisiting the same initial program as in the first novels here—Megri, M'am, Assèze, or Saïda's determination to *Become*) and to function entirely in the present place. These women's literacy classes, as already suggested by *Maman a un amant*, immediately threaten the traditional power and absolute authority of men. In fact, these lessons are an opportunity for Saïda to assert her identity alongside the other women who, like Ngaremba, educate her. These male and female characters' plurality partly also allows them to play a role in the deconstruction of dominant discourse by proving that representations of Africans/the African community as a homogeneous whole are stereotypical and inaccurate. One-way images break down here to make room for a multiplicity of faces, voices, and discourses.

The issue of authenticity nonetheless remains at the very heart of this discourse as a paradox seems to occur, which results from the fluidity between dominant and dominated discourse. Indeed in a sense, Beyala's characters, particularly in *Le petit prince de Belleville* and *Maman a un amant*, sometimes appear fixed in a set of predetermined and predictable behaviors and speech. It is less the case in *Les honneurs perdus* where the surrounding characters have more depth. Should one thus speak of authenticity or of a discourse more or less corresponding to readers' expectations? There is indeed a danger, which we will discuss in greater detail in chapter 3, of a discourse where the representation of the community blends dominant and dominated discourse through the very fusion of certain stereotypical images and the shattering of these stereotypes. Or is this fusion instead to be perceived as the subversion of the usual representations of the immigrant and of immigration, and through the reflection they offer, of French people's stereotyping gaze? The use, for example, of a certain mode of speech by immigrants, much like the *"petit nègre"* speech of colonial literature, of expressions such as "La tribu nègre" ["the negro tribe"] runs the risk of confusing the reader, of reinforcing prejudices and preconceived notions about immigrants in his mind, because the discourse is not decoded as a subversion of stereotypes and racist images.

At this point I would like to remind the reader of what Rey Chow wrote on the topic in "Where Have All the Natives Gone?": "The hasty supply of original 'contexts' and 'specificities' easily becomes complicitous with the dominant discourse, which achieves hegemony precisely by its capacity to convert, recode, make transparent, and thus represent even those experiences that resist with a stubborn opacity" (133).

Indeed, Rey Chow broaches crucial points with regards to the authenticity of "natives"[33] that are entirely pertinent in the framework of our analysis. In particular, she discusses the image of this "native," how we (postmodernist Westerners: here I am adopting the position that would correspond to my profile from an ethnological viewpoint) expect a certain image, a certain behavior from immigrants (she cites the example of the disconcerted, almost uncomfortable Henri Levi-Strauss at the sight of a Native American conducting anthropological research at the New York library and using a Parker pen, whom Levi-Strauss would have expected to be dressed a certain way; Chow discusses the fact that witnessing the individual's interest both in anthropology and in his own culture from an objective perspective disturbed Levi-Strauss). In a sense, this Westernized image of this Native American individual indicates the risk of disappearance of the "authentic," of the "pure" as Levy-Strauss imagines it. In a sense also, such a reaction is a testimony to the resilience of a priori and of clichéd images with regards to the notion of natives and its representation.

Why are we so fascinated with "history" and with the "native" in "modern" times? What do we gain from our labor on these "endangered authenticities" which are presumed to be from a different time and a different place? What can be said of the juxtaposition of "us" (our discourse) and "them"? What kind of *surplus value* is derived from the juxtaposition? (137)

Chow then broaches the issue of un-translatability of "third-worldist" discourse into that of the "first world." Later on, she draws our attention to the
dangers of projecting a certain mode of thought and of "first-world" representation onto a discourse presented as third-world. In the same manner—and consequently—the danger occurs of seeing a stereotyped discourse imposed onto the
subaltern party since this discourse risks being interpreted as fake. In the same
frame of mind, Chow addresses the central issue of authenticity, of what this
(currently very fashionable) term means depending on the origins of the one
speaking it, and discusses this fascination on the part of the Western world for
the myth of purity, of a return to origins.

> . . . the native, the subaltern and so forth are used to represent the point of "au-
> thenticity" for our critical discourse, they become at the same time the place of
> myth-making and an escape from the impure nature of political realities. (139)

If we place ourselves back into the perspective of the African novel/of the
novel of the diaspora and of our example of Beyala's Parisian novels, this question takes on critical importance: indeed, in this analytical context, Abdou's discourse embodies this issue of "authenticity," as the epitome of the African immigrant's native discourse. Through his gaze onto the past, on an immemorial
pre-colonial time, Abdou creates a magical space, the place of a mythical Africa,
which allows him to escape the weight of his surrounding milieu and to thereby
escape the difficult confrontation of the political reality of immigration. He is
par excellence the one whose gaze indicates an identity gap between there and
here, between before and now. But his discourse is also in a sense the imagined
one, almost expected of his immigrant status. The evocation of his past will inevitably be elegiac in comparison with a dark and uncertain future. We may thus
pose the issue of the narrator's gaze and of the exploitation of this gaze, in other
words, of the author's intentions. If we keep the same example of Beyala's Parisian novels and of her choice of African immigrants as protagonists, we may
question the gaze she directs as the author. By giving voice to an African immigrant, which gaze does she adopt? With whom does her own gaze coincide? Is
her experience parallel, or should we speak of an exploitation of the gaze,[34]
based on the very fact that Beyala's readers have a certain fascination with emigrants and the evocation of their origins; for they are sure to find in her texts a
certain Africa, a certain representation of the African community in Africa but
also an image/counter-mirror, which in turn offers a reflection of French society.
In a way, the represented African immigrant's discourse exhibits new values in
that he becomes a displaced native, allowing, through his textual voice, the superposition of two discourses: "theirs" and "ours" (in our reading and interpretation of who "they" represents.) All throughout her "Parisian" novels, Beyala
incontestably plays on the superposition and juxtaposition of these two possible
discourses, in the duplicity and duality of the potential reader, "I" or the Other.
As an intermediary, she offers a mediating gaze between the image of the Other
who has become "I," no longer as an object, but as a subject, all while knowing

that s/he is the object of the gaze of the "I" who has become Other. In particular, Beyala plays on the very subversion of this dichotomy, Self and the Other, invalidating it through its very representation.

This same issue of an African community, of the I and Other, appears in varying degrees and angles in most of the novels of the new generation. Biyaoula's *L'impasse* and *Agonies* also examine the African community's discourse on the topic of its homogeneity through a set of zoom effects. The setting here is no longer Belleville or central Paris, but rather the *banlieues* of the Parisian region. Through this change in landscape and decorum, the new writings subvert the traditional representation of Paris, of the myth of Paris as the city of lights.

On this topic, Michel Laronde notes in his study of the *Beur* novel a change in the Parisian landscape—in other words, a landscape where the *banlieue* and certain specific zones are concentration points for immigrant communities, while Paris, the center, is where the nationals reside. Indeed, Laronde shows how the peripheral ring of the *banlieue* surrounding the vital center of Paris can, in a subversion of discourse, be inverted. An infiltration of the center occurs, a displacement of the *banlieue* towards the center. Inversely, the margins close up completely in a choice of auto-exclusion and the rejection of the central vertical gaze. Only Tierno Monénembo's *Un rêve utile* and Daniel Biyaoula's novels send the reader back to an image close to the oppressive and/or closed universe of the *banlieue* as rendered in the *Beur* novel. The described environment is rarely oppressive and the hardening of the gaze visible in the *Beur* novel does not apply. *Agonies* nonetheless introduces this very dimension, that of the urban space of the *banlieue* and of what comes with this "ZUPean" universe, in other words, a stifling feeling, but also the difficulty in leaving, in "tearing oneself out" of the space, and the fear of "rotting" in this universe of grayness and impasse.[35] Furthermore, the characters' actions, through their gossip, their attempts to stigmatize newcomers, revert to Taieb's observations, and before him, to those of Norbert Ellias on the formation of racist sentiments within immigrant groups and the notion of ethnic exclusion.

The Family

Through the example of Loukoum's family (Abdou and his two mothers, M'am and La Soumana) and its interaction with the immigrant African community of Belleville, *Le petit prince de Belleville* poses the issue of the redefinition of family in the context of immigration and of the renegotiation of power dynamics within the family and within the community in which the family evolves. We are brought to ponder questions of cultural fragmentation and displacement. Due to the circumstances, the issue arises of who shapes whom. Indeed, as we saw in chapter 1, the power of the husband and father disintegrates once it comes into contact with Western society, as Abdou's wives and son discover another mode of thought and life—although the woman (through the characters of La Soumana and M'am) initially displays the usual conservative image associated with the immigrant mother/wife (Maghrebi in particular) who is confined to the interior space and has difficulties with the host society's language.[36] Consequently, the notion of what is familiar and internal is in constant redefinition for the father, the mother(s), and the son.

In "Mother Tongue and Other Strangers: Writing 'Family' across Cultural Divides," Angelika Bammer raises questions on the redefinition of the notion of "family," the notion of permanence, its function with regards to the social environment, with regards to knowing if "the family affords protection, for example, or if it is an ominous place."

One of the factors notably contributing to modifying the profile of the family in its evolution relates to the child's schooling and the arrival of a second language competing with that of the house.[37] "Which/whose languages shall the family speak, literally and culturally?. . . How does family even translate across such a divide when the very meaning of 'family' within the family differs?" (96)

Life in a different milieu brings with it consequences in terms of reassignment of the formative role with regards to the language and the society. Because the child enrolled in school learns a new language and through it, a new culture, a new way of seeing life that is based on the values of others, he is the one to establish the link between the family and the outside world; he is also the one who risks imposing another language on the family; he is thus the one bringing a new knowledge, and thereby, a new authority into the family. Hence the possibility of an additional conflict in the family, which has already been upset by its spatial, and particularly, cultural displacement.

> In this process, language plays a complex role, both binding and dividing the family members. For not only do parents and children often end up with different native languages, their different relationships to these languages can have notable social consequences. For example, the traditional position of authority can be confused or even reversed depending on who does—or does not—master a given language. . . The children come to master the very cultural codes (language, mode of dress, forms of social interaction), ignorance of which functionally reduces the parents to children. (100-101)

In *Le petit prince de Belleville*, Abdou certainly comes into contact with the outside world, but this world is beyond him, incomprehensible; it is a world that rejects him and renders him transparent, annulling his position of authority in his family. Consequently, as it evolves, the story shows a loss of Abdou's authority over his wives and his son, and *Maman a un amant* opens on an inversion of family roles where it is M'am who assumes the position of authority and initiative in the family for some time. Her authority erodes from the moment she begins a romantic relationship with Monsieur Tichit and leaves the conjugal home to move in with her lover. From that point on, as the community expresses its disapproval, power within the family returns to its origins, with Abdou regaining his position as authority figure. *Maman a un amant* is proof of the persisting interrelation between family and community and the de facto predominance of the community's authority over the family and its modus vivendi. M'am returns to her family because she has been shunned from the Malian community of Belleville.[38] Here once again, Angelika Bammer offers pertinent insight on the notion of power in the family and its redefinition in the face of a doubly exterior environment (society, a foreign cultural reality where the word power is negotiated with difficulty).

> As the locus of cultural authority in such families tends to shift, the sites of power and security are often dispersed and multiply situated . . . The question is then: given the displacement of the locus of familial identity and authority, what happens to the notion of family? Does it disintegrate, itself displaced onto a variety of dispersed sites (of which the family in our sense—nuclear, heterosexual, patriarchal—is only one)? Is it affirmed with a reactionary vengeance? Or is it rewritten, recast not in the preset mold of one particular tradition but in the form of a sketch that can be erased and (re)drawn, depending on what—then and there—is called for? (104-105)

Biyaoula's *L'impasse* broaches some of these topics (the rapport between family, power, and environing milieu) from a different angle, and the notion of an African community takes on a completely different light. Indeed, family in this framework undergoes a series of transformations, first in France, and then in Africa, and then retrospectively in France once more. For Joseph who has been settled in France for some ten years, family has become an almost foreign concept—at the least, a secondary one. His links with Africa remain in the epistolary realm, and the reader very soon discovers that the relationship before his departure was characterized by tensions, notably the impression that Joseph was neither very important, nor very loved in his family (as a result of his very dark skin color and the indifference of his mother who even came up with his nickname, "goudron" [tar]). In France, he does not have a family. One could expect the African community to serve as a familial substitute for him, but it turns out that he avoids most of the other Africans living in his city or neighborhood. He is thus essentially alone, cut off from his family and practically cut from his cultural links. This solitude establishes propitious ground for the feeling of *malaise*, of marginalization which progressively invades him. His vacation in Africa contributes to this feeling, because of his failure to re-establish a relationship with his family and even his friends. The feeling of distance grows and leads to the appearance of a wall, an insurmountable void between the two parties judging each other unfavorably with respect to each side's ways of life. Joseph disapproves of the disproportionate power granted to tradition which regulates family and community life in its smallest details, including in what he would deem to be his intimate life. These tensions and conflicts between his family and him are at the root of his psychosis upon his return to France. At that point, he breaks ties with all his African friends, his colleagues from work,[39] and Sabine, as he sees each individual or group as a representative of a racial community, and all irritating him equally, although for different reasons. The overall tone of *L'impasse* plays off the dark humor reigning in the rapports between the protagonist and his family or his friends, whether in Africa or in France. On the other hand, his confrontations with the various groups—in particular with his compatriots in France—are an opportunity to deconstruct the idea of a single and homogeneous community and to outline the stages in the process of alienation affecting Joseph.

The third phase (which we described and analyzed in the first part of chapter 1) recounts his radical transformation and his adherence to the very principles he initially abhorred. The process of auto-exclusion discussed by Laronde in his analysis of the *Beur* novel functions here, in both directions,[40] to the extent that Joseph's mental health is in question. He isolates himself not only from French society, but also—and firstly—from African society. He returns to his countrymen after a stay in a mental institution where he undergoes therapy, which is reminiscent of the incarceration parameter. This therapy, performed by a French doctor reputed for his "knowledge" of Africans, illustrates the modulating, regulating, and official discourse of the two central powers (France/Congo). This discourse does not deal with the singularity of the case per se. Rather, it should be read as an attempt at bringing the prodigal son back; as a patent "demonstration" of the difficulty for Africa/the African to define it/himself, to conceive it/himself outside the definition and the role prescribed by the West, as evoked by Achille Mbembe in his analysis of African writings of self. Once again we encounter the discourse of centrality and power incarnated by the doctor. In fact, by being to close to the Foreigner (the Other in an inversion of normative, meaning French, discourse), Joseph has become aware of his Foreignness. On the other hand, healing from his alienation consists in quieting all feelings of foreignness, of being a foreigner, and in completely assimilating into his community, and thereby including himself anew into French society: becoming African and French.

> Je ne me frotte pas "impunément" à l'Etranger car il se produit une sorte d'osmose, de renvoi alternatif, de dédoublement selon lesquels l'Autre et Moi sommes intimement mêlés . . . C'est cette distance qui installe en moi la conscience de l'Etrangeté de mon identité. (. . .)
> Alors pour me distancier de l'Etrangeté que l'Etranger me fait pressentir en Moi, je vais me refondre dans le collectif qui me rassure. En me resolidarisant avec mon Semblable, je retrouve la carapace de mon identité collective qui m'aide à repousser l'Autre, envahisseur et persécuteur dont je vais à mon tour me venger en l'envahissant (en l'assimilant) ou le persécutant (le rejetant) soit dans son identité privée (individuelle: sexuelle, psychique, familiale), soit dans son identité publique (collective: professionnelle, politique, nationale). (Laronde 35)

> [I do not carelessly rub myself against the Foreigner, as a sort of osmosis, of alternative rejection, of doubling occurs, according to which the Other and I are intimately involved . . . It is this distance that creates within me a consciousness of the Foreignness of my identity. (. . .)
> So, to distance myself from the Foreignness that the Foreigner makes me anticipate in Myself, I will melt back into the reassuring collective. By reestablishing a solidarity with my Like, I one again find the protective shell of

my collective identity which allows me to push the Other—the invader and persecutor—away. I will avenge myself by invading him (through his assimilation), or persecuting him (through rejection) either in his private identity (individual: sexual, psychological, familial), or in his public identity (collective: professional, political, national).]

An inversion of discourse clearly occurs here, where the gaze of the Other becomes the enunciating Me and the Me becomes the Other, the Foreigner. A subversion of the discourse of assimilation and resistance to the Foreignness of his own identity thus occurs. For Abdou in *Le petit prince de Belleville* for example, a sort of osmosis occurs in his constant dialogue with "l'Ami," he who has become the Other. This osmosis is double-edged, because in his search for intimacy and similarity, Abdou has also gained awareness of his Foreignness, which is at the root of his burgeoning insanity. The following statement, analyzed by Laronde in the case of the *Beur*, applies perfectly to Abdou's situation, and through him, to that of the African immigrant.

Je me reconnais alors partiellement et en même temps différent de Moi et de l'Autre et semblable à Moi et à l'Autre! Je ne me sens pas seulement "étranger à l'autre" mais aussi "étranger à moi-même" (d'après l'expression de Julia Kristeva : "étrangers à nous-mêmes") à cause de la présence de l'Autre. (35)

[I thus recognize myself partially but at the same time differently from Me and from the Other and similar to Me and to the Other! I no longer only feel "foreign to the other" but also "foreign to myself" (from Julia Kristeva's expression: "foreign to ourselves") because of the presence of the Other.]

Le petit prince de Belleville and even more so, *L'impasse*, gravely illustrate this topic of the loneliness of the individual who has chosen to settle in a different place and culture. This loneliness is linked to choices: whether or not to lean towards integration, certainly, but also whether or not to adhere to the principles of life for the community of origin present in the host society, even if these principles do not necessarily correspond to his/her own. Traditional power (or its conception) thus changes, not to disappear but rather to take on a substitute form: that of the power of the community in the host society. *African Gigolo* is another illustration thereof: the delicate issue of individuality for those implanted in France. Because he or she is pointed at, but also classified as Other by the other inhabitants of the place (French people), the individual is forced to choose between a life of solitude and life among the semblance of an African community[41] with the restraints it can present. *Agonies* and *Bleu-Blanc-Rouge* emphasize these restraints in their most extreme manifestations, where the community imposes itself with force in order to "protect" its cohesion. The fact that Ghislaine has a relationship with a member of the rival ethnic group, that Maud goes out with a young French boy (*Agonies*), or that Massala-Massala (*Bleu-Blanc-Rouge*) is forced into a vicious cycle as a result of the ways of life, not in Paris, but on the continent, are all examples—as in *L'impasse, African*

Gigolo, Le petit prince de Belleville, Maman a un amant—of the protagonists' dilemma on whether or not to link themselves to the present African community and examples of how this "host" African community is neither homogeneous nor necessarily united or liberating and how it can be an element of resistance in the African writing of self.

Literary *Métissage* and Transculturation

Even though transformations in identities linked with the experience of immigration for individuals leaving their country and culture of origin to settle in another country and culture are generally acknowledged, much less thought tends to be given to the impact of the arrival of the person/group on the host country and culture. When such thought does occur, however, it is unfortunately in a very precise framework: that of a racist language of rejection towards what is perceived as a danger. In reality, individual and collective transformations do not limit themselves to the migrant group, but rather exert an influence on the society in which this group integrates itself. The preface of *Un regard noir* attests to this fact:

> *Un regard noir* est un livre écrit par des Africains sur les Français. Il ne s'agissait pas, en fait, de reprendre les *Carnets du Major Thompson*, version noire, mais bien plutôt de *montrer comment la France se transforme grâce à l'influence exercée par les immigrés qui la peuplent.*
>
> [*Un regard noir* is a book written by Africans about French people. The idea was not, actually, to write a Black version of *Major Thompson's Diary* but rather *to show how France is transformed as a result of the influence exerted by the immigrants that populate it.*]

The part I emphasize introduced a new topic in the 1980s: the impact of immigrants and of the phenomenon of immigration on French society and the transformations that come along with it. Similarly, Mar Fall reminds us in *Des Africains noirs en France* of the role of immigrants as an ethnic community within French society, of how immigration "interpelle les états concernés" (52) [calls on the mother countries] and constitutes a remembrance of the past. It plays, he says, "un rôle de révélateur dans la mesure où elle permet de saisir l'impact du passé et du présent dans les stratégies qui sous-tendent les rapports entre l'Etats français et les Etats africains" (52) [a revealing role in that it allows for an understanding of the past and the present through the strategies that underlie the relationship between the French state and African states].

But with the growth of unemployment in France and economic difficulties in the 1980s, rightist political forces have pushed for a policy of reduced immigration, trying to limit entries into the country, encourage people to return "home," and establish rigorous barriers to illegal settlement in the country. Consequently, as highlighted by Fall, the issue of immigration, but also that of the presence of emigrants in French society, of their rights (or lack thereof, particularly the right to vote) has become contentious.

> Les Africains noirs sont aussi acteurs dans le champ des luttes politiques et culturelles: c'est une dimension capitale pour qui veut comprendre le processus d'intégration conflictuelle engagé qui fait que les Noirs font aussi la France. (52)

> [Black Africans are also actors in the field of political and cultural battles: this is a fundamental dimension for anyone wishing to understand the ongoing conflictual process of integration through which Black people also define France.]

Today Fall's analysis remains completely valid. More than ever, issues of naturalization, of nationality, of the presence of immigrants are inscribed at the heart of social and political life in France. The issue of wearing a headscarf at school that became an issue in the late 80s and is central again to national debates, the scandal at the beginning of the 1990s around the question of family allocations for immigrant families,[42] and then the issue of the "sans-papiers" [clandestine immigrants] in 1996 and the repeated attempts to pass anti-immigration laws all attest to the gravity of the situation.[43]

Also, paradoxically, Europe's progression towards a single entity ultimately symbolized by the single currency also favored a return to nationalist sentiment and the need to redefine a national identity. Concurrently, however, a multiplicity of counter-waves, of counter-voices also feeling the need to define new identities representative of communities living throughout Europe has also arisen.

A phenomenon of trans-culturation has thus occurred. It manifests itself on one hand through the peripheral and central discourses' urgent need to redefine themselves, particularly as a result of the presence of the Other. It is also manifested on the other through the fact that neither discourse is strictly impermeable, but that instead a sort of osmosis or a two-way infiltration of culture occurs.

On this topic, Françoise Lionnet uses the notion of *métissage*[44] in *Postcolonial Representations: Women, Literature, Identity* (1995) to show the result of interactions between central and peripheral discourses.

> Dominant systems are more likely to absorb and make like themselves numerically or culturally "weaker" elements. But even the "inferior" or subaltern elements contribute to the evolution and transformation of the hegemonic system by producing resistances and counter discourses. (9)

Contrarily to the usual discourse on the inevitable assimilation of the immigrant and the idea of passive resistance, Lionnet highlights the creative force of African and Antillean literatures and their diaspora.

> It is not assimilation that appears inevitable when Western technology and education are adopted by the colonized, or when migration to the metropole severs

> some of the migrants' ties to a particular birthplace. Rather, the move forces
> individuals to stand in relation to the past and the present at the same time, to
> look for creative means of incorporating useful "Western" tools, techniques, or
> strategies into their own cosmology or *Weltanschauung*. (11)

Inversely, the West absorbs certain elements from the various migrant groups. Lionnet therefore advocates—despite, as she emphasizes, the fact that some of these influences and interactions are obfuscated through the medium of the central discourse's self-representation—a new vocabulary that better translates this phenomenon of contact and movement between the two spheres, in other words, the phenomenon of trans-culturation. Lionnet demonstrates the usefulness of such a concept, since it puts an end to the usual binary and dichotomic analyses (Self and Other, nationalism and internationalism, Africa and Europe), instead leading to the emergence of a multilingual and multicultural dimension, not only for literature, but also for society and culture. In so doing, discourse on difference collapses, whether it is one advocating the migrant group's assimilation (through the artificial recourse to a sort of preservation of the original culture's "purity") or one of reaction, advocating a return to a more "authentic" pre-colonial Africa. Lionnet shows how both discourses lead to artificial creation by both leading to the exoticization of the other: "Difference then becomes—on both sides of this binary system—the reason for exoticizing, 'othering,' groups that do not share in this mythic cultural purity" (14). Now beyond the binary dichotomy, we end up with a third entity, which is the result of a "*métissage* of forms and identities" (Lionnet 14). In the same manner we end up with a new *métisse* literature, where the French language reflects the multicultural diversity.

> To write in French is thus also to transform French into a language that be-
> comes the writer's own: French is appropriated, made into a vehicle for ex-
> pressing a hybrid, heteroglot universe. The creative act of taking possession of
> a language gives rise to the kind of linguistic *métissage* visible in many con-
> temporary Francophone and Anglophone works. (13)

Basing herself on the work of anthropologists Arjun Appadurai[45] and especially Jean-Loup Amselle with *Logiques métisses: Anthropologie de l'identité en Afrique et ailleurs*, Lionnet shows that the old dichotomous divisions must give way in the face of a growing interrelation between local and global. Behind the directions taken by today's society—in other words the results of an interculture[46]—emerges "the profile of a post-colonial literature shaped by nomadism, exile, and movement, where the characters, particularly the women, illustrate the unavoidable nature, but also the advantages and disadvantages of intercultural exchange" (cf. Lionnet 17).

Assuredly, the novels of our study fit squarely in this framework and Beyala's writing corresponds perfectly to this profile. Describing Loukoum's way of being in Beyala's *Le petit prince de Belleville*, Mireille Rosello points out the character's ambiguous complexity through his behavior, his speech, and his being:

> At one level, [he] is perfectly at home in the larger entity called France. [He] is perfectly at ease with the language, and is at home in the French urban and even Parisian culture. [He] does not correspond to the post-colonial image of the diasporic traveler. The only environment [he has] ever learned to decipher is [his] banlieue . . . At another level, [he is] completely dejected, marginalized, rejected by this very same society that treats [him] as foreigner. [His] language is the only adequate representation of this constant motion between being inside and being outside, between being a native and being a foreigner. (Rosello 133)

Even more so than a manifestation of duality, his behavior is evidence of a constant back-and-forth motion between his original culture and the culture in which he is immersed. The character alternately suffers and draws pleasure from the interferences and interrelations between the two cultures and the two languages. A symbol of evolution for writing from the new diaspora, this phenomenon of cultural interrelation and transculturation has taken an increasingly central place in the work of Beyala, but also in the works of other African writers as a whole. The result is a writing that serves as evidence for the simultaneous modification of language and of literature: Africanized French, "Gallicized" African writing. This writing is also reflexive, at once representative of the discourse by and on the immigrant/immigration. A constant reflection of both discourses, of both cultures, it also becomes the reflection of its own representation and writing.

At this point, an issue seems to arise naturally: faced with a *métisse* language serving as a vehicle to convey *métisse* concepts, and a more significant interaction with the Western addressee (as we saw earlier in this chapter), the reader's profile is also likely to be altered, possibly to become *métisse*. This is the issue I propose to explore further in the following chapter: that of the readership and of its impact on a post-colonial writing written within France.

Notes

1. Her first name is indeed closer to Arabic—rather than Cameroonian—onomastic, as Saïda would not even be part of the common first names for a Muslim woman in Cameroon (which would instead be Aminata, Abiatou, or Binetou, for example). We must also specify that Saïda is Fulani, and that her family, being from the northern regions of the country, probably did not encourage her education, nor her dreams of leaving for France (these aspirations are much more common among people from the south). Apart from the primary importance she grants to virginity—a primordial value for the Fulani people—

Saïda's character refers the reader to an imaginary universe and to the author's creativity.

2. This roundtable was part of the third edition of the Lille Arts Festival, Fest'Africa (November 7 to 16, 1996), and addressed the emergence of Negro-African women's voices ["Voix/Voies de femmes négro-africaines"]. It brought together Calixthe Beyala, Gisèle Pineau, Aminata Sow Fall, and Véronique Tadjo.

3. Similarly, this shift in writing extends to the depiction of Africa, the "grimy Africa" ["l'Afrique crasse"] mentioned on the back cover.

4. Cf. Rangira Béatrice Gallimore, *L'univers romanesque de Calixthe Beyala* (Paris: L'Harmattan, 1997).

5. I make this specification because her use of slang, vulgar, and obscene language has allowed her to appropriate an area widely deemed to be men's prerogative. Furthermore, her depictions of violence or horror in her first three novels have allowed her to reach, as I showed in *Femmes rebelles*, a passionate and open critique of post-colonial Africa's issues. In this sense, she also appropriates the area of political criticism, another male bastion. Her audacity therefore manifests itself through her use of language and linguistic areas, including the domains generally considered male.

6. This same type of shift is to be noted in the title of her second essay, *Lettre d'une Afro-française à ses compatriotes* [Letter by an Afro-French Woman to Her Compatriots] (1999) when compared to her first, *Lettre d'une Africaine à ses soeurs occidentales* [Letter by an African to Her Western Sisters] (1994). The change in the addressee indicates her choice of a readership is no longer primarily French and the realities of a double culture and identity with regards to Africa and France. Her shift from African to Afro-French marks a change in her self-identification, in terms of how she sees and defines herself.

7. For a detailed study of the role of writing in the work of Beyala, see Cazenave, "Calixthe Beyala's 'Parisian Novels': An Example of Globalization and Transculturation in French Society," in *Sites: The Journal of 20th Century/Contemporary French Studies*, special issue on "Women/Femmes," 3, no. 2 (Spring 2000): 119-127.

8. We will return to this aspect in Chapter 3 when we look at the impact of the readership on Afro-Parisian writing.

9. See Winnifred Woodhull, "Ethnicity on the French Frontier," *Writing New Identities: Gender, Nation, and Immigration in Contemporary Europe*. Gisella Brinker-Gabler, G. and Sidony Smith, eds., 31-61 (Minneapolis, University of Minnesota Press, 1997).

10. Cf. Cazenave, " L'exemple d'une écriture décentrée," 123-148.

11. The fact that the narrator's de-doubling follows gender lines to which corresponds a particular subsequent audience ("L'Ami" [the male Friend] for Abdou, "L'Amie" [the female Friend] for M'am), allows us to later refine the viewpoint of the gaze.

12. The terms in italics refer to the terminology used by Laronde about the Beur novel.

13. The term *roman de formation* refers to the classification of French-language African novels established in *Littérature nègre* (1984) by Jacques Chevrier.

14. For example, see Salah Rimani, *Les Tunisiens de France* (Paris: L'Harmattan, 1988); Mohammed Mazouz, *Les Marocains en Ile-de-France* (Paris: L'Harmattan, 1988); Mohammed el Moubaraki, *Marocain du Nord: entre la mémoire et le projet* (Paris: L'Harmattan, 1989).

15. Numerous texts were published at the end of the 1980s through the beginning of the 1990s on the issue of the *Beurs* in France such as for instance, Abdel Aïssou, *Les Beurs, l'école et la France* (Paris: L'Harmattan, 1987); Smaïn Laacher, *Questions de nationalité. Histoire et enjeux d'un code* (Paris: L'Harmattan, 1987).

16. Bernard Lorreyte, *Les politiques des jeunes issus de l'immigration* (Paris: L'Harmattan, 1989); Maryse Tripier, *L'Immigration dans la classe ouvrière en France* (Paris: L'Harmattan, 1989); Paul Oriol, *Les Immigrés devant les urnes* (Paris: L'Harmattan, 1992); Emmanuel Todd, *Le destin des immigrés: assimilation et ségrégation dans les démocraties occidentales* (Paris: Seuil, 1994).

17. Using Frantz Fanon's analysis for the *Beur* novel, Laronde speaks of a transposition of the dichotomist system of Colonizer/Colonized onto a new system: Overseer/Overseen. In both cases, the discourse remains a racist one looking to constrain the Foreigner/Overseen in the role of a deviant character, one which encompasses all relating to delinquency and incarceration, the punitive outcome of this process. Even though the notion of the dangerous individual only appears very occasionally in the Afro-Parisian novel, abnormal development (as linked with dangerousness) as a result of insanity is more frequently broached. As demonstrated by Laronde, both revert to a sort of causality that is the result of racist discourse's tautological approach which ends up with an equation of the Foreigner with deviance. This transposition is also visible in colonial discourse and in the similar deconstruction of racist tautological discourse in numerous novels by the new generation, notably those by Simon Njami and Calixthe Beyala. The emphasis, however, is somewhere else, primarily placed on the discourse of the Overseen, on his reactions, his inner feelings in the face of the Overseer's discourse and the discourse that he or she knows the Overseer expects of him/her. The supposed dialogue between Abdou (the Overseen) and his interlocutor (the Overseer) is founded on the basis of this very principle.

18. In *La France raciste* (1992), Michel Wieviorka shows that social exclusion has been coupled with the appearance of the theme of ethnicity. Patrick Simon remarks on this topic that initially "le tissu urbain en France façonné par une stratification sociale, contrairement aux Etats-Unis où le 'color line' détermine en partie la localisation résidentielle" (28) [the urban fabric in France [was] shaped by a social stratification, contrarily to the US model where the color line

partly determines residential location]. But with the increase of xenophobic behavior and racism (partly linked, according to Wieviorka, to the decline in in-
dustrial society and the implications for housing provided for the factories), a
certain gentrification has occurred in some *banlieues* while inversely, some
neighborhoods have essentially decayed. In *Immigrés: l'effet generations*
(1998), Eric Taieb pursues this idea of the devalorization of neighborhoods and
shows that the fear of social devalorization has become ethnicized, that adjacent
neighborhoods fear being perceived in the same manner because of their proximity, and thus that a phenomenon of ghettoization looms ahead.

19. Ben Jelloun also cites the Tunisian philosopher Hichem Djaït who notes
that "les préjugés médiévaux se sont insinués dans l'inconscient collectif de
l'Occident à un niveau si profond qu'on peut se demander avec effroi, s'ils pour-
ront jamais en être extirpés" [medieval prejudices have insinuated themselves
into the collective subconscious of the West on such a deep level that we may
fearfully ask ourselves if they can ever be extirpated].

20. In the 1990s, the author pursued this interest in the situation of immi-
grants/emigrants in his novels. After *Les raisins de la galère* (which portrays the
problems of integration and of construction of an identity for a young *Beur* girl
in her family on one hand, and in French society on the other hand), his essay,
Le racisme expliqué à ma fille (1999) uses the medium of a dialogue between an
adult and a child, his daughter in this case, to whom he undertakes to explain
what racism is, in an attempt to help to stunt the growing phenomenon.

21. In *Immigrations: l'effet generations*, Eric Taieb recalls Pierre Bourdieu's
analysis which emphasizes "le lien entre la segregation spatiale et la place que
tient aujourd'hui, dans les champs politique et médiatique, l'opposition simpliste
entre "nationaux" et "immigrés" qui est venu supplanter l'opposition jusque-là
de premier plan entre dominants et dominés" (314-315) [the link between spatial
segregation and the space taken today by the simplistic opposition of "nationals"
and "immigrants" in the fields of the media and politics, and which has sup-
planted the previous predominant opposition between dominating and domi-
nated].

22. To the contrary, novels such as *Cercueil et Cie* or *African Gigolo, Assèze
l'Africaine* or *Les honneurs perdus* attempt to move beyond such a construction
to show that the question of identity is posed in different terms today and is
linked to a search for inner balance in the face of confrontation between two
geographic and cultural spaces tied to two distinct times: the past and the present. In this case, the narration highlights the precariousness of such a balance,
with the outside harmony and the protagonist's initial feeling of satisfaction being no more than a mask. The crisis's resolution relies on the success of the protagonist in negotiating his or her own geographic or cultural dislocation and in
resituating him or herself and filling the initial inner void.

23. Textually, it is important to note that the woman loses her narrative voice
at the end of *Maman a un amant*. Indeed, Loukoum takes over and becomes the
sole narrator. While a childlike voice, it is nonetheless distinctly male in the

spirit it conveys. The alternation between male and female voices, the presence of one, at the detriment of the other, sanctions the different stages of the verbal game and of what corresponds to a struggle for power.

24. The preface documents a project initiated by the Ministry of Foreign Affairs: "Cette idée de regard à rebours a été d'abord mise en pratique par des chercheurs sénégalais et français, qui ont lancé en 1983 (à la suite d'un colloque à Brest sur la "culture de l'oralité", en juin 1982) un programme d' "ethnologie inverse," invitant plusieurs chercheurs africains et malgaches à venir étudier certaines categories de la population française" [This idea of reverse gaze was first put into practice by Senegalese and French researchers, who launched a program of "inverted ethnology" in 1983 (following a colloquium in Brest on the "culture of orality" in 1982), which invited several African and Malagasy researchers to come study some categories of the French population].

25. On the way that Bessora uses and subverts the representation of immigrants who are victims of administrative hassles, and thereby breaks away with a miserabilist image of the non-European immigrant by notably working off the autobiographic dimension of her text and her belonging to a privileged milieu, see Patricia-Pia Célérier, "De la gaulologie à l'impéritie" in *Présence Francophone* 58, *Francophonie, Ecritures et immigration*, edited by Odile Cazenave (Mai 2002): 73-84.

26. Since *Les deux mères de Guillaume Ismaël Dzewatama, futur camionneur* (1983) and its sequel, *La revanche de Guillaume Ismaël Dzewatama* (1984) by Mongo Beti, hardly a handful of novels have included a French character and given him vital agency in the progression of the story; we may for example cite *Les baigneurs du lac rose* (1994) by Tanella Boni, but even there the character of the White woman remains in the background, physically disappearing at the end of the text. Mongo Beti's last two novels, *Trop de soleil tue l'amour* (1999) and *Branle-bas en noir et blanc* (2000) also portray a White character. See also *Sorcellerie à bout portant* (1998) by Achille Ngoye, where an English businessman living in Africa contrarily takes on a pivotal role in that he offers support to the protagonist, an African living in Paris and freshly arrived in Kinshasa. After the young man faces many problems, the Englishman takes it upon himself to "re-educate" him to life in Kinshasa, with roles here, notions of familiar, internal and external thereby becoming inverted. Interestingly, even though this novel is situated on the continent, the novelist lives in France.

27. In his lexicon of important terms associated with questions of immigration, Eric Taieb defines the word community as follows: "regroupement par origines nationales (et/ou religieuses)" (19) [regrouping according to national (and/or religious) origin]. He further specifies and distinguishes the notions of community, of communitarianism, and of regrouping: "Pour les uns (école de Chicago), c'est un cas vers l'intégration, une médiation entre le nouvel immigrant et la société d'accueil. Mais pour d'autres, quand la communauté devient la référence sociale principale, voire unique d'appartenance, comme aux Etats-Unis, on risque de basculer dans le communautarisme et alors de dériver vers la ségrégation

(l' 'hyperghetto' américain), voire le séparatisme . . . Il ne faut pas confondre le terme de communauté 'ethnique' avec celui de community, regroupement plus local (de biens ou d'intérêt) sans dimension forcément ethnique" (19-20) [For some (Chicago school) it is a case for integration, a mediation between the new immigrant and the 'société d'accueil.' But for others, when the community becomes the main social reference, or even the sole reference of belonging as in the United States, we risk falling into communitarianism and thereby drifting towards segregation (the American "hyperghetto"), or even separatism . . . The concept of 'ethnic' community must not be confused with the simple term 'community,' which refers to a much more local grouping (of goods or interest) which does not necessarily have an ethnic dimension].

28. In *Immigration et situations postcoloniales. Le cas des Maghrébins en France*, a sociological analysis of post-colonial minorities in France as seen through the Maghrebi example in particular, Abdelkader Belbhari emphasizes respect for traditions as a characteristic of the immigrant community's attempts to anchor itself: "Les valeurs islamiques sont rigidifies, le sacré devient plus sacré ... Les rites alimentaires sont scrupuleusement respectés" (153) [Islamic values are reinforced, the sacred becomes more sacred ... Food rituals are scrupulously respected].

29. See Angelika Bammer, ed., *Cultural Identities in Question: Displacements* (Bloomington: Indiana University Press, 1994).

30. Doreen Massey "Double Articulation: a Place in the World," in *Cultural Identities in Question. Displacements*, ed. Angelika Bammer, 110-121 (Bloomington: Indiana University Press, 1994).

31. Inversely, Taieb shows that mixedness is a factor determining integration into French society.

32. *Amours sauvages* (1999) once again focuses its gaze on Belleville, offering a new variation on the life of the Bellevillean African community.

33. The term refers to Native Americans.

34. In this regard, the example used by Rey Chow in her analysis is thought-provoking. She discusses Malek Alloula's study, *The Colonial Harem* (Minneapolis: University of Minnesota Press, 1986), where he examines postcards of Algerian women sent by the French during the war. She notices that "Alloulah is intent on captivating the essence of the colonizer's discourse as a way to retaliate against his enemy, his own discourse coincides much more closely with the enemy's than the women's" (135).

35. The expressions in quotation marks refer to Azouz Begag's analysis in *Ecarts d'identité*, where the three terms define a new space and the delineation of its perimeter.

36. Abdelkader Belbhari makes the same observations in his study *Immigrations et situations postcoloniales. Le cas des Maghrébins en France* (1987) on the immigrant Maghrebi woman (within the context of a woman following her husband and coming to settle in France). In addition, he notes changes in modal-

ity and power within the family and in its evolution in the midst of the new host society.

37. On the topic of schooling as a significant factor in integration into the host society, see Taieb, *Immigrés: l'effet générations.*

38. Her love for her children should however not be minimized, as she does miss them; she also eventually realizes that Monsieur Tichit played her and that he is in no way different from her husband, in other words, that she left an unequal patriarchal structure for another just like it.

39. His confrontation with colleagues following a televised program on excision illustrates and confirms in a fictional framework observations made by Philippe Bataille in his study, *Le racisme au travail* (1997). Bataille notes the following point in particular: "dans ces discussions, il s'agit pour l'essentiel de démarquer la culture française, et au-delà européenne, des cultures africaines, surtout maghrébines, et de dénoncer les particularismes religieux. (. . .) Ce temps passé à converser a clairement une fonction de réaffirmation identitaire qui trouve sa voie avec l'annonce d'incompatibilités irréductibles des cultures européennes et des cultures africaines, et surtout arabo-musulmane" (18) [in these discussions, the goal is essentially to demarcate French—and beyond that, European—culture from African, especially Maghrebi, cultures, and to denounce religious particularities. (. . .) This time spent on conversing clearly plays the role of reasserting one's identity, using the proclamation of irreducible incompatibilities between European and African—particularly Arab-Muslim—cultures as a justification]. As for Joseph, he comes to reject the French model after repeated altercations with his colleagues and with Sabine. Simultaneously, he also rejects the African model; the conflation of the two rejections necessarily leads him to a crisis.

40. As a logical follow-up of his analysis of the modification of the Parisian urban landscape, Laronde comes to examine geopolitical spaces and their synchronic and diachronic variants, based on a binary opposition on the level of referential codes. In this regard, referential codes and geographic polarizations (France/Africa; Europe/Africa; and West/Africa) as well as political polarizations (French/African; National/Foreigner; Westerner/Easterner) remain intact in the new African writings of self. The same applies to the diachronic field of sociocultural polarizations: French/immigrant; French/African; Afro-Parisian/immigrant. In the framework of our study, we could thus refer to the interaction among three collective discourses by making the necessary term substitutions: the question is that of the adoption of a collective discourse where the individual recognizes himself as African and French (in an equipollent position), or as French and African, or lastly, demarcates himself from this position by choosing double exclusion: neither French nor African. This search—not only of identity balance between the two discourses, but also of belonging—is at the heart of *L'impasse*, as well as of Simon Njami's novels, *Cercueil et Cie* and *African Gigolo*.

41. Speaking of an African community may cause us to lose sight of the fact that the expression refers to a gigantic continent composed of a multiplicity of languages and cultures, rather than a single culture. Considering the African community as a whole, just like the Maghrebi community, is a way for the dominant discourse to erase cultural differences, simplify them, ignore them, and ultimately, to somehow domesticate the notion of community, by rendering it homogeneous and single.

42. Numerous government representatives protested against the fact that children were from different mothers, adding that polygamy is illegal in France and that allocations should therefore be regulated differently and reduced, because—according to them—French working class families received less than their immigrant counterparts. The issue facilitated a racist discourse where a number of arbitrary stereotypes reappeared in the daily language of individuals, but also in public language through the media, until a counter-wave occurred, which highlighted the racist dimension as well as the danger of such statements.

43. For details on these stages, see Sami Naïr, *L'Immigration expliquée à ma fille* (Paris: Seuil, 1999).

44. On the notion of *métissage* in French society, see also Amadou Gaye, *Génération métisse* (Paris: Syros/Alternatives, 1988), a collective text with contributions by Leïla Sebbar and Yannick Noah.

45. See "Disjuncture and Difference in the Global Cultural Economy," *Public Culture 2* (Spring 1990): 1-4. Arjun Appadurai particularly shows the impossibility of returning towards a pure and unique past, whether that is in so-called dominant Western culture or in third-world cultures: "The past is now not a land to return to in a simple politics of memory. It has become a synchronic warehouse of cultural scenarios."

46. On this point, Lionnet cites Amselle: "The definition of a given culture is in fact the result of a ratio of intercultural forces ... The modification of the ratio of forces ... along with the appearance and disappearance of cultures explain the changes which occur in each subcultural system when one looks at them in isolation" (55).

Chapter 3

The Addressee: Africa or the Seine?

C'est à partir de leur façon d'inventer leur propre liberté,
c'est-à-dire de perpétuer, ou de transformer, ou de refuser, ou
d'augmenter, ou de renier, ou d'oublier ou de trahir leur
héritage littéraire (et linguistique) national que l'on pourra
comprendre tout le trajet des écrivains et leur projet littéraire
même, la direction, la trajectoire qu'ils emprunteront pour
devenir ce qu'ils sont.
Pascale Casanova, *La République des Lettres mondiales*

[It is by starting with their way of inventing their
own freedom, in other words, of perpetuating,
or transforming, or denying, or rejecting,
or forgetting, or betraying their national literary
(and linguistic) heritage that one will be able to
understand the journey of the writers and of their
literary undertakings, the direction, the path they will
take to become what they are.]

Quand un monde ne nous est pas (ou plus) tout à fait
familier—qu'il se situe en dehors de notre quotidien, notre
relation à cette étrangeté peut-être de trois ordres: exotique,
folklorique, amoureuse. Trois attitudes immédiates et
irrationnelles qui annulent la distance.
Catherine N'Diaye, *Gens de Sable*

[When a world is not (or no longer) completely familiar
to us—when it lies outside our daily life, our relationship
with this strangeness can either be exotic, folkloric,
or one of love, all three, immediate and irrational attitudes
that annul the distance.]

Before broaching the topic of the potential readership for the novel from the diaspora per se, it would be appropriate first to remember the *initial* potential readership for the French-language African novel. By opting to write in French, the writer potentially granted him or herself access to a double audience: the African community, but also the French, and by extension, the European/Western community. During colonization, but also after the Independences of Francophone and Anglophone African countries, a paradox occurred whereby the writer reached mostly Western readers, as opposed to a low percentage of Africans, due to low literacy rates. Indeed, the mastery of French or English remained a privilege of the few. Nonetheless, regardless of his/her origins, both the African and the European reader had certain expectations. Phanuel Egejuru writes on this subject in *Black Writers, White Audience* (1979):[1]

> Equally in choice and presentation of subject, the writer is influenced by his double audience. The choice of subject has been limited to Africa because the audience seems to be interested only in Africa although for different reasons. The African audience wants to read a balanced if not all too good account of Africa. The European prefers novels which present Africa as an exotic land. The writer is thus under the pressure to produce something acceptable to both audiences. (243-244)

We must also admit, however, that the authors did not "limit" themselves to Africa and Africans simply for the sake of their double audience. Their need to speak of Africa also answered to a tacit pact of political commitment on their part, whereby African literature could not be conceived as other than socio-realistic and *engagée*.

Through the years, the reader's desire to read about a true, "authentic" Africa changed into a desire to understand today's Africa in its politics and culture. The African readers' desire to find Africa and Africans in these novels was associated with a need to see their cultures, their history, re-evaluated and revalued. This desire still holds true today, though it has been accentuated by the desire to find a mirror that displays reflections of current African society in its achievements and its pitfalls, in its social and political life.

The arrival of Francophone women in the field of writing in the early 1970s broadened literary space. Using the autobiographical or semi-autobiographical mode, these earlier voices corrected women's portrayals from within, addressing issues of women's place in their social, public, and private roles as daughter, wife, and mother. In the 1980s, a new feminine, more overtly rebellious, novel emerged, searching for a constructive view of tomorrow's Africa. A potentially double and even quadruple readership responded to this new feminine writing: female African and European readers and male African and European readers.

At the end of the 1980s, and then of the 1990s, even though the novel from the continent no longer necessarily engaged itself in the realm of socio-realism, the writing remained centered on a space that can be defined as African, or in the case of a foreign space (France, Europe, the United States), on African characters, both male and female, confronted by these new environments. When the writer engages himself/herself in the realm of myth, of legend, the story draws from the imaginary realm, to capture a facet of collective history and to confront the present with a past that was glorious but also occasionally laden with contradictions and weaknesses.[2]

With the novel of the new generation and the writing of self and postcolonial identity, the distance and the perspective take a new turn as a result of their nature: (1) The novel is anchored in the Parisian/French environment, and the protagonists, if they are African, are in constant interaction with French culture and society, with French people; (2) The reader, if s/he is African, is often implanted in France as well. Due to their cost, books often remain unavailable to most African readers from the continent. Through a gaze not necessarily turned toward Africa and Africans, novels offer a different perspective dependent on the reader's age group.[3] As for the French readers, they become much more significant. On one hand, the very fact that the novel is either published in France by a publishing house not necessarily aimed towards an African audience attracts readers with varied interests, who might not initially have a specific interest in Africa. On the other hand, the very milieu of the novel, a combination of African and French cultures, a partially known environment which is nonetheless different due to its African component, leads the readers to participate more actively in the story. Something they know is presented to them, to which they are thus able to oppose their own personal reading of the environment—of the representation of Paris, of the broached subject or the evoked question. If there is a desire for exoticism, it is the desire for an exoticism internal to French culture. Occasionally, the narration will introduce a French addressee and invite him to enter the dialogue, thereby creating an active interaction between writer and receiver. This is the case of Calixthe Beyala's *Le petit prince de Belleville* and *Maman a un amant*.

Ultimately, we come to the redefinition of a multifaceted audience: the French reader, the African reader in France, the African reader in Africa, the Francophone reader (Canadian, Antillean, Maghrebi, etc.). We must of course also take into consideration the gender component (male/female), which doubles the possible number of readers of the novel from the African diaspora in Paris. In other words, the reader's profile has changed along with the novel's premises: his or her profile is in constant motion as the readers no longer belong to a fixed category, no more than the texts themselves can be classified under a single label. Whether French or not (and "French" does not necessarily mean with Franco-French roots), the reader is in turn subject to the phenomenon of globalization, where the parameters of age, social status, and degree of urbanization play a primary role. The issue thus becomes to determine the extent to which this evolution of the reader's profile exerts an influence over the writer's thematic and/or his/her writing.

In turn, the term "Francophone" deserves some thought. Strictly speaking, Francophone literature encapsulates all French-language literatures written outside of continental France, the "hexagon." The extension of the readership to geographical regions far from the hexagon might suggest more open-

mindedness, annulling some of the effects of the often ambiguous relations between Africa and France resulting from their common history. Nonetheless, the
term Francophone also evokes by association that of *francophonie*, a concept
also somewhat ambiguous, which often masks a French policy of more or less
strong intervention or a policy at times close to paternalism.[4] French people,
forever convinced of France's intellectual superiority through its culture, its art,
and in particular, its literature, tend to consider Francophone literatures as unified under a single banner, that of their love for the French language, forgetting
all too soon the historic reasons leading to the use of the French language in
certain regions of the globe. We should thus speak of the dangers, or at least, of
the pitfalls (of the curse), of *francophonie* and thereby, of Francophone literature.[5]

But beyond the potential impact of the substitution of names (Francophone
literature in favor of French-language African literature) on the reader, the
change in nomenclature poses the issue of belonging and of recognition. The
novel's identification finds itself masked by the Francophone label, drawing
attention first to the use of the French language. In other words, what used to be
a tool now becomes the primary criterion for classification, simultaneously erasing the immediate implicit cultural and literary characteristics. The title of Francophone literature in turn evokes, through its implicit absence, that of French
literature. Is there more than a geographic distinction in the mind of the readers?
What are the implications of the non-recognition of these literatures as French?
Furthermore, how should, for example, Calixthe Beyala's novels be characterized: Francophone or French literature? Several of her latest novels have received literary awards, notably the *Prix de l'Académie Française* in 1996 for
Les honneurs perdus. Apparently, receiving such an award should be the ultimate certificate of the French-ness of the author's writing, if not of the author
herself. Does the fact that Beyala lives in France and has French citizenship necessarily lead to the following equation:

Calixthe Beyala = French author = French novel?

Inversely, do her more recent novels, often qualified as "Parisian novels,"
belong entirely to African literature? The issue arises all the more now that the
author is experiencing major success, with her books on "new releases" and
"bestsellers" racks. Which leads to the following question: in which aisle of the
FNAC bookstore in Paris or in other cities, or of Le Furet bookstore in Lille—
considered to be one of the largest in Northern Europe—are Calixthe Beyala's
novels found? In the *French literature* section under the letter B, or in the
Francophone literature, or the *Foreign literatures* section?[6] How does a novel
or a writer come to be classified in one rather than the other section? What is the
determining criterion? The author's profile, that of his/her writing, of his/her
anchorage in French culture and space? Or that of his/her publishing house, of
what it prints, of its orientation?

Determining what distinguishes French literature from Francophone literature or from French-language literature or again from new diasporic African
writings is not a case particular to France. The same sort of issue indeed arises

for German literature with regards to the various categories that have appeared over the past few years: *Gastarbeitliteratur* (literature of temporary workers), *Gastliteratur* (guest literature), *Ausländerliteratur* (foreign literature), *Migrantenliteratur* ((im)migrant literature). In "Migrants' Literature or German Literature? *Torkan's Tufan: Brief an einen Islamischen Bruder,*"[7] Leslie Adelson addresses the issue of categorization and of defining literature of non-German origin. Next she addresses the issue of defining what intrinsically constitutes German literature and of the legitimacy of these literatures as German literatures. In the same mindset, it seems critical to reflect on the relationship between so-called peripheral literatures and central literature, in this particular case between the novel of the diaspora and the French novel, as well as the relationship between the French-language African novel and the novel of the diaspora.

In this regard, Pascale Casanova's analysis in *La République des Lettres mondiales* sheds valuable light on the issues of power, on the hierarchization of literatures in the realm of global literature, and thus on the domination of certain literatures over others. The aforementioned categorizations, the distinctions made between French and Francophone literatures, revert to the initial notion of domination, itself partly the result of the domination of the French language as *the* literary language, reminding us of the place of French literature on the world stage until the end of the nineteenth century and of the heritage of the historic relationship between France and the other European nations, as well as between France and its former colonies.

The goal of the following section is not merely to speculate on the possible reader an author could choose, but rather to examine the implications of this virtual readership—linked in a sense to the space of writing and publication—with regards to the writing and reception of the text. In so doing, our goal is to reflect more elaborately on the issue of terminology and belonging of the novels we study, and to return to the issue of the outlining and the perception of the literatures.

Paradox of the Readership

To an Uninformed Reader, the Risk of Uninformed Interpretation

In *Le paradis du Nord*, J.R. Essomba denounces with brio and humor the myth of the West as the land of success and easy living by exploring the hidden sides of illegal immigration, where illegal immigrants are exploited by both their compatriots and by Europeans from the *"pays d'accueil."* For a novice reader, however, uninformed or perhaps reading the text a little too fast, *Le paradis du Nord* poses the risk of a counter-sensical interpretation of the text. By "uninformed reader," I mean a French/European/Western reader with superficial knowledge of Africa, mainly limited to media reports and to the "shock images" shot during armed conflict in some part of the continent or another. The novel presents the danger of reinforcing certain stereotypes that French people, and

Westerners in general, might have with regards to Africa and Africans. For instance, certain readers might infer from the text that most Africans come into France illegally, that their daily life is a succession of frauds and of all sorts of illegal activities. A second risk arises: that of seeing this text and other so-called novels of immigration become valued for their *para*-literary value and the informative sociological input they provide with regards to the experience of legal and illegal immigration. It is thus the risk—as was the case of the Maghrebi and Franco-Maghrebi novel of immigration and second-generation—of seeing these texts relegated to the periphery. A third risk arises: that of taking the reader in the direction of a current spreading through France, that of systematic suspicion of non-European foreigners, in particular those from Africa, one whereby every foreigner tends to be seen as an illegal immigrant. In other words, there is a risk of a racist current exploited by the political forces of the extreme right.

The issue of the potential for misreading echoes the primary question: ultimately, to whom are these books addressed? In *Le paradis du Nord*, who does Essomba address? If he is addressing the African reader, it is obvious that such a novel could only have a beneficial effect through its denunciation of the "*miroir aux alouettes.*" On the other hand, for a French reader, the novel could lead to a misunderstanding (in the literal sense). The reader could move right past the text's ironic dimension, overlook its ambivalence, read the account on a superficial level, and risk confounding the limits between fiction and reality, and could therefore risk arriving at a conclusion that all African immigrants share the same experience, that their experience is necessarily the same, and that clandestine immigration is in turn almost a *sine qua non* condition.

Nonetheless, the identity of the publishing house, Présence Africaine, attenuates the risk of misreading to the point of nullifying it, in that it determines a certain context for both reading and the readership. In other words, it caters to readers with a certain level of knowledge of and interest in issues relating to Africa and African literature.

As a matter of fact, Essomba speaks on this topic in a special issue of *Africultures* 15 (February 1999) focusing on writers' experiences of exile. He broaches the subject from the angle of the author's desire for recognition by the reader. He first considers this desire to be one of the important factors in a writer's decision to move out of his country and to implant himself in Paris, London, or New York.[8] He highlights the paradox of the readership whereby his compatriots, his African brothers, the readers with whom he would primarily be concerned, cannot for the most part read his work, either because of the cost of the book published outside the continent or because of the context of illiteracy in which they operate. He will therefore be read by more Western readers. But "African writers," Essomba tells us, "are conscious of the fact that what they write is not primarily directed towards an African readership. Still, when they are asked who they write for, most reply without the least hesitation that they are writing for Africans" (16). Here the second paradox occurs, notably the fact that on one hand, readers expect to find Africa and Africans in the text, while on the other hand, the author, locked in the quasi-obligation evoked at the beginning of the chapter, finds himself confronted with the task of evoking a mostly unfamiliar reality to the (Western) reader, and if he wants to be read—in other words, if he wants to please this reader—the writer must succeed in capturing him through what may be a sort of selling out with regards to what could have been his original writing: "and because we want to exist, because we must exist, we are willing to compromise a great deal" (16). Essomba then broaches the topics of guilt, obligation, and freedom of creation from two angles:

> Ce n'est pas un crime de ne pas écrire pour son peuple. On peut ne pas écrire pour l'Afrique et faire honneur à l'Afrique. Le crime serait de discréditer l'Afrique, de se renier ou de se moquer de ce que l'on est, dans le seul but d'amuser l'Occident et de vendre des livres. (...) L'écrivain africain n'a pas à se sentir coupable s'il ne parle pas de l'Afrique. Il y a des occidentaux qui écrivent sur l'Afrique, pourquoi des Africains n'écriraient-ils pas sur l'Occident? Seraient-ils moins doués? . . .
> Pourquoi donc l'écrivain africain, lorsqu'il est parti, éprouve le besoin de clamer haut et fort qu'il écrit pour les siens? N'est-ce pas simplement pour atténuer le poids de la culpabilité qui l'écrase? Car, à moins d'être sans âme, on se sent toujours un peu coupable d'être parti, d'avoir démissionné, d'avoir abandonné les siens à leur triste sort. (16-17)

> [It is not a crime to not write for your people. It is possible to honor Africa without writing for her. The crime would be to discredit Africa, to deny yourself or to mock what you are, only for the sake of entertaining the West and of selling books. (. . .) The African writer does not have to feel guilty for not speaking of Africa. There are Westerners who write about Africa, why wouldn't Africans write on the West? Are they any less talented? . . .
> Why then does the African writer, once he has left, feel the need to proclaim loud and clear that he writes for his people? Is that simply not attenuating the weight of the guilt which crushes him? Because unless you are without a soul, you always feel a little guilty for leaving, for quitting, for leaving your people to their sad fate.]

In this sense, the notion of guilt—made all the stronger, as Essomba reminds us, by the fact that leaving was voluntary—is the motivation for writing. Essomba, a novelist, thus consciously chooses to speak of Africa, to situate *Le paradis du Nord* in France, and to deal with the issue of illegal immigration, conscious not only of the parameters and of the risks governing his writing and its reception, but also of what makes its complexity.[9]

Gaston-Paul Effa: An Invocation of Africa for a Convocation of the Past

To the contrary, a writer such as the Cameroonian Gaston-Paul Effa, who lives in Lorraine, has built most of his novels—*Tout ce bleu* (1996), *Mâ* (1998), and *Le cri que tu pousses ne réveillera personne* (2000)—on an African, even national, anchorage. The caveat is that the Cameroon in question, the Cameroon of his childhood, of the child he was in the 1960s, no longer exists. The Cameroonian woman, the mother, and the Cameroonian family as he evokes them are gazes onto the past, the restitution of a facet of life appearing in his essentialized[10] writing. In fact, this anchorage in a given geographic space, in a culture that is defined or given as such appears all the more important because this is the only way for him to really anchor himself in a cultural and familial space that he was denied or that he misses. As in *Mâ*, where the narrator-protagonist is taken from his mother at age five to be offered to the Church, where his only father and mother figures are priests or nuns, and the absence of real formative figures equates with the absence of his own cultural references—the author was also deprived of his roots. Consequently, writing grants the writer the possibility of recreating the missing cultural and familial roots and thereby, of recreating himself. Hence a writing which essentializes Cameroon.

This undertaking thus appears to be contrary to that of the new African writers settled in Paris in that the space of writing, Paris/France, seems almost completely absent. But if the French/Parisian landscape is absent from the frame of writing, its impact is nonetheless key. Indeed, the Cameroonian landscape and frame the writer evokes reveal to the reader an attempt to remember, to tell of a space of nostalgia linked to absence and lack. If indeed, as in the case of writers from the previous generation of the diaspora, Effa's gaze remains turned towards the continent, his is a gaze breaking in continuity with historic time. The Cameroon he evokes is no longer. One of his recent novels, *Le cri que tu pousses ne réveillera personne* (2000), refers to mythical times. In so doing, it ressembles the writing of exiled authors who attempt to recreate the missing landscape and *cadre* through the act of writing, even if in the present case the purpose is before all else to express the pain of the child's separation from his mother, of the mother from her child, and to explore how each separately survived this breach of love.

Unlike a Marie Ndiaye who stands out by her complete effacement of *métisse* cultural origins and roots—with occasionally subtle traces of the *métissage* of the writing piercing through—Effa convokes the origins, the lost mythical space and times. His writing gets its strength in the art of invocation. His often complex style shows an elaborate quest for aesthetic value, betraying the problematic of a new African writing of self for a writer located in the French space of writing, of publication, and of reading.

Calixthe Beyala's Mediatization and Success

The risk of misreading, of the paradox of the readership which we have discussed, can be found to a much greater extent in texts such as those of Calixthe Beyala, because the publishing houses where her texts were published—Stock, Albin Michel—aim for the masses of French readers.

Many of the images generated in these novels, in particular in *Le petit prince de Belleville* and *Maman a un amant* are reminiscent of French clichés of African immigrants. Certain words and expressions can lead to misunderstandings, such as in the following quoted excerpt:

> Comme un seul homme, les Nègres se lèvent. Ils applaudissent pour la bouillotte de paix. Les femmes crient: "Youyouyou!"
> (. . .)
> Seul l'esprit de la tribu compte. (MAM 297-298)

> [Like a single man, the Negroes arise. They rejoice over the renewed harmony. The women cry: "Youyouyou!"
> (. . .)
> Only the spirit of the tribe matters.]

> Je ne m'inquiète pas, la bonne humeur proverbiale des Nègres est là et tout finit toujours par s'arranger. (MAM 299)

> [I don't worry, the proverbial good humor of Negroes is there and always ends up fixing everything.]

The second example, especially, dangerously evokes several enduring stereotypes in Western society: that of the *"Banania* smile," the image of "good-natured Negroes" and all other relics of the colonial era. Even though the author's humorous tone may thus be blatant to someone familiar with Beyala's writing or with the Cameroonian novel, where humor and irony are common tools and where the authors play with ambivalences,[11] this humor will however remain imperceptible to the uninformed reader. Indeed, these words and expressions risk being taken literally, in turn reinforcing certain racist prejudices anchored in French society. We saw in chapter 1, however, the role of these stereotypes and clichés in Beyala's work, how they constitute a writing strategy aiming to subvert the very nature of the existing expressions. The issue is thus to determine whether the author's intention and the subversive nature of a writing, which appears deceptively simple at first glance, are appropriately decoded.

Calixthe Beyala has experienced tremendous success in France after receiving a number of literary awards: the *Grand prix littéraire de l'Afrique Noire* for *Maman a un amant* (1992), the *Tropiques* award for *Assèze l'Africaine* (1994), which was also awarded the Best African Writer's Prize in 1994, and finally, the *Prix de l'Académie Française* for *Les honneurs perdus* (1996). Her popularity deserves specific attention. She was one of the first African authors to have published her first novel through a wide distribution publishing house, Stock. Stock published her first two novels, *C'est le soleil qui m'a brûlée* and *Tu t'appelleras Tanga.* Her highly colorful writing, with its raw and direct language replete with erotic scenes, was initially rejected by African readers and Africanist literary critics, or was at the very least examined with circumspection and caution. For some, notably male critics, she appeared to overuse the cheap spectacle of sexual scenes, of vulgar language, of an environment of prostitution.[12] Starting with *Seul le diable le savait*, the wind changed. Critics of African literature began to recognize her and, retrospectively, to reconsider her first two novels. The release of *Le petit prince de Belleville* by Albin Michel had immediate success. Very soon, the novel was published in paperback, becoming available in the *tabacs* of France and Navarre, in supermarket aisles, in train station kiosks, etc. About how many Francophone African writers can the same be said? Pushing the question further still, how many *female* African writers?

From an unknown writer, Calixthe Beyala has become the female African voice heard on the airwaves, the recognized face featured in women's magazine articles, appearing in numerous shows on television, engaging herself today in the struggle for a greater representation of minorities on television and in other media.[13] Her case exemplifies the paradox of the readership: on one hand, Beyala is the object of multiple controversies within the African community, mainly outside of France, due to opinions she has expressed during interviews on television or on the radio. Numerous Africans, notably women, have blamed her for the portraits she paints of Africa, of the African woman, and of Africans in general.[14] To the contrary, she is perceived by the French as the representative voice par excellence of Africans, especially African women, even more so than that of the African diaspora in France. At the very root of this duality in reception was the publication of her essay, *Lettre d'une Africaine à ses soeurs occidentales* (1995) [Letter from an African woman to her Western sisters]. The title in itself merits a moment of thought in that it automatically indicates a choice of audience on the part of the author: Western women. Secondly, the fact that it is an African woman who addresses them plays on the ambiguity, notably, that she is *one* African woman, one African woman among so many others, and thus that this letter implicates her and her individual opinion alone; on the other hand, that as an African woman, she speaks as such, as a representative of her African sisters. But the essay discusses a number of delicate issues and subjects concerning the African woman in the assertion of her identity in today's world. For the reader (both female and male) of this essay, what is written not only takes on testimonial value, but also that of a reference document, a sort of guide to African culture and to women. Indeed, the subjects of dowry, polygamous family structures, and genital operations are discussed. The last two topics are even explained without solid sociological or historical references.

The year 1997 was tumultuous for Beyala as the agitation surrounding her increased due to allegations of multiple instances of plagiarism.[15] The printing of her novels, however, remained unimpacted by the controversy. Regardless of the current status of the plagiarism allegations and the extent of this plagiarism, one must recognize that Beyala has produced thirteen novels and that outside of the pages in question, there still remains an impressive output that cannot be disregarded.

For my part, more than the issue of plagiarism,[16] what is important is to reflect on the evolution of her writing, on the significance of the multiple decenterings and slips that appear in her last novels, the marks of the author's progressive shift from Africa towards France, as she turns her gaze towards the African community implanted in France. That also implies a redirection of her writing:

when Beyala speaks, who is she ultimately addressing foremost: her compatriots in Africa, her Afro-French compatriots—as she identifies herself in her second essay—or French readers, or again Francophone readers? This question is not a given in that it breaks with the basic premises of the duality of the African novel's readership (in this particular case, of the *French-language* African novel). Currently, it seems to me that Calixthe Beyala writes primarily for French society. That obviously does not necessarily mean French readers with French roots. We saw in the preceding chapter how today's society is multifaceted, how emigrants influence the evolution of French society, no longer single, but rather multiple and cosmopolitan. It still remains that readers from France are not necessarily versed on African history, cultures, or literature and will not notice the shifts occurring in her most recent novels. Slips such as the fact that the Muslim Cameroonian protagonist Saïda calls herself "Me, the Arab" as she bakes Arab pastries for Loulouze and Ngaremba will undoubtedly be overlooked and most readers will not be aware of the *métissage* of such a representation or of the contributions of such shifts from a literary perspective. In fact, these shifts represent a central point in the evolution of Beyala's writing, as seen through her interaction with the reader, but also through the extent of the negotiations between the writer and her environment, or in other words—to return to Essomba's analysis—through the compromises made to please the (French) audience. Beyala's success is meaningful in that she was able to negotiate this interaction successfully, thereby attaining her current level of recognition on the French and international literary scenes.

These issues of negotiation, of interaction with the Western reader, and of recognition do not only apply to Calixthe Beyala's writing or person. They arise for every author from the diaspora in France. But the greater the author's presence in the media, the more success he or she experiences, the more significant these issues become. More important than the risk of potential misreading, Beyala's writing, as well as that of several authors in Paris, calls before all else for reflection on the nature and the function of these successive shifts and decenterings. Reflections of the evolution of the society in which these writers live and compose, these shifts in writing lead to a *métisse* literature, creating its own *métissage*. The fact that Saïda's character loses her Cameroonian nature to become interchangeable with a Maghrebi woman accounts for the similarities between experiences of immigration as lived by a Cameroonian and a Maghrebi woman in Belleville. As for the shifts in writing, they suggest a phenomenon of trans-culturation between center and periphery occurring within what is given as peripheral. The potential for misreading in itself is not important. What is important is the tension between the paradox of the readership and the textual shifts indicating the decentering of these African writings of self in a space of writing, publishing, and reading different from the writer's original one.

Therefore this tension is an indication not only of a change in the context of writing-reception within the framework of French-language African literature, but also of a gap between the new African writings of self in France and the novel written on the continent. Moreover, Calixthe Beyala's success with a greater public, which does not specialize in African literature, signals a certain fascination with the author's flamboyance certainly, but particularly, for Africa and the African diaspora in Paris, or *l'Afrique sur Seine*.

Indeed, we could perhaps speak of a transposed return to exoticism. On this subject, Catherine N'Diaye defines exoticism as follows, in *Gens de sable*:

> L'exotisme, c'est la curiosité qui fige tout de suite les choses dans une altérité radicale, absolue; et qui ne dérape (ni névolue) jamais vers un quelconque rapport heuristique. Aucun désir de résoudre l'énigme, de réduire la distance, ni de lever le voile. (. . .) Ce rapport est aux antipodes de la quête, de la recherche.
> L'exotisme est une forme de rencontre avec l'Autre qui se situe à l'opposé de la connaissance (être content sans savoir). La relation exotique est contradictoire avec la recherche de la vérité.
> Elle bascule donc facilement dans le folklore, dans la vision énorme et fixiste. (13)

> [Exoticism is the curiosity that immediately sets things into a radical, absolute otherness; and a curiosity that never slips (nor evolves) towards some sort of heuristic rapport. No desire to solve the enigma, to reduce the distance, to lift the veil. (. . .) This rapport is unfavorable to investigation, to a quest. Exoticism is a form of meeting with the Other, located at the other end of the spectrum from knowledge (unconscious happiness). The exotic relationship is contradictory with the quest for truth.
> It thus tips easily into folklore, into generalizing and fixed views.]

But it is also more than that. The infatuation with the African diaspora in Paris is not devoid of a somewhat narcissistic dimension, whereby the French readers find a reflection of themselves in the depiction of the French/Parisian milieu in the context of the African immigrant's daily contact with the Other. By delving into these new (African?) writings of self (of an African self?), the reader also finds a little about him or herself: a fascination not only with discovering the Other (I in the textual framework of the novel) and the I (textually, the Other), but with encountering internal depths from an outside-inside perspective.[17] The fluidity in the interaction between the two discourses (the discourse of I and of the Other, in inverted positions for the Western reader) not only offers the possibility of capturing a little of the Other, but also, of capturing a little of oneself, a self not very well known, that may even be refuted. It is a reverse anthropological gaze proceeding in the same mindset as that of Blaise N'djehoya in *Un regard noir* or of Bessora in *53cm* (1999). Inversely, these novels should not be reduced to their anthropological value alone or discarded into the para-literary realm, as their primary goal is first to express the individuality of their voice, precisely outside of all missions of engagement and affixed labels.

I would like to add another possible interpretation to the arguments already presented with regards to the fascination of French/European readers with any foreign French-language literature. The success of a number of Francophone authors—not only Calixthe Beyala, but also Tahar Ben Jelloun, Maryse Condé,

Patrick Chamoiseau, or Gisèle Pineau, in fact opens the debate on a larger issue. We have evoked the idea of a renewal of exoticism, of a sort of voyeuristic curiosity for the Other (in his intimacy, his sexuality, his desires, his pains), as well as a narcissistic desire to look at oneself. But could we not also understand this success as the sign of a phenomenon actually affecting contemporary French literature, as a means of compensating for what could be perceived as its boringness? A possible hypothesis would be to return to historic causes and to the evolution of the French novel since the end of the Second World War. Indeed, if we examine the lasting impact of this international conflict on artistic and cultural expression, we remark—and other critics of French literature must have already pointed this out—that the *Nouveau roman* was in a way born from this traumatic period, when confidence in basic notions, such as that of the hero, re-emerged eroded. The development of a literature placing the emphasis on the object, on the objectification of actions and of their description, in a sense signifies the death of not only the hero, but also of imagination, no longer allowing the reader to dream, to let his mind wander. If we follow this argument through, it seems logical that Francophone novels would come about during those same years to fill a void in this area and feed readers' hunger for a freer imaginary realm. Inversely, the readers' fascination with the African diaspora in Paris indirectly poses the problem of representation and of the part of Africa in new writings of the diaspora.

Representations of Africa. Which Africa, for which Audience?

We showed in chapter 1 how these new writings favored a gaze which was not necessarily turned towards Africa, and which, when it was, came from the outside, from Paris/France. This was not true in every case, as certain authors, such as Yodi Karone, Bolya Baenga, J.R. Essomba, Achille Ngoye, or Calixthe Beyala alternate the direction of their gaze, opting to "tell Africa" in one text rather than another. The issue thus becomes to reflect on this "need for Africa," on the nature of the depicted Africa and its function, on the confrontation between various representations of Africa, as well as on the expression of an internal Africa which, in the case of authors living in France, evolved outside the continent, in the midst of the confrontation between their selves and their imaginations. The following table features a number of African writers living in France who either look at Africa in all their texts—as in the case of Abdourahman Waberi, or in an alternating fashion, at times looking at it, at times looking away from it—as with J.R. Essomba or Bolya Baenga, or who play with the alternation, as did Kossi Efoui with *La fabrique de cérémonies* (2001) and Essomba with *Une Blanche dans le noir* (2001).

AFRICA	YEAR	PARIS/FRANCE	YEAR
Beyala			
CSB	1987	PPB	1992
TTT	1988	MAM	1993
Seul le diable	1990	Assèze	1994
La petite fille du réverbère	1998	Les honneurs perdus	1996
Les arbres en parlent encore	2002	Amours sauvages	1999
		Comment cuisiner. . .	2000
Karone			
Le bal des caïmans	1980	A la recherche	1986
Nègre de paille	1982		
Beaux gosses	1988		
Bolya			
Cannibale	1986	La polyandre	1999
Ngoye			
Kin-la joie, Kin-la folie	1983	Agence Black Bafoussa	1996
Yaba Terminus (short stories)	1999	Yaba Terminus	1999
		Sorcellerie à bout portant	1998
Waberi			
Balbala	1997		
Moisson de crânes	2000		
Essomba			
Le dernier gardien de l'arbre	1998	Le paradis du Nord	1996
Destin volé	2003		
Efoui			
La Polka	1998	La fabrique de cérémonies	2001
Mabanckou			
		Bleu Blanc Rouge	1998
Les petits-fils nègres de Verc-ingétorix	2002	Et Dieu seul sait comment je dors (Situated in Martinique)	2001

Aesthetics maintain the link between the two geographic spaces created. For a gaze turned towards the continent, we mark the same use of irony and self-derision, and of fragmentation in particular, as in Kossi Efoui's *La Polka* or in Abdourahman Waberi's *Balbala*. Moreover, we may note the increasing number of collections of short stories at the end of the 1990s: *Cahier nomade* and *Moisson de crânes* by Waberi, *Le Preux* et *Rêves sous le linceul* by Jean-Luc Raharimanana, Achille Ngoye's *Yaba Terminus*, *La Préférence nationale* by Fatou Diome, as well as collective texts.[18] The short story's brevity, its instantaneous aspect in a photographic sense, its gaze going back and forth between the two continents, somewhat like a spectator continually "zapping" between television stations,[19] contributes to the feeling of fragmentation of life in our postmodern and post-colonial societies. In addition, the assertion of the police mystery which also favors a back-and-forth gaze between Paris and Kinshasa, Paris and

Dakar, Douala, or Brazaville through investigations and mysteries to be solved, is another characteristic of the new diasporic generation's writing.[20] This is the case for Abasse Ndione's *La vie en spirale* (1998) for example. The police investigation lends itself perfectly to this sort of internal-external gaze rummaging through and penetrating the world of the urban underground. These writers' heroes, like the protagonists of the texts written against the backdrop of the Parisian landscape, do not belong to it; instead, they attempt to face the preoccupations and dangers linked to this urban world as they evolve in Paris or in any African city.

The alternation in the direction of the gaze shows that the new writings do not subscribe to a particular, fixed thematic of immigration in particular, but rather that these variations in the writer's gaze speak of a need, that of telling Africa, corresponding to the need to tell of one's own bicultural variations in which the continent remains an undeniable dimension, although it is experienced differently, due to distance.

Inversely, the diasporic character of these new writings is not simply limited to a French/Parisian space.[21] Instead, a set of specific traits gives these new writings their identity. First is the fact that this is a different generation, born after the Independences, which did not directly experience colonization and which therefore does not have the same relationship with French culture or to the language. Its relationship with the French language is necessarily different, since the polemic has changed. Second, there is also the writer's choice to settle in France. Third, there is a different gaze which, when turned towards Africans, first evokes an urban, French/Parisian space, which is in turn filtered and subverted through the gaze's new nature. There is Belleville, the *banlieue*. Literary Paris, the Paris of literature is decentered, demystified, transformed. Finally, there is the desire for individual expression, free from the implicit constraints of sociopolitical involvement for the African writer.

Some writers' resistance to being reduced to creating politically engaged novels exclusively, manifested through their choice of literature of detachment and disengagement, and of one-way accounts of the experience of immigration, fits into this attempt to freely express themselves. In so doing, they also challenge the act of locking the immigrant into a certain representation, what Homi Bhabha summarizes in *The Location of Culture* (1994) as follows:[22]

> To be amongst those whose very presence is both "overlooked"—in the double sense of social surveillance and psychic disavowal—and at the same time, overdetermined—psychically projected, made stereotypical and symptomatic. (236)

In another sense, these writers are also trying to counter an attempt to domesticate writing as seen in the application in academic and journalistic discourse of fixed categories and a sort of compartmentalization of literature—French literature/Francophone literature/etc., as seen earlier. They no longer want to be identified by a collective attribute, but rather demand to be recognized through the expression of their individual voices. They want to create and make their mark in the current of literary modernity and thus completely enter global competition. Nonetheless, it remains that even if the writer is interested in Africa or Africans in Africa, s/he is still in France, looking at the situation through lenses marked by the geographic, cultural, and temporal distance.

Having a predominantly French audience/an audience residing in continental France further creates a link between the writer and the receiver. Choosing to satisfy or instead ignore the audience's expectations is a personal choice. In response to a French audience, the writer is likely to create an image closer to the French imagination's representations of today's Africa, an image which does not necessarily conform to the reality of the situation, an image no longer necessarily presented as a depiction of reality, but nevertheless read and interpreted as such. That is notably the case of Beyala's "Parisian novels." In this sense, the post-coloniality of such a literature would initially be denaturalized, as the internal quality of the gaze and of the perspective is shattered. The previous approach of differentiation from the French literary space would evidently emerge minimized.

Inversely, this gaze is also attached to a multiple, urban, and cosmopolitan environment with its own dynamic, benefiting from globalization (or enduring it, depending on the viewpoint we adopt), leading to a more cosmopolitan and *métisse* writing. It is thus by extension a *literally* post-colonial literature betraying through its writing a growing globalization, where writers and readers no longer identify with a single environment, but rather with a multiple world nourished by diverse influences, where cultural currents meet and mix in continual transmutation, where the Africa of today and its diaspora offer a multiplicity of faces, inscribing the need to redefine the notions of modernity and tradition, and subsequently, to revisit the concept of post-coloniality.

The fact, for example, that this literature wishes to stand apart from all collective engagement in favor of emphasizing the individuality of its expression is actually the result of a postmodern and post-colonial approach. Just as some protagonists such as Yebga (*Cercueil et Cie*), Moïse (*African Gigolo*), Philippe (*Discopolis*), and Joseph (*L'impasse*) attempt to distinguish themselves from the stigmas attributed to the collectively devalued immigrant by adopting an approach of individualization and demarcation with regards to their compatriots, on the level of writing, the novel becomes singular, gaining the freedom to simply be. Nonetheless, several of its distinctive traits, notably the combination of the text's hybridity and its reception, its *métissage* of language, its subversion of idiomatic or clichéd images challenging cultural perceptions of the African immigrant or of sub-Saharan immigration, remind us of the definition of this literature in terms of discourse, ideology, and power (in the sense formulated by Michel Foucault and Homi Bhabha). The writing space, which in this sense is decisive since it represents the cultural, and thus, ideological receptacle in which the writer immerses himself, creates a framework and contours which must be redefined by the post-colonial text on its own terms: whether or not to adhere to the emanating ideological discourse, and evolve as a grafted entity, or instead,

refute it without necessarily standing in the margins, and undo the common dichotomy between center and periphery.

Addressee, Writing space, and Post-colonial voices

Here I will start from Pascale Casanova's theory of a literary heritage where
"chaque écrivain entre dans le jeu muni (ou démuni) de tout son 'passé' littéraire" (64) [every writer enters the game armed with (or disarmed from) his
literary "past"], whether or not s/he is conscious of doing so. In this context,
"chaque écrivain est situé d'abord, inéluctablement, dans l'espace mondial, par
la place qu'occupe l'espace littéraire national dont il est issu. Mais sa position
dépend aussi de la façon dont il hérite de cet inévitable héritage national, des
choix esthétiques, des choix linguistiques, formels qu'il est amené à opérer et
qui définissent sa position dans cet espace" (65) [every writer is inevitably first
situated in the global space according to the place occupied by his original national literary space. But his position also depends on the manner in which he
inherits from this unavoidable national heritage, on the formal aesthetic and linguistic choices he comes to make and which define his position in this space].
Casanova subsequently notes the need to situate the writer twice: "selon la position de l'espace littéraire national où il est situé dans l'univers mondial, et selon
la position qu'il occupe dans ce même espace" (65) [according to the position of
the national literary space in which he finds himself in the global universe, and
according to the position he occupies in this same space]. Beyond a reiteration
of the structure of literary domination and of the fact that "chaque écrivain
n'hérite pas de la même façon de son passé littéraire" (65-66) [every writer does
not inherit from his literary past in the same manner], appears the notion of the
original importance of this heritage, the fact that it plays the role of a sort of
"destiny," and that it becomes each writer's responsibility to determine how he
will situate himself with regards to this heritage (either in its continuation or in
opposition to it) and to the national and linguistic space from which he draws his
inheritance. Although this theory holds true for French-language African writers, it is modulated by a number of paradoxes and specificities. Indeed, the concept of national literature only comes in a largely secondary position, as the idea
of African literature is evoked before that of Ivorian, Cameroonian, or Congolese literature. With this label (which refers to a geographic space no smaller
than an entire continent), the primary linguistic distinctions will refer to the languages of former colonizing powers, thereby once again reasserting the predominance of the historic link between political power and linguistic power, and
the literary domination linked to this language: French literature, English literature, Spanish and Portuguese literature.

To speak of Francophone African literature is equivalent to inscribing this
literature in a subspace linked to the French language, where the term "subspace" immediately refers us to notions of dependence and hierarchization. The
previous generation of French-language African writers both on the continent
and in Paris as a whole attached themselves to writing in reaction to this frame-

work, to making their literary mark in order to in turn enter the global literary scene. The previous generation also spent significant time evaluating the ambiguities of French as their language of literary expression. Paris as "un carrefour mondial de l'univers artistique" (50) [a "cosmopolis," a global crossroads of the art world], encouraged greater freedom in writers and intellectuals from the 1930s to the 1950s. Another paradox arises, however, where Paris's "neutrality" should not mask, as highlighted by Casanova, "a constant political and national use of the literary capital," the fact that "La France et les Français n'ont cessé d'exercer et de faire subir, notamment dans leurs entreprises coloniales, mais dans leurs relations internationales, un 'impérialisme de l'universel' (55) [France and French people never stopped exerting and imposing—notably in their colonial undertakings, but in their international relations as a whole—a certain "imperialism of the universal"]. As Casanova reminds us, "Il ne nous faut donc pas oublier l'importance et le rôle de la langue, surtout dans le cas de la France, comme symbole primordial d'identité, le capital littéraire étant d'abord national et la langue "à la fois affaire d'Etat et matériau littéraire" (56) [We should therefore not forget the importance and the role of language, particularly in the case of France, as a primordial symbol of identity, where the literary capital is before anything else national, and language is "both State matter and literary material"]. The previous diasporic generation highlighted that aspect as well, posing the issue of dependence on one hand and of its marginality on the other hand. It was ultimately able to take its distance with regards to the centrality of French language and literature, and to make itself more visible by entering the scene of global literature.

But Paris as the city of literature plays a doubly magnetic role with regards to expatriate writers. As the locus of both formation and freedom, Paris served throughout the twentieth century as a crossroads and an inspiration for this renewal and represented the possibility for these expatriate writers coming from "minority," "lesser" literary spaces to break with their own national and linguistic space and to provide it with the markings of modernity.[23] Inversely, for some foreign writers, Paris has become synonymous with assimilation, with the desire of fitting a certain mold, of "becoming" a French writer. To this effect, Casanova cites the examples of the Belgian Henri Michaux, the Romanian Cioran, and the Swiss Ramuz, all fascinated from various angles with the characteristic of "strangeness" (Michaux). She also provides the example of V.S. Naipaul, originally from Trinidad, now living in London and today considered an English writer. By striving to be more English than the English in his writing, he renounced the whole of his national literary heritage.[24] In the case of Francophone African writers from the new generation though, the following question could be posed: by inscribing their writing in the time and space of Paris (as the capital of literature), should their approach be understood as an attempt to centralize themselves, to leave the periphery and properly enter global competition? Does it imply compromises in their writing, or instead, a new autonomy and advancements in their efforts to innovate?

Subsequently faced with a writing space anchored in the French landscape and a writing defined as hybrid—"Afro-Parisian," "Afro-French"—the question arises of these authors' participation in a post-colonial literature. How should their contribution be defined with regards to the post-colonial African novel?

The expression "post-colonial literature" is problematic and has been the object of several debates,[25] particularly in the Anglophone world, while French and Francophone critics have remained timid on this topic. Issue 28 of *Africultures*, entitled "Postcolonialisme: inventaire et débats" (May 2000) summarizes the issue. Abdelwahab Meddeb's article and the interview with Jean-Marc Moura regarding his essay *"Littératures francophones et théorie postcoloniale"* (1999) explore the lack of enthusiasm on the part of French academics for using this critical apparatus. Its Anglophone origins and the subsequent extrapolation of the theory to a certain distrust of anglophony explains, as highlighted by Moura, the reservations in academic discourse in France. Very often, the lack of distinction between postcolonialas a historical concept and post-colonial as a critical concept—breaking down colonial codes through literature—adds to the confusion. Meddeb finds another reason for the French silence or lack of enthusiasm for post-colonial theory, one he links to partiality towards *francophonie*:

> A la place du post-colonialisme, on a inventé la francophonie, devenue une francophonie académique et officielle. Dans le cadre de la francophonie, on continue de fonctionner dans le topos centre/périphérie—la France étant le centre et l'origine de la langue et du pouvoir qui octroie, la périphérie n'étant là que pour recevoir. La notion de post-colonialisme implique la destitution du centre, l'idée même de centre se trouve dissoute. (30)

> [In place of post-colonialism, *francophonie* was invented, becoming an academic and official *francophonie*. In the framework of this *francophonie*, we are still functioning in the center-periphery paradigm—where France is the center and the origin of language and of the power it exerts, while the periphery is there only to receive. The notion of post-colonialism requires the destitution of the center, the dissolution of the very notion of the center.]

Hence a "fear of destitution" (Meddeb), the refusal to confront French history, particularly to rethink colonization, and by extension, the lack of enthusiasm for studies. Similarly, in "Littérature et postcolonie," Lydie Moudileno remarks that all too often, practical applications of isms are mere inventories reproducing former categorizations and labels: "au lieu de s'inscrire comme dépassement des catégories, la 'postcolonie' maintient et confirme une historiographie consensuelle" (11) [instead of going beyond categories, the 'postcolony' maintains and confirms a consensual historiography]. In this regard, the essay responds to arguments presented in Abdourahman Waberi's essay "Les enfants de la postcolonie," which emphasizes the confusion we mentioned in the introduction between the terms "generation" and "literary movement." These two articles place the new African writings at the heart of the debate and pose two issues, that of their belonging to one generation, while, as highlighted by

Moudileno, it is the plurality of their voices and writing that emerges, and that of their relationship with the post-colonial novel, when they define themselves as writers "period" before they define themselves as Africans.

Our own analysis of these writings allows us to extract the following points: as we highlighted in the introduction, these writers, due to their age, literally belong to a post-colonial generation which has only known colonization through the memories of their parents, grandparents, uncles, etc., or at most, through memories of their early childhood. These novels primarily aim to express an individual voice, which simultaneously demarcates itself from any mission of political engagement or of testimony with regards to Africa. Nonetheless, precisely because this is strictly speaking a post-colonial generation, the issue of its relationship with the place of writing as the former *métropole* and their country as the former colony arises. We may thus infer a renegotiation of the former colony-*métropole* relationship in that the place of writing coincides with the former colonizing power. This renegotiation could either take the form of an unwillingness to consider this relationship or that of a need to evoke it through its transformations and experiences on an individual level.

But the age parameter intervenes, as highlighted in chapter 1, as a key factor in the generation's relationship to France and to the French language. The generations born soon after the Independences had a hope, a motivation not necessarily experienced by youth born between 1975 and 1980. They were all confronted with a new context in terms of the birth of nations, of national sentiment, of sociopolitical issues linked to the aftermath of colonialism. Today, the twenty-something are experiencing the terrible propensity of AIDS, growing unemployment and the air of crisis in European countries leading to a rise in racism towards non-European immigrants in France particularly, and heightened nationalist sentiment in the face of a unified Europe.

Each author will approach these questions depending on his/her age and experience with the subject matter and, depending on that, is likely to show a different approach with regards to political commitment. An author like Etoké, for example, deals with the issue of today's young Africans confronted with the future in Africa. While her older brothers and sisters—Mabanckou, Essomba, Biyaoula, and Beyala—denounce the myth of France as the land of success, Etoké poses the question of what other alternatives, what other dreams of success exist for these young Africans.[26] What she actually shows is her generation's distress at essentially being caught between a rock and a hard place. Faced with the desperate situation in Africa, leaving for France, along with the risks, administrative annoyances, and frustrations that entails, can only seem enviable when compared to the impasse in which the youth finds itself. In her case, even though she published her book in Paris, her readership remains double because she appeals to the African youth in France and on the continent.

Etoké's writing actually signifies a renewal in engagement, not in the form of Mongo Beti-like activism, but rather through the issues she poses, her appeals, and the depiction she makes of today's post-colonial urban youth. She illustrates the road traveled between a Njami and an Etoké: from a rejection of engagement to a re-adoption of engagement, from an aspiration to universalism to a desire for particularization and for cultural anchorage, the novel of the diaspora makes its post-colonial mark on the French literary scene, notably in its way of undoing the false dreams promoted by the neocolonialism still existent in Africa.

Nationalism, the creation of a nation, assessments of African governments, all central to the writing of numerous African novelists on the continent, are either completely absent with this new generation of writers, or at the very least, largely secondary. The notion of nomadism, of wandering, of "the African writing of (a post-colonial) self," to use Mbembe's expression, moves to the forefront through an important concern for aesthetics.[27] In this regard, the issue of an ambiguous use of the French language as the language of writing, visible with numerous Francophone writers, is completely absent here, both with men and women.[28] What is central, however, is an effort to bend the French language through the subversion of idioms and idiosyncrasies.

The issues of aesthetics as well as both the plurality and the singular quality of these voices are not without their share of paradoxes. In this regard, Lydie Moudileno poses the question of writers' paradoxical discourse: "d'un côté, revendiquant le 'tout court,' et de l'autre s'identifiant à un mouvement" (12) [on the one hand claiming the "writer—period," and on the other hand, identifying themselves with a movement]. She cites Achille Mbembe, for whom "cette tension entre l'universel et le particulier est caractéristique des 'écritures africaines de soi' au vingtième siècle" (Moudileno 12) [this tension between the universal and the particular is characteristic of "African writings of self" in the twentieth century].

It seems to me, however, that this tension is not specific to African writers. It is instead an aspect of writing characteristic of the modern nomadic experience linked to economic, political, and cultural considerations of the day. This reaction is found for instance with German-language Turkish authors. They do not want to be reduced to their national origins and to a false homogeneity by which German-language Syrian or Libyan writers are assimilated to Turkish writers. Inversely, as pointed out by Leslie Adelson in her analysis of foreign German-language literature, the risk arises of witnessing a rejection of the heritage of the writers' origins. Doing so is equivalent to ruling out what made the individual in his/her experiences prior to his/her arrival in the *pays d'accueil* (France, Germany, Italy, Sweden, etc.). The act of classifying all these literatures as literatures of immigration, for example, with all the associated images that such a classification conjures, implies the preclusion of all historical, social, political, or religious specificities which preceded the author's settlement in his/her new space.

Similarly, Adelson remarks that the categories of gender, class, and ethnicity become fixed operators, not really leaving room for individual specificities. The characteristic assumption with regards to "*Migrantenliteratur*" (immigration literature), Adelson shows, is that it can be identified as such so long as it depicts "displaced foreigners struggling with a loss of a personal identity, cultural homeland, and political orientation in the face of German 'coldness,' hostility and bureaucracy."

Consequently, continues Adelson, the fact that academia and publishing houses extract the common trait as that of being between two cultures actually reinforces some of these "parameters." We can thus identify the following characteristics:

> (1) power emanates from a "German" center (however negatively assessed), and all "marginal" positions are structurally the same, such that any differences among or within these positions are not seen as making a difference worth reorganizing as such. (2) Questions of personal identity, cultural homeland, and political orientation arise only once a foreigner enters Germany. The multidimensionality that has shaped such a person's development even prior to arriving in the federal Republic is ignored or negated, as is the condition of nonsynchronicity that characterizes the lives of the authors and their characters. (220-221)

Beyond the risks of such a myopic literary approach, Adelson draws our attention to the dangers of academic/journalistic critique when it projects a Western reading and interpretation that proves reductive. An obvious example would be that of a female Muslim Turkish writer whose text necessarily is read as an illustration of the oppression and victimization of women in Islamic communities.

Such actions reveal the desire on the part of the central society (and its readers), to generalize and reduce the diversity to one or two entities with the aim of domesticating the difference in a sense. It is thus operating in a certain optic of assimilation, this time, on a literary front.

The issues of the European audience's fascination with foreign literatures of a particular language (French, German, English, Italian, etc.) on one hand, and of its attempt to reduce/channel the differences into a few entities, as well as the author's reaction to these two forces necessarily carry certain implications for the notion of post-colonial literatures, considering the fact that these literatures, in the cases we study in this text, are created in France.

The subversion of the non-European immigrant's representation, of self-questioning, and the writing of a bicultural self, illustrate the decentering of the African novel, of French literature, of terminologies, contributing to a post-colonial spirit of systematic decentering of contexts, categories, and writings.

It seems to me that due to their desire for singularity and their quest for individuality, these new writings first position themselves *not* with regards to their national space, but instead with regards to what could be denoted continental space. In so doing, they inscribe themselves in the current of expatriate writers in search of modernity and exhibit the same aspirations for the center. If assimilation to the great literary centers actually occurs, a hyper-identification whereby the writer would attempt to "become" a *French* writer does not necessarily ensue. To the contrary. Besides the case of Beyala—who plays the card of the proximity of language/of representation between writer and receiver and the fusion of imaginations, all while operating through a subversion of language and idioms—the new African writers in Paris, in their writing of self, assert themselves and impose the following criteria.

They are no longer "stealing" fire,[29] but rather *selling* fire. Through their subversion of the French language, the orientation of their gaze on Paris, on French society, on Africans in Paris, they are no longer "translated" authors (in that they borrowed the language imported by colonization), but rather, authors who translate. And what are they translating? Not only the answer to the question: what is a real African? A real African in Paris? Or, what is an African writer? But rather: how to write about oneself? How to write about oneself without being relegated to the periphery and managing to break from historical literary (and political) domination? How to impose oneself in the game of world literature?

Through the very attempt to liberate themselves from criteria of analysis hailing from Western critique and not only associated with a geographical space (the Third World, post-colonial Africa) or a cultural space, but also with an ethnic/racial visibility dating back to colonial perceptions of the Other, these new African writings of self force a re-conceptualization of the norms of literary critique and of the meaning of the term "post-colonial." In so doing, they render us more sensible to the ideological process taking place in the outlining of literatures, their delimitations, their naming, their perception. The concluding chapter should in this sense allow us to better grasp the ensuing implications.

Notes

1. Phanuel Akebueze Egejuru, *Black Writers, White Audience: A Critical Approach to Literature* (Hicksville, NY: Exposition Press, 1979). On the topic of the audience's demands and its double composition, also see Mohamadou Kane, *L'écrivain africain et son public* (1966).

2. I am referring to novels by Boubacar Boris Diop, particularly *Les Tambours de la mémoire* (1990), *Les Traces de la meute* (1993) and *Le Cavalier et son ombre* (1997); also Aminata Sow Fall's *Le Jujubier du patriarche* (1989) and *Les Baigneurs du lac rose* (1994) by Tanella Boni.

3. Due to the nature of the problems evoked, these new writings respond directly to the youth's questions and expectations. With today's Paris and France in the background, they also paradoxically represent a form of access to their dream, that of leaving and trying their luck in France, right as the authors concurrently attempt to denounce this very myth of Paris/France as a *terre d'accueil* and the land of success.

4. See Gérard Guillot, "Francophonie. Moyen de développement ou gadget politique?" *Journal France-Amérique*, 8-14 mars 1997, 19.

5. For an in-depth analysis of the dangers and pitfalls of *francophonie* with regards to post-colonial Africa, see Ambroise Kom, *La malédiction francophone* (Hamburg: LIT, 2000). Also see Guy Ossito Midiohouan, *Du bon usage de la francophonie. Essai sur l'idéologie francophone* (Porto-Novo [Bénin]: Editions CNPMS, 1994).

6. The same issue arises for Antillean writers living outside of continental France, such as Maryse Condé, or for African writers living on the continent such as Boubacar Boris Diop, or in France, as in the case of Henri Lopès. Diop and Lopès are plausible examples, having both been published by important French publishing houses (Diop published *Le Cavalier et son ombre* [1997] and more recently, *Murambi, le livre des ossements* [2000] with Stock, and Lopès published *Le Lys et le Flamboyant* [1997] and *Dossier Classé* [2002] with Editions Seuil).

7. Leslie Adleson, "Migrants' Literature or German Literature? *Torkan*'s Tufań: Brief an einen Islamischen Bruder" in Brinkler, *Writing New Identities*.

8. Here we return to remarks Pascale Casanova made in her own analysis; she notably cites Octavio Paz, for whom access to modernity on one hand, and to recognition on the other hand, occurs through the space and time of large capital cities: "My time was a fictional time [. . .] Thus began my expulsion of the present. For us Hispanic Americans, this real present did not live in our countries: it was the time in which others lived, the English, the French, the Germans. It was the time of New York, Paris, and London" (*La quête du présent* 18-20).

9. We must remember that he is one of those authors whose gaze is not strictly limited to France and to the African community in France. His novels display an alternation in the gaze. *Une Blanche dans le noir* (2001) for instance links the two thematics and scopes of the gaze. Through his choice of an interracial couple, of addressing the issue of fake marriages as a means of obtaining residency documents, of the return to the continent, and particularly of the paralyzing effects of belief in witchcraft for those living in Africa but also those abroad, Essomba takes into account two possible audiences and their respective interests.

10. The word is a reference to Patrica-Pia Célerier's analysis and her paper "Gaston-Paul Effa: essentialisation d'une écriture Cameroonaise" presented at the ALA, (Fès, Morocco, March 1999). Célerier shows precisely how, through its poetry, Effa's writing accounts for the essentialization of the country, of its culture, of the woman-mother, and of the woman-spouse.

11. This is particularly evident in Mongo Beti's last novels, *Trop de soleil tue l'amour* (1999) and *Branle-bas en noir et blanc* (2000).

12. For example, see Oumbi Fakoli's report of *Tu t'appelleras Tanga*, *Présence Africaine* 148 (1988): 147-148.

13. This is at the core of her second essay, *Lettre d'une Afro-française à ses compatriotes* (2000), where she reflects on the issue of racism in France and on the weak representation of visible minorities in the media.

14. This reaction could also be partly due to jealousy in light of the author's spectacular success. There are currently very few Francophone African or

French writers, particularly among the women, who can live from writing exclusively. As a matter of fact, this is the argument Beyala uses herself in her responses to the various attacks made against her. In particular, see Rachid N'Diaye's article, "Dans sa nouvelle maison, un nouveau roman," *Africa International* 311 (February 1998): 76-80.

15. On this topic, see the following articles published in the newspaper *Le Monde* : "L'écrivain Calixthe Beyala est de nouveau soupçonnée de plagiat" (November 26, 1996); "L'écrivain franco-Cameroonaise Calixthe Beyala accuse à son tour Ben Okri" (November 28, 1996), Pierre Assouline's article, "L'Affaire de Beyala rebondit," published in the February 1997 issue of the magazine *Lire*, as well as Beyala's own response, "Moi, Calixthe Beyala, la plagiaire!" published in *Le Figaro* (November 26, 1997).

16. For a detailed analysis of Beyala's plagiarisms and the press and critics' reactions, see Kenneth Harrow's work in *Less than One and Double*. He has a very interesting take on how her writing has been sweetening the original texts she borrowed from; likewise, her essays are fairly conventional; what is destabilizing and subversive is her plagiarizing.

17. The determination of this perspective, outside and/or inside, is directly related to the issue of the narrator/protagonist's status, whether he or she considers him/herself to be an insider of French society on one hand, and on the other hand, whether he or she is initially *seen* as a foreigner or instead considered to be integrated in French society.

18. I am referring to *La voiture est dans la pirogue* (Limoges: Encres vagabondes/Le bruit des autres, 2000), for example, in which among others, Waberi, Ngoye, Bessora, and Efoui participated.

19. Here, I am referring to the theme of the first short story "Le sofa," in Raharimanana's *Rêves sous le linceul*.

20. One could object that Mongo Beti also uses—particularly in his most recent novels—the police mystery genre although he writes from Cameroon, and that this tool is thus not specific to writers outside the continent. That would be accurate. But we must remember that his return to Cameroon is recent and is responsible for the fresh gaze he casts on his country, precisely because he takes the inside-outside perspective, thereby discovering internal traits and changes that are striking to him as a result of his long absence.

21. In this sense, Alain Mabanckou's second novel, *Et Dieu seul sait comment je dors* (2001) demonstrates the extension of the gaze beyond the habitual trajectories and destinations (France, Africa) with a story and characters implanted in the Antilles and Africa only appearing very marginally in the background. Likewise, Sami Tchak's *Hermina* (2002) departs from the habitual trajectory, bringing in Cuba and the Caribbean, but also Miami and the US.

22. Here Bhabha alludes to Frantz Fanon's analysis of what it means to be Black (following an insult uttered at a street corner in Lyon). By extension, he uses the same designation for all those who have been displaced and exiled into the diaspora. Despite the specific nature of the occurrence and its link to the

history of the Black man, Bhabha notes a certain temporality of modernity, a reminder of what is "allowed," accepted by society—White society. For more details, see his concluding chapter, "'Race,' Time and the Revision of Modernity" (236-256).

23. Here Casanova also provides the example of numerous expatriate Latin American writers such as the Mexican Octavio Paz or the Uruguayan Alejo Carpentier. "Du seul fait de son crédit littéraire, Paris aussi attire des écrivains qui viennent chercher au centre le savoir et le savoir-faire de la modernité, et révolutionner, grâce aux innovations qu'ils importent, les espaces nationaux dont ils sont issus" (138) [Simply because of its literary credit, Paris also attracts writers who come to the center in search of the knowledge and the know-how of modernity, and who come to revolutionize, through the innovations they import, the national spaces from which they hail].

24. Casanova analyzes the example of Naipaul's extreme assimilation with regards to his adherence to the values of the British empire, his English vision of the world, and the absence of all traces of (his original) Trinidadian culture or of his partly Indian roots.

25. The expression is often contested in that it seems to suggest, through the "post-" prefix, that all links with colonization have been erased, eradicated. In reality, the current difficulties of political and social life on the African continent sadly suggest that "postcolonialism" proper is still of the realm of the imaginary.

26. Starting with Etoké's example, I evoke the same topic in the framework of an analysis of new writings by women, "Vingt ans après Mariama Bâ, nouvelles écritures au féminin," *Africultures* 35 (Février 2001): 7-15.

27. As a matter of fact, this is what Moudileno proposes in an attempt to resolve the dilemma of the often paradoxical position of writers: to return to the text and pay attention to aesthetic creation.

28. I emphasize this point because in the case of the African novel from the continent, whereas men displayed a certain ambiguity in their use of the French language, with the tension of language sometimes playing the role of a thematic thread among the texts, female writers have not shown a preoccupation with this issue; language has simply been a means for them to express themselves and to gain access to writing and to the literary scene.

29. Here I borrow Casanova's expression (*"voleurs" de feu*) ["stealing" fire] from her analysis of African and Caribbean writers' use of the other's language, where those refusing to use the language as it stands must either translate their context by manipulating the language of domination, by contorting it, or instead resort to their mother language and then be translated, as in the case of N'gugi Wa Thiongo.

Chapter 4

Specificities of the New Writings of Self

Over the past fifteen years, cultural studies in the United States in particular have broadened the scope of the notion of "diaspora": we are no longer just dealing with African diasporas, but also with Jewish, Asian, and Indian diasporas. This phenomenon is indicative of greater attention to the presence of the tropes associated with these diasporas, notably those of ethnic and religious identity, including exile, as shown by Maeera Schreiber in her study of Jewish identity and of the theme of exile in Jewish-American poetry.[1] Concurrent to the extension of the notion of "diaspora," the implantation of non-European immigrants in France and in Europe as a whole requires us to acknowledge the writing of new identities. These new writings, sister literatures, exhibit similarities with regards to the (re)definition of "central" literature (French, German, British, Italian, Swedish, etc.) on one hand, and with regards to writing strategies on the other hand. In this last chapter, I would like to further define the specificities of these new writings—in terms of their delimitation, their perception, and their reception—through a comparative study with literature of exile.

Literatures of Exile

As highlighted by Ambroise Kom in "Une littérature plurivoque; pays, exil et précarité chez Mongo Beti, Calixthe Beyala et Daniel Biyaoula," African literature is often primarily a literature of exile and exiled. Consequently, I felt it was important to consider the meaning of the term "literature of exile" in its strict sense. In his introduction to *Les littératures de l'exil: des textes sacrés aux oeuvres profanes* (1993), Jean-Pierre Makouta-Mboukou defines exile as follows:

> L'exil a toujours été au coeur de la création littéraire, comme il a toujours été une des marques des sociétés humaines. Dès le premier couple humain, dès le premier groupe social, l'homme a connu l'exil. (. . .) comme si par essence l'homme n'était destiné qu'à être déplacé, déchu du jardin originel, chassé de

son pays, de sa maison, coupé de sa culture, de sa civilisation, de sa langue; comme s'il était perpétuellement destiné à être dans les territoires et l'histoire des autres; dans les idéologies étrangères (économique, sociale, financière); dans les humanismes, c'est-à-dire dans les visions du monde des autres; dans la foi et la spiritualité des autres; pire dans la langue des autres. Comme si en un mot, la vie de l'homme était une permanente *a-culturation*, à défaut d'être une heureuse *acculturation*. (9)

[Exile has always been at the heart of literary creation, as it has always been a mark of human societies. From the first human couple, from the first social group, man has known exile. (. . .) As if man were by nature destined to be dis-placed, expelled from the original garden, thrown out of his country, of his house, cut off from his culture, from his civilization, from his language, as if he were perpetually destined to be in others' territory and history; in foreign ide-ologies (economic, social, financial); in the humanisms, meaning in visions of others' world; in others' faith and spirituality; worse, in others' language. As if, simply put, man's life was a permanent *a-culturation*, for lack of being a happy *acculturation*.]

In his study, Makouta-Mboukou refines his definition of exile by delineating three distinct types: deportation-exile, escape-exile, and banishment-exile. The distinctions he makes depend on the spatial position of the exiled-victim and of the reason for his/her exile, in other words, of his/her persecution and his/her persecutor. In the first case, the two spheres are combined, with the victim and the persecutor sharing the same space.[2] Contrarily, in the second case, the rap-port between victim and persecutor is characterized by the distance between the spheres, with the goal being to maintain this distance. The third case, banish-ment-exile, distinguishes itself from the previous case in that the persecutor is the one deciding on the distance and its perpetuation, leading to a different situa-tion in that the runaway's fear of being caught is not found in the banished char-acter; it is instead substituted by a fear of forgetting.

Regardless of the type of exile in question and of whether or not it is pre-sented as eternal, the literary motif of nostalgia for the native country appears as a constant because, as highlighted by Makouta-Mboukou, "toute aspiration à la liberté doit nécessairement signifier un retour au pays natal" (220) [any aspira-tion to freedom must necessarily imply a return to the native country]. In this framework, the exiled's space is in constant confrontation with the desired, dreamed, and occasionally mythified space; the difficulty lies precisely in the evocation of this lost space.

In *Literature in Exile* (1990),[3] the Polish author Jan Vladislav notes the im-possibility of finding the homeland as it was at the time of departure, not only because of the impact of time on the space and culture left behind, but also, and mostly, because of the impact of time on the self:

With some effort or nostalgia, we can evoke our country's true geography. Slowly, but correctly, we can redraw its faded contours. But it is impossible to return there in reality. Not only has everything changed, but we ourselves are also different, and above all, time has changed—ours, as well as everyone else's. (14-15)

The accuracy, or instead, the haziness of the memories remains linked to the time factor, and by association, to the effort one makes to remember. But the difficulty lies in this very point according to Vladislav: the memories in question are not simply individual; rather their evocation refers to a collective memory, and personal memory is a bundle shaped by the country of origin's history and culture.

> For man, the immaterial time of mathematicians freezes and realizes itself in memory. This is not only a question of individual memory, for a man's home, fixed in time, is shaped not only by his history, but also by the histories of those who surround him, by his family and tribe, and by the palpable history of tilled fields, of ancient villages and new cities, and above all by that unfathomable, mythic reservoir of his native language. (15)

Transposed to the case of the new African writings of self in France, the issue becomes the representation of Africa and Africans from the continent as an internal representation linked, as shown in the last chapter, to a time which does not necessarily coincide with the present time of French space, no more than it does synchronically with that of Africa. But it is also, through the confrontation of two spaces and two times, the notion of a modern wandering, a post-colonial nomadism.[4]

Numerous exiled writers gathered for a colloquium on the issue of exile (The Wheatland Conference) joined their voices to underline this need to return and the nostalgia inevitably associated with the forbidden place left behind. The invited writers (originally from Poland, former Czechoslovakia, former USSR, Somalia, Turkey, etc.) chose the topic of the philosophical meaning of exile as the starting point for their discussions. In particular, the Somali Nuruddin Farah said:

> What is the topic of literature? It began with the expulsion of Adam from Paradise. What, in fact, writers do is play around either the myth of creation or with the myth of return. And in between parentheses, there is that promise, the promise of return. While awaiting the return, we tell stories, create literature, recite poetry, remember the past, and experience the present. Basically, we writers tell the story of that return . . . It's a return to innocence, to childhood, to our sources. (*Literature in Exile* 4)

Subsequently, the writers decided to debate more specific points and more sensitive issues around the following axes:[5]

a) History. Has the role and meaning of exile changed? Whom do the exiled writers regard as their predecessors?
b) Leaving. Do writers leave their native countries out of admiration for a different country or culture, or are they usually driven out by negative

      pressures? Once they have left, what are their obligations to and relation-
ships with colleagues and readers back home?

c)   Politics. What role does the émigré play? What are the taboos of the new
society?

d)   Literary tradition. Is the exiled writer primarily concerned with preserving
his national tradition or opening up to new influences? What are the fa-
vorite topics of the exiled writer? Is he part of the avant-garde of an in-
cipient "world literature"?

e)   Language. Does living abroad undermine or, at the very least, influence
the writer's language? Can the writer change languages? If he does so, is
this an enrichment or an impoverishment? If the writer translates his own
book, does he create a new book?

f)   The émigré condition. How does the new society treat the émigré? What
is his role in this new society? Is the condition of exile a curse or a bless-
ing? How different is the situation of the émigré who only began to write
once he was abroad from that of the writer who had already established his
literary credentials at home? Should the émigré writer strive toward liter-
ary/social integration in the new community? What is the nature of a creative process doomed to be ignored, given the conditions of exile? What
sort of ego must an author have to accept such odds?

g)   Commonalities and difference. What do exiled writers have in common,
regardless of their country of origin, and what are the factors that differ
from one national group to another? Are there national literary traditions
that exercise a greater influence on the exiled writer than do others? (Preface, xii)

Some of the discussion topics chosen by the writers at this conference appear
at the heart of works by the authors we are studying. To take a few steps back,
several of the characteristics of exile literature as defined by Makouta-Mboukou
can also be found in the new diasporic writings. If the protagonists live in Paris
or elsewhere in France, it is generally by choice. Nonetheless, the feeling of
being displaced, of being in the territory, the ideology, the culture, and the language of the other appears at the heart of most of the studied texts. The protagonist's space is one, as in the case of the exiled, marked either by a certain wandering, or at the very least by loneliness and an undefined feeling of lack,
heightened by the feeling of not belonging to the new environment. This condition is also par excellence that of the post-colonial subject today, in other words,
one where nomadism and identitary wandering are the premises of his identity.
In this regard, it is necessary to establish a distinction between male and female
characters, and between male and female writing. Male characters in the work of
male and female writers express a marked feeling of nostalgia, the need to look
back, to look towards the past and the place left behind.[6] Female characters, absent or relegated to the background in the work of male writers, instead occupy
the foreground in female writing and emphasize the situation of limbo between
two cultures. For example, in *Kesso, princesse Peuhle*, Kesso says the following:

Aujourd'hui, je ressens la nécessité de me regarder, de parler de moi, et de re-
mettre en question, pour mieux les comprendre, ce que furent mes choix: vivre
à l'occidentale. J'ai trop joué le jeu des Blancs, j'ai, comme on dit, poussé ma
balle trop loin dans leur camp, et me voilà vivant comme une soi-disant civili-
sée. Je raisonne, je m'inquiète à l'idée de ne plus savoir où je suis. Je me sens
écartelée entre deux mondes, avec, d'un côté, mes racines brûlées, et de l'autre,
un mari, des enfants, et cette vie agréable qui me satisfait, mais qui parfois, me
semble dure à supporter. (36)

[Today I feel the need to look at myself, to talk about myself, and to question—
in order to better understand them—the choices I made: to live in a Western
way. I have played the White game for too long, I have, as people say, pushed
my ball too far into their side, and here I am, living as a so-called civilized
woman. I reason, I worry at the thought of no longer knowing where I am. I
feel torn between two worlds, with, on one side, my burned roots, and on the
other, a husband, children, and this pleasant life that satisfies me, but which I
sometimes find hard to bear.]

Similar echoes can be found in Calixthe Beyala's work, for instance, in
Assèze l'Africaine:

En France, j'appartiens encore à une minorité. Jamais je ne serai considérée
comme une Blanche. Je n'appartiens à rien. Une hybride! Un non-sens! (A, 339
[Sorraya's voice])

[In France, I still belong to a minority. I will never be looked at like a White
woman. I don't belong to anything. A hybrid! A nonsense!]

Nonetheless, this stage is merely transitory. Novels by female writers, particularly works by Beyala, display the desire of female characters to move forward, to *become*, and to assess immigration through the potential for individual
accomplishment it offers them. Whether in *Le petit prince de Belleville, Maman
a un amant, Assèze l'Africaine*, or *Les honneurs perdus*, the emphasis is always
placed on the transformation of gender roles in the African community in Paris.

Male writers, whether a Njami or a Biyaoula, place greater emphasis on the
feeling of individual *malaise* which increases until the explosion of an identity
crisis, showing that the male character's stability was only an illusion, a voluntary blindness through which he attempted to attenuate feelings of lack and aspirations towards his homeland and tried to quiet all feelings of exile. The extreme
version of this behavior consists in immuring all feelings of nostalgia in silence.
The most patent example thereof is Tierno Monénembo, who only addresses the
topic of Guinea and of his exile in *Cinéma*, where he takes the voice of the autobiographical "I" for the first time, after six novels. The shift in Monénembo's
writing reveals a long process of maturation through which the writer chose to
quiet his voice as an exile in favor of focusing on the surrounding world, such as
the French world/the world of immigrants in Lyon in *Un rêve utile* (1991) or the
intricacy of African and Latin-American influences in Brazil with *Pelhourino*

(1995). For Monénembo, the issue of the free or forced choice (following exile) to settle in France operates in reverse. Speaking of the self, remembering a time which is no longer—that of childhood, but also of a national and historical context in the development of Guinea—required years of writing, during which he went from a caustic critique of Africa to a gaze turned away from Africa in favor of the diasporas, to finally return to Africa and contemporary Guinea, and most recently, to Rwanda, with *L'Aîné des orphelins* (2000). The wandering of his writing is unusual: through silence—by silencing his feelings—Monénembo retrospectively speaks of his lack and nostalgia.

The undefined feeling of lack, of a wandering, the par excellence attribute of exile literature, can also be attributed to immigration literatures. We saw in chapter 1 how these new writings of the self—whether they focus on detachment, displacement, or on the phenomenon of immigration as such—refer, through their variants, to the immigrant African community in France. We also saw that through their subversion of the usual clichés, they decenter both the so-called immigration novel and the terminology commonly used to frame literature in France.

In the same manner, whether the issue is addressed from the angle of a feeling of *malaise* in the protagonist due to his displacement—not necessarily with regards to Africa, but rather with regards to his identity as an African in Paris (as in Simon Njami's novels for example), or whether it is more an issue of internal exile rather than actual departure and the nostalgia for a return, the notion of displacement remains at the heart of the problem.

Indeed, immigration literature, like exile literature, looks at the phenomenon from the angle of displacement, what Jean-Pierre Makouta-Mboukou defines as "déplacement physique et social dans le temps et dans l'espace; déplacement culturel, moral et spirituel, déplacement linguistique, idéologique et économique" (255) [physical and social displacement in time and space; cultural, moral, and spiritual displacement, linguistic, ideological, and economic displacement].

> Dans tous les cas d'exil, de l'intérieur ou de l'extérieur, il s'agit de l'expulsion de ce fœtus qu'est l'homme, de la matrice sociale, de la matrice maternelle qui correspond à une perte d'identité. Cette expulsion se traduit-elle nécessairement par une *aliénation*, l'individu cessant de s'appartenir et devenant esclave de ce qui l'entoure, loin du milieu originel? Y'a-t-il nécessairement *a-culturation*? Ou au contraire constate-t-on une véritable *acculturation*? (255)

> [In all instances of exile, whether internal or external, what occurs is the expulsion of this fetus that is man, of the social matrix, the maternal matrix, corresponding to a loss of identity. Does this expulsion necessarily manifest itself in an *alienation*, whereby the individual stops belonging to himself and becomes a slave to his surroundings, far from the original milieu? Is there necessarily *a-culturation*? Or do we instead witness an actual *acculturation*?]

In his general conclusion, Makouta-Mboukou summarizes the central point of literature of exile: the outcome of any exile, regardless of the *form* of exile, is lived as a loss of identity. Departure is never experienced as a gain of freedom, but rather, as a constraint and as suppression. This aspect is the central nerve of most Afro-Parisian novels, whether we speak of novels by Njami, Beyala, of *Kesso, princesse peuhle* or *L'impasse*. Contrary to novels of exile, however, the protagonists either do not really intend on going back to their native country, or when they wish to do so, they are in no position to realize their wish.[7]

Finally, the fundamental issue posed by Makouta-Mboukou must also be posed in the case of immigration: does being far from one's original milieu necessarily lead to alienation and to the loss of culture? To an *a-culturation* or an *acculturation*, to use Makouta-Mboukou's terminology?

Specificities of the Novel by the African Diaspora in France

The new African writings are not to be simply analyzed in terms of their similarities with literatures of exile or with sister literatures such as *Beur* or Antillean literature, Italophone literature in Italy, or in the case of Great Britain, writings from the African diaspora in London. A number of differences must be pointed out. Indeed, contrarily to the Antillean novel, the Afro-Parisian novel rests on a national experience.[8] As we saw in the introduction, contrary to the *Beur* novel or, in another context, the African-American novel, the large majority of Afro-Parisian novels are written by immigrant African writers remembering their place of birth and childhood.

A first difference lies in the objectives of their methodology. Indeed, with the exception of Calixthe Beyala who, through her characters, considers African immigrants as a community, though she does not really give them a collective voice, the Afro-Parisian novel does not voice claims for the right to be different, as seen in *Beur* literature. The authors' main concern is instead to have some sort of individual impact which would not only justify detachment from the community, but also render it worthwhile. This obviously contests the idea that individual writing is impossible without the backdrop of a collectivity.[9] But, contrary to the *Beur* novel, the literary creation in question here does not necessarily speak of a need to differentiate oneself from national identity. A priori, there are no Afro-Parisian political claims, let alone an Afro-Parisian discourse as found with the *Beur*, for example. The case here is one of voices expressing themselves, rather than the creation of a single homogeneous discourse. If a discourse does exist, it is a doubly composed discourse, which uses otherness as a strategy without necessarily attempting to depict a social situation of extreme otherness, which would be synonymous with ghettoization. Indeed, contrary to the *Beur* novel, which often speaks of a lack of identity through the rejection of bilingual, bicultural, and even biracial ties, the Afro-Parisian novel defines itself through a *métissage* at its core. This does not mean that identity crises do not occur or that characters' development occurs simply and harmoniously. Daniel Biyaoula's *L'impasse* is the most probing example of this phenomenon. Balance in one's identity as linked to the surrounding global culture and place is to be redefined for each individual, without the necessary intervention of a collective voice (and thus a mission imparted on the author). This is a discourse at once rejecting the central African discourse and that of the peripheral collectivity (here, diasporic), which attempts to impose yet another identity. As we saw in the first part of this text, this is also the rejection of an engaged literature, which limits the African writer to writing about Africa and Africans. Phillipe Camara's novel, *Discopolis*, is certainly the most patent illustration thereof.

On the other hand, this novel also demarcates itself from the immigration novel as generally defined by the *Beur* novel, which speaks of the integration issues faced by immigrant communities, such as generational challenges, delinquency, incarceration, the central power's control mechanisms, the ghettoization of *banlieues*, the racial and racist tensions between Maghrebi immigrants/young *Beurs* and White French people, and between immigrants and the surveillance system (police, social workers, etc.). Some of the same characteristics are also found in the Afro-Londonian novel. The central power control mechanisms and the community's ensuing reactions remain rare in the new African writings of self, however. Indeed, the police practice of checking identification documents, and the world of ghettos or of illegal squatter settlements figure very little in the Afro-Parisian works, right up until the 1990s. These topics have only arisen over the past five years, as seen with Essomba's *Le paradis du Nord*, Alain Mabanckou's *Bleu Blanc Rouge*, Luc Léandre-Baker's *Ici, s'achève le voyage*, as well as Nathalie Etoke's *Un amour sans papiers* and Bessora's *53cm* for the female writers. The presence of squatter settlements corresponds to an infiltration of the Parisian place/center and to a redefinition of the squatter: "le réenclavement a ainsi valeur de différence (décalage social, culturel, politique) mais aussi de *subversion* (affirmation des décalages comme lieu d'ancrage)" (Laronde 125) [the redefinition is thus indicative of difference (social, cultural, or political shifts) but also of *subversion* (assertion of shifts as spaces of anchorage)]. However, this notion of anchorage does not appear in *Le paradis du Nord*, for example. Indeed, the protagonist does not experience a warm environment where a community comes to life, but rather a stifling environment where the individual is denied minimal living space.[10] In this sense, this novel also stands apart from the Italophone novel, written by immigrant writers, generally originating from the Maghreb, who wish to transcribe their experiences of migration and immigration in Italian society.[11] Closer to the *Beur* novel, the Italophone novel is the expression of a collective voice, that of the African immigrant (from the Maghreb or from sub-Saharan Africa) in Italian society. The relationship between the writer, the space of writing, and writing is different due to the relationship the writer has with the Italian language. Indeed, Italian was not a colonizing language for the Maghreb, and the choice of immigrating in Italy as opposed to France, of learning the language and wanting to write in Italian is interesting in itself. The phenomenon clearly indicates new tendencies, where immigration towards a country in Europe no longer necessarily corresponds to criteria of historical colonial heritage, such as the mastery of a common language of expression and writing. German-language Lebanese writers or the new writers of Maghrebi origins settling in Italy are testaments of a new international map of writing and linguistic expression in Europe. The new African writings are an integral part of this phenomenon, adding their own material to French literature.

Another point to underline is that, although these new writings use the transposition of colonial discourse and of a Dominant/Dominated, Surveying/Surveyed, or National/Foreigner discourse on one hand, on the other hand, they move away from the other habitual contours of the immigration novel, particularly contours in which classes are in opposition, with the subaltern figure of the immigrant worker relegated to archetypal, if not stereotypical jobs (city cleaning services), and thus, from a rather fixed representation of the immigrant.[12] The characters in the new African writings of self in Paris display a variety of occupations: from journalism to modeling, music, factory work, office work, homelessness, all the way to the life of a gigolo, thereby covering a wide range of social, cultural, and religious paradigms. For several of these novels, the difficulties encountered by the protagonists are psychological, linked to internal conflict and to an identity quest. As we have repeatedly seen, the hero by no means has a heroic profile. Through his marginality and marginalization, he emblematizes the post-colonial context's fragmentation and globalization as they relate to migration from the African continent to the "first world." This literature, however, differs from exile literature in that the exile is internal rather than actual, and is linked to a voluntary, rather than forced, departure. As I highlighted previously, the resolution of this internal conflict lies in the renegotiation of individual identity in light of a new geographical and cultural space, and of an African community different from that of the country of origin. Particularly, the issue of return is not posed in the same terms. If there is some nostalgia with regards to the space left behind, the protagonist is often in a position where returning to his or her country is not really an option, even if it is a desire. Paradoxically, when there is a return, it is often a forced one, the result of some recent development in government policies regarding illegal immigration, as in the case of Salif's return to Mali, when he left without a trace, unable to contact Malaïka.[13]

Contrary to the Antillean novel, these new writings do not deal with the issue of identity in terms of replenishment and anchorage through the search for a restituted past.[14] Most protagonists in the novels studied here direct their gaze towards the present and the future, on the "here" rather than a hypothetical "there" to which they cannot return. In the case of Joseph (*L'impasse*), it was precisely the return to this other place and the confrontation with an African life surpassing him that precipitated an identity crisis. Similarly, Moïse (*African Gigolo*) became aware of his life's artificiality through references to Africa and his family in a letter from his mother. Yegba (*Cercueil et Cie*) also came to confront his present life in Paris and to face the void within him after his encounter with the two African-American police officers, through their questions on Africans in France and on the relationship between Whites and Blacks. That still did not lead him to think about returning to Cameroon or to glorify his past life in his country though; his replenishment had to occur from his life in Paris.

The new diasporic writings in Paris also exhibit distinctions with regards to the Anglophone novel in London. Even though their gaze is certainly geared towards auto-contemplation, it is a gaze devoting ample time and space to French society. As we saw with Buchi Emecheta, Afro-Parisian writers are not at a point, unlike their Afro-Londonian counterparts, where they can use characters belonging to a non-African community (Antillean or *Beur* for example).[15] Afro-Parisian novels also offer a different transcription of the society *d'accueil*. They do not speak of physical violence as do the novels in London. It is instead the *Beur* novel, as mentioned earlier, which serves as the vehicle for similar accounts of the rapport between immigrants and the society into which they come. One would have to revert to Sembène's *Docker Noir* or *La Noire de. . .* to find violence of a similar sort, although it is not of the same level; in this case, it is portrayed as a *reaction* to extensive violence and racism. Moreover, the gaze onto British society is above all one of disdain and disgust, certainly not a humorous one as found in the works of N'djehoya or Beyala, for example.

Some of the questions posed by the exiled writers gathered at the Wheatland conference[16] may allow us to better frame specificities of the new African writings of self. The idea of predecessors and peers suggests that these young writers stand apart from the previous generation of intellectuals from the African diaspora in Paris. Here again, historical reasons bring a particular difference to light, notably the fact that the previous generation's stay in France coincided with the awakening of a collective consciousness, with a movement around the notion of Négritude. Today, even though a group of diasporic, Afro-Parisian writers does exist, even though they know and occasionally socialize with each other (which is neither automatically nor necessarily true as it was between the 1930s and the 1950s), they do not constitute a movement, nor do they claim a common cultural heritage, whether that of their contemporary peers on the African continent, or that of the previous generation making up *Afrique sur Seine*. If a heritage or influence does exist, it must be that of Black American writers from the Harlem Renaissance in Paris (in this aspect, the writers are reminiscent of the Négritude generation). In particular, I am thinking of Blaise N'djehoya, Simon Njami, and Yodi Karone. Besides his interest in jazz, for instance, N'djehoya co-produced *Un Sang d'encre* (with Jacques Goldstein), a documentary on the generation of African-American writers and artists in Paris between the 1930s and the 1950s. The documentary deals with the possible parallels between a Cameroonian writer coming to Paris in the 1970s-1980s like N'djehoya, and a writer coming to the same city forty years earlier, like Baldwin.

Simon Njami was also attracted and influenced by African-American literature from those years. In fact, his first novel *Cercueil et Cie* showcases characters directly inspired by Chester Himes's novels. Chester Himes himself becomes a character in the novel (*in absentia*, since he is either absent, dying, or dead). Furthermore, the title of his second novel, *African Gigolo*, is an implicit reference to American culture, as it is immediately evocative of the movie *American Gigolo*. And then of course, there is the biography Njami wrote of James Baldwin. In *A la recherche du cannibale amour*, Yodi Karone indirectly evokes the United States when his character sets out in search of his manuscript and the search points him in the direction of the US.[17] Other writers also display in one way or another the same interest for the other side of the Atlantic, as in the case of Léandre-Alain Baker in *Ici, s'arrête le voyage* or, more recently, Henri Lopes's *Dossier classé* (2002).

As we have seen, the notion of departure has also evolved. Let us remember that when it is construed as an integral part of the narrative fabric, it is conceived from the angle of the motivating factors for leaving, of what the space of arrival—France or Paris—evokes. Differently from the previous generation, the departure is conceptualized as a situation of migration rather than as a stay for educational purposes. When looking at the condition of emigrants in the new society, the author not only individually but also collectively deals with issues of identitary transformation with regards to the changes they suggest due to the presence of Africans/an African community in current French society. Questions regarding the evolution of the writing itself arise through the theme of migration/immigration. How does being immersed in the Parisian milieu and the French language influence the creative process? We may note for example that most of the writers who place their fiction against the backdrop of the Parisian landscape are those living in Paris or in its *banlieues*; that inversely, the writers living in provincial cities, in Bretagne, Vendée, or in Lorraine, such as N'Diaye, Waberi, Monénembo, Effa, etc., first turn their gaze towards the African continent. We could, of course, speculate on possible causes: that the cosmopolitan and multicultural urban Parisian environment paradoxically invokes Africa, makes it more present. It could be that this universe confronts the writers more imperatively with the issues of identity and with their compatriots living in the same universe. Inversely, the absence of the Parisian universe, unique in its own way, leads to a greater need to evoke Africa, to turn one's gaze towards the continent; in this sense, Paris as a space of living and writing is determinant in the creation of a so-called Afro-Parisian novel. All of these claims, however, remain in the realm of speculation and intuition. What to me seems more interesting and meaningful is to consider if and how these writers are interested in the preservation of an African literary and cultural heritage and how, on the flip side, the issue of literary integration in the new community can attract and influence them. But even if and when the writers identify themselves as African writers, they still do not make any specifications that refer the reader to a national literature. Inversely, they do not necessarily identify as Afro-Parisians. If they do identify themselves, it is simply as writers, thereby marking an aspiration to belong to a so-called "global" rather than "third-world" literature. Here we return to the issue of equal recognition and participation in global literature.

In all these texts, the issue of authenticity, of what it means to be a "real" African man or woman transplanted in a foreign space in modern society, remains central in that it refers readers to the notion of auto-definition and by extension, to the writing of self. Here I revert to Mbembe's analysis in "A propos des écritures africaines de soi": how to define oneself, think of oneself outside of the definitions formed and prescribed by the West, how to break with the "liturgical

mode of victimization" (16) and manage an equilibrium of "représentations africaines qui se forgent à l'interface de l'autochtonie et du cosmopolitisme" (16)
[African representations created at the intersection of autochthony and cos-
mopolitanism]. The narrative becomes an African writing of self, standing apart
through its singularization. As such, these writings pose the issue of belonging
on a literary front. To pose one's individuality as a primary principle is already
to detach oneself from the African novel. How to define, on the other hand, the
fictive and invisible frontier between African and French novel and African and
diasporic novel? In this case, open-mindedness with regards to new conceptions
of the novel and to the writer's role prevails over open-mindedness towards new
influences, notably French influences. The issue of the author's literary integration is to be conceived in terms of the reception of his or her text and of the audience's reaction. The fact that the French reader is interested in a particular
author or a particular novel does not necessarily mean that he therefore characterizes it as "French."

Inversely, by simply claiming their identity as writers, these men and women
are illustrative of a characteristic phenomenon, notably the aspiration towards a
globalization which would allow them to break from the habitual French-
African literature dichotomy. Through their efforts towards universalization and
their aspirations to individual expression, many of these writers are able to
"rompre le cercle du doute et de l'angoisse identificatoire" (Mar Fall 41) [break
the circle of identitary doubt and anguish] and to move beyond the common
alternative of isolation-assimilation facing the African diaspora in France.[18] But
they are also challenging the notion of "Francophone literature" and the principles of categorization and classification among literary works. Parallel to the
trans-culturation of French society, the literature also reflects a trans-culturation
whereby the French language absorbs terms borrowed from African languages,
and where African writing Gallicizes itself. Far from being negative, the resulting hybridization proves the existence of a dynamic creative current by losing its
pejorative connotation. In so doing, it breaks down the usual center-periphery
dichotomies and lies in the scope of a writing methodology in the post-colonial
spirit.

The fact that these new writings primarily correspond to individual expressions demarcating themselves from the idea of a movement, of collective claims,
and of some imparted mission, is at the very root of this literature's success,
when compared for example to the now out-of-steam *Beur* novel. Much like
Jean Baudrillard's claims in *A l'ombre des majorités silencieuses* (1982) that
today's masses can no longer be represented, much less spoken for, these writings show that it is fragmentation and fragmented, prismatic discourse that
grants access to the immigrant's voice and to his rapport with the so-called
hegemonic discourse. The fragmentation and subversion of the dominant discourse in the work of Beyala, Bessora, and N'djehoya demonstrate that point.
Through their amalgamations, these texts show, contrary to Gayatri Spivak's
analysis, that the "subaltern" can effectively speak and articulate his or her vision of the society to which he or she belongs as a subject.

Moreover, the subversion of a single representation of the non-European immigrant aims to nullify this fixed vision of the subaltern. On one hand, it shows and highlights the persistence of a resilient collective imagination laden with clichéd derogatory images of the immigrant, mostly referring to Maghrebi immigration. On the other hand, it facilitates the breakdown of the parameters determining the interaction dynamic: factors of class, gender, biculturalism, race (and biracial-ness).[19] Thus the writers whose gaze lingers on the rejection of Africa/Africans show the role played by the class parameter. For example, in Njami's novels, Moïse and Yegba intend to distinguish themselves through their professional success from representations of the unemployed immigrant or the immigrant working for the city's cleaning services and who are confronted with controls of identification documents in public transportation. To the contrary, in *Les honneurs perdus*, Saïda's character, who identifies herself during her process of adapting herself to her new universe as "Me, the Arab," tells of the experience of a character's decentering, the new generic and stereotypical representation of the immigrant Maghrebi woman, which has become that of the immigrant woman by extension. The subversion of these representations and the confluence of discourse on immigration, as well as experiences of immigration, when taken in their multiplicity, shatter the dominant central discourse. The reader is now forced to reconsider the non-European immigrant individually, according to the historical and cultural baggage the immigrant brings along, and consequently, to the wealth he or she brings to the society he or she enters. In this sense, the writers of the new diaspora renew the post-colonial discourse, in the way that they redefine the basic parameters.

The new writings rest on the very principle of this current and of literary transculturation. These novels reveal profound work on language and aesthetics, characterized by a fluidity and the birth of a third dimension, of a *métisse* and bicultural writing by definition and by nature, which draws its sources from the wealth of two cultural and literary heritages, African and French. Eventually, this type of writing refers the reader to deep transformations not only of French literature, but also of French culture and society, no longer single, but multiple.

Notes

1. See Maeera Schreiber, "The End of Exile: Jewish Identity and Its Diasporic Poetics," *PMLA* 113, no. 2 (March 1998): 273-287.

2. Makouta-Mboukou defines deportation-exile through the persecutor's concurrent presence: "le persécuteur n'aura qu'une idée, tout au long de l'existence: opprimer le plus possible l'exilé pour tuer en lui toute velléité de révolte. L'exilé n'aura de cesse qu'il n'ait trouvé de faille dans le système de l'oppression pour renverser le bourreau ... Les exemples types seront sans doute: le peuple élu en Egypte, *Tamango* de Prosper Mérimée, *Bug-Jargal* de Victor Hugo, *Racines*

d'Alex Haley" (14) [the persecutor will have but one goal throughout his whole existence: to oppress the exiled as much as possible in order to kill even the slightest desire of revolt within him. The exiled finds no rest until he has found a crack in the oppressive system that could allow him to overthrow his persecutor. ... Typical examples are undoubtedly: the chosen people in Egypt, Prosper Mérimée's *Tamango*, Victor Hugo's *Bug-Jargal*, Alex Haley's *Roots*].

3. See *Literature in Exile*, ed. John Glad (Durham, London: Duke University Press, 1990).

4. The space of the exiled is characterized by wandering, loneliness, and even temptation, that is, faced with a feeling of abandonment, the exiled is tempted to give in to the best offer to find a little human comfort.

5. See *Literature in Exile*, ed. John Glad. (Durham, London: Duke University Press, 1990).

6. Joseph and Moïse's characters in *L'impasse* and *African Gigolo* respectively are exceptions to this perspective.

7. Moïse in *African Gigolo* and Malaïka in *Un amour sans papiers* are exceptions. Moïse sees his return as a solution to his identity crisis, while Malaïka goes home after her studies, hoping to change daily life through her activism.

8. Evidently, authors born in France such as Marie N'Diaye, in Switzerland like Simon Njami, or in another country are exceptions.

9. Laronde comes to a similar observation regarding the *Beur* novel: "Dans le discours identitaire, la part individuelle du discours ne fonctionne [donc] pas en relation d'opposition systématique à la part collective mais en relation de dépendance: sans fond collectif, il n'y aurait pas de discours identitaire individuel" (17) [In discourse regarding identity, the relationship between the individual and collective components of the discourse is [therefore] not one of systematic opposition, but rather one of dependence: without a collective backdrop, there would be no individual discourse on identity].

10. *Un amour sans papiers* is an exception in this regard. The notion of warmth is present and contiguous with the stifling feeling and disregard for minimal living space: over thirty people are crammed into Salif's apartment, as in the rest of the building doomed for destruction, living in the most precarious situation. Nonetheless, the first thing the protagonist, Malaïka, notices upon entering, is the feeling of being back in Africa, with the market, the businesses, the different languages, the various dishes being prepared, all of it going full force with people facing their situation in good humor and in a united struggle.

11. Italophone literature also encapsulates immigrants from former Italian colonies (Eritrea, Somalia), often sent by their parents to gain a "Western" education. See Graziella Parati, ed., *Mediterranean Crossroads: Migration Literature in Italy* (Madison, NJ: Fairleigh Dickinson University Press, 1999), Azade Seyhan, *Writing Outside the Nation* (Princeton: Princeton University Press, 2000).

12. Beyala's characters, particularly in *Le petit prince de Belleville*, *Maman a un amant*, and *Les honneurs perdus*, have this somewhat fixed, archetypal aspect and are exceptions compared to other Afro-Parisian novels.

13. This theme is also starting to appear in novels from the continent, as in the case of *Douceur du bercail* (1998) by Aminata Sow Fall.

14. On the topic of differences in the rapport with memory and the past in the works of female African, Maghrebi, and Antillean writers, see Cazenave, "Francophone Women within France in the Nineties," in *Beyond French Feminisms: Debates on Women, Politics and Culture in France, 1980-2001*, eds Jean-Roger Celestin, Eliane Dalmolin and Isabelle de Courtivron, 129-145 (New York: Palgrave at St. Martin, 2002).

15. We saw that in cases where the novel displays an attempt at detachment, the characters' identity no longer matters and the world of foreigners/immigrants disappears. Beyala's characters, notably Saïda, who loses her Cameroonian-ness to become first and foremost an immigrant Muslim woman, is a counterexample in this sense.

16. On this topic, see the first section of this chapter on literatures of exile.

17. It is worthwhile to note that all these writers are of Cameroonian origins. This reminds me of a debate on the great literary currents of the twentieth century that marked African literature, in which Mongo Beti participated (Fest'Africa, seventh edition, Lille, November 1999). He remarked that the Négritude did not influence him, nor did it influence Cameroonian intellectuals of his generation in general, as most of them were engaged in Marxist debates. On the other hand, he added, novelists such as Richard Wright had inspired him. Another aspect N'Djehoya brought forward during his contribution in a debate organized on *Un sang d'encre* (at MIT, November 16, 1999), and which may explain this Cameroonian attraction for African-American writers (or musicians), was that the presence of American Protestant missionary groups in Cameroon might have given young Cameroonians easier access to African-American literature or music.

18. On this topic, see Mar Fall, *Des Africains noirs en France. Des tirailleurs sénégalais aux . . . Blacks* (Paris : L'Harmattan, 1986).

19. The biracial-ness of characters becomes food for thought, but also a reflection of the pressures of central society (French and African) which expect the individual to position him or herself with regards to one culture or the other, often denying him or her the option of *métissage*. In this sense, it incarnates the polarization of identity issues faced by the other characters, who are *cultural métis*.

Conclusion

All too often, the term diaspora is simply associated with dispersion and scattering, causing one to lose sight of its original meaning, "to sow," in the sense of spreading, but also of planting. This second meaning of the gathering of fruit from what was planted is frequently relegated to the background. On a literary level, the new diasporic African writings fit in this perspective: as the fruit of dispersion, they add a new dimension to French-language African literature, offering their hybridization to French literature.

At the end of our study, I would like to review some of the most important traits of the writings in question. We noted that the gaze has changed directions and now looks towards continental France as a living space, more so than Africa, questioning the present and the future more than the past. Contrary to the Négritude phenomenon, these writings do not constitute a movement and the voices remain the expression of their individuality rather than that of a collective agenda, with their singularity being their primary characteristic. While the previous diaspora was made of intellectuals who all shared the experience of colonization and saw it as their unifying link, the experience of today's diaspora is primarily marked by individual choice. Although the choice is certainly singular and individual, it still responds to shared situations: the lack of opportunities on the continent leading to a departure towards Europe or the United States, the need for recognition which still manifests itself through Parisian space, and the aspiration to enter the scene of global literature with a writing which dissociates itself from the African novel. The writing space consequently offers the solution of continuity with regards to the contemporary novel from the continent through a change in the direction of the gaze and through a disinterest in the past, in the place/memory, and in the quest for origins.

In chapter 1, I outlined some points of focus according to authors' interest in issues of being African in France. I uncovered three main directions: (1) a novel marked by the lack of focus on Africa/Africans, at the heart of which—as in the work of Camara, N'djehoya, and Njami for instance—lies the desire to distance oneself from the original literary and cultural matrix; (2) an axis of reflection over the implications of departure from a particular place and culture in favor of

others on an individual level in terms of alienation and of the dislocation of acquired reference points. *L'impasse* and *Ici, s'achève le voyage* are patent examples thereof; (3) the phenomenon of migration considered in its entirety as a
collective phenomenon, affecting both the community left behind and the one
which is found in the new space.

Through the novels we analyzed, issues of identity, insertion and assimilation, or rejection and exclusion are posed in the context of an "African" community in Paris, France and the sometimes artificially "traditional" components of
its relationship with the central group (generally French, but also at times African). Although the feeling of precariousness, of a frailty of the male or female
protagonist, emanates from novels of displacement as from novels of
(im)migration, a distinct dynamic force is nevertheless exuded with regards to
the possibilities this individual or collective displacement offers in terms of a
character's future.

As we have seen, the initial reading axes offer numerous variations around
the issue of migration in France. Some authors display through their characters
the desire to dissociate themselves from other African immigrants, refusing to
engage themselves with regards to immigration as a phenomenon, and to follow
the path of the politically committed novel for fear of seeing it considered solely
for its para-literary value. To the contrary, others offer a critical depiction of
compatriots on the continent or of fellow immigrants. Finally, still other authors
and novels offer a gaze embracing the condition of the African community
through its daily life and the challenges it faces, including issues of illegality,
thus presenting a positioned gaze. These variations have allowed us to reflect on
the perception of African immigrants held by French people and by other Africans. The act of dissecting pejorative connotations associated with immigrants
and negative perceptions of African (or non-European as whole) immigration
has allowed us to outline the contours of current French society. As the writing
of new identities in France, the novel by the African diaspora forces us to rethink not only immigration, but also the definitions of literature, what defines
immigration literature or rather immigration *literatures* in France, what distinguishes French literature and French-language literature when the two are written within the same space. It thus brings us to reconsider literature in terms of
power and of domination.

In this regard, chapter 2 allowed us to further examine the interrelation between language and identity in the writing of these new identities. The new identities, but also the multiple faces of French society, were revealed through their
inscription in the texts. We explored the variations within the narrative fabric to
reveal some of the strategies utilized by the authors to subvert normative and
peripheral discourses and deconstruct the myths and stereotypes they conveyed.

Novels such as *L'impasse*, *African Gigolo*, *Le petit prince de Belleville*,
Assèze l'Africaine, and *Les honneurs perdus* particularly touch on the identity
transformations linked to a new geographical and cultural environment. They
challenge the basic values of the original system. Notions of family, power, and
gender roles take on new form in both the microcosm (the family unit) and the

macrocosm (the African "community," Belleville, French society), with poles of authority moving from parents to children and from the man to the woman in the new world order. The woman, as shown in Beyala's work, also gains the ability to conceive of her future in new terms.

We also attempted to show how the notion of "community" needs to be reconsidered, how through the very fact that it serves as a substitute for what was left behind, it forms—and even fixates—itself around rituals and traditions, alternatively resisting or participating in the globalization of French society. The deconstruction of "dominant" discourse, but also that of the "community," allowed us to identify the manifestations of daily trans-culturation. What we found is that through globalization, so-called peripheral cultures are not doomed to uniformity, but rather they display a diversification, not only within the group, but also with regards to "central" French society. Consequently, new relationships indicative of a new order are established between the periphery and the center, among *Beur*, African, and Asian cultures and French culture, and among diasporic, Antillean, and French literature. A redistribution of elements ensues, where the imported material is integrated in everyday life and language and inversely, exported elements soon figure as local elements in the new environment.

In chapter 3, we posed the issue of readership and of its possible impact on a writing that often primarily addresses itself—through the place of publication and particularly through the choice of publishing houses—to French, and occasionally, European society. The changes in the reader's profile have repercussions, as we saw, on a writing feeding off of "Western" images while subverting them, and drawing from a collective whole of re-orientalized representations of the Other, of the foreigner. The impact of the readership also particularly touches on the possible interpretation of the texts due to a reading shaped by cultural habits and perceptions.

In this context, several of the writers favor their identity as writers, choosing to neutralize the usual label imposed on them of the writer's tacit mission of engagement. Consequently, several of them refuse to take into account the premises of a double readership. Nonetheless, those who still publish with *Présence Africaine*, *L'Harmattan*, and *Le Serpent à plumes* publishing houses particularly aim to confront the weaknesses, unrealistic dreams, and utopic myths of their compatriots, whether in France or on the continent, through a critical gaze. As in the case of Biyaoula, these authors primarily favor the African reader even if, as we highlighted, their writing space—France—and their choice of publishers in France determine the readership and imply that their audience will first be made of French people, and then of Africans living in France. This is particularly true because publishing costs are such that most African readers on the continent are unable to afford the texts. The paradox lies in the fact that, because of their pointed critiques, these authors incur criticism for depicting representations of Africans that might be misinterpreted by French people. Inversely, for a writer like Beyala, her visibility on the French literary scene and in the media leads to the risk of a literal interpretation of her work and of a general overlooking of the irony and subversion operating in her texts. African readers, on their part, are divided as to the portrait she draws of Africa and Africans.

We also addressed the danger of misinterpretation of the texts as a testament of a dynamic interaction between readers and writers in favor of the Africanization of the French language and the Gallicization of African literature. We consequently end up with the creation of a third *métisse* dimension. Moreover, we evoked the issue of these new writings' literary success with French readers. Different hypotheses were offered. A return of exoticism, albeit in the new form of a voyeuristic gaze onto the Other, but also of a narcissistic gaze finding pleasure in discovering oneself through the reflected image of French society and of the self, figured as a possible hypothesis. These aspects brought us to explore more in depth the implications of the writers' approaches and of the literature's success with regards to post-colonial African literature.

We saw how, contrary to initial assumptions, the act of writing from France inscribes itself in the spirit of a literally post-colonial literature which, due to this generation's age and its way of challenging norms, has led to the shattering of certain categorizations by referring the reader to a terminology inherited from colonial perspectives, and thereby rendering it obsolete. In the same spirit, we also saw how post-colonial writings cannot be seen as a single, monolithic block and how the parameter of the writer's age intervenes in a predominant manner over gender, class, and cultural or national origin determinants.

Finally, we tried to capture the parameters of new African writings in Paris more specifically. In particular, we highlighted the fact that it is not a movement claiming a right to difference, as in the case of the *Beur* novel, or setting out on a quest for origins and a historic past as with the Antillean novel. This novel does not speak of the ghettoization of society, as is occasionally visible in the Anglophone novel in London or in the *Beur* novel in France. When racism occurs, it is manifested essentially on an internal, psychological level or as a verbal externalization which does not necessarily lead to physical violence as it does in Anglophone literature. Although there are still relatively fewer women than men writing this type of novel, a well-known figure such as Calixthe Beyala ensures visibility for the genre that her colleagues in London do not necessarily enjoy although they are more numerous and have been on the British literary scene much longer. Even though a wandering quality is still at the heart of these writings, the nostalgia for a geographic and temporal "elsewhere" characteristic of exile literature or of the previous diaspora is gone; returning to the country of origin is no longer envisaged. On a writing level, the strategies of subversion used by writers force us to rethink the terminology of critique with regards to African and French literatures.

The writing of new identities and the need to recognize a space for them in the face of a so-called "central" literature (French, German, Italian, British) demand the redefinition of literary contours. Resistance to rethinking what intrinsically constitutes "purely" national literature is symptomatic of a societal phenomenon of national resistance to the expansion of physical, geographic, and cultural frontiers.

But as I stated in the introduction, Europe's frontiers have changed and been re-drawn. The writing of new identities corresponds to the broadening of these societies, not only in France, but also in Germany, in Italy, in Sweden. These literatures are Turkish, Syrian; they are German-language Lebanese literatures; they are the work of Jewish writers dedicated to claiming their literary space in German, Italian, English, or Spanish literature; they are also the work of Maghrebi, Eritrean, and Somali immigrants adding their creations to Italian literature. They are finally *Beur*, Antillean, Vietnamese, Indian Oceanic, and Afro-Parisian literatures changing the profile of French literature by introducing a *métisse* dimension, without necessarily being hybridized in the usual sense of the word. French society's expansion has implications with regards to its own definition, and by extension, to the definition of the concepts of nation/ality and literature. Trans-culturation, as I showed in chapter 2, testifies to new fluidity in circulation and influence, no longer unidirectional, but instead, reciprocal. No supermarket or convenience store aisle can today be devoid of a variety of couscous or *taboulé* offerings, of Vietnamese *nems*, or of Antillean *accras de morue* or *boudin*. Whether on the level of cuisine, music, fashion, or any form of art, French society experiences a *métissage* drawing from Africa, the Maghreb, the Antilles, and Asia.[1] The multicultural French soccer team's victory at the 1998 World Cup is a thought-provoking illustration of this phenomenon. Victorious through the unity of its game and adulated by the French public, the French team was a testament to the multiple faces of the French society which adores and celebrates players; indeed, Zinedine Zidane became the new "national" hero overnight. The spirit of celebration following the team's victory also marked a reflux in nationalism with over eight hundred people invading the Champs Elysées some twenty-five minutes after the end of the game to unanimously chant "We won, we won" and celebrate the colors of France. With the tricolor flags flying above, this was also indirectly an opportunity to celebrate France's greatness. Inversely, the French team's multiethnic composition was celebrated only because the team was victorious. This fact points out a paradox: such spontaneous joy, where people of all origins embraced and smiled at each other, does not change the fact that the idea of French nationality remains based on notions of citizenship, of common ancestry and history. Each French athletic victory renews the paradox of athletes who are considered entirely French regardless of their origins, while rightist political discourse simultaneously evokes the dangers of immigration.

French euphoria following the soccer team's victory temporarily quieted the traditional French *mal-être*, the growing pessimism in light of a constant crisis. In fact, the collective athletic victory spread to the economic and political realms throughout the whole summer of 1998.[2] Whether they were *Beur*, Antillean, or African, young French people benefited from a sort of tolerance as a result of the new order through the possibility for some of entering certain nightclubs where they had often been rejected in the past, for example, and a sort of overall loosening of feelings towards youth from the *banlieues*, which became associated for a short time with the country's triumphant multicultural face. The celebration of multiculturalism and of a multiethnic French profile came into fashion. The arrival of the New Year in 1999 marked the end of this hiatus as the collective memory forgot and returned to its habitual fears of a "delinquent and difficult" youth, or of illegal immigration cases to be terminated. The following victory of the same soccer team in the spring of 2000 at the European cup once more created a new wave of *bien-être*[3]—but for how long? Was a report not published which revealed discriminatory practices in real estate at around the same time?

The last presidential elections and the spectacular success of Jean-Marie Le Pen in the first round proved the increasing extreme right-wing conservatism of France and unmasked uneasy feelings and racism about foreigners and second-generation children, born from non-European immigrants. The fear of seeing an extreme right-wing government ruling France did spur demonstrations and feelings of solidarity among the French. But it also exposed the fact that France was living in denial[4] by refusing to recognize internal transformations and by continuing to consider immigrants as second-class citizens, when in fact French society is experiencing a *métissage* on a daily basis. The theory of assimilation, long the cornerstone of French history and of the French colonial system in particular, and which continues to makes its way into rightist political discourse, appears completely obsolete in light of today's realities, in light of the current globalization. Indeed, as shown by Mireille Rosello in *Declining the Stereotype*, it would be entirely ludicrous to consider certain Parisian, Lyonnean, or Marseillean *banlieues* as enclaves of idyllic fusion between foreign and French cultures. In fact, some of the texts in our study speak of the difficulties of adaptation for immigrants settling on French soil particularly with regards to identity transformations due to the new environment and rhythm, or with regards to experiences of blatant or latent racism, as broached under the cover of humor in Bessora's *53cm* and *Les taches d'encre*. Novels such as *Bleu-Blanc-Rouge* broach this issue of a dichotomous France, which on one hand aspires towards universality at the time of the Euro, yet, on the other hand, is unable to embrace the idea of non-European immigration. In this sense, the new writings from the end of the 1990s move closer to the novel of Maghrebi immigration, using a similar landscape—no longer limited to Paris, but now expanding to the *banlieues* and to other big cities such as Lille—and situations: the underground life and work, legal difficulties, and the "système D" [the art of getting by] as a form of survival.

Much like the transformations experienced by French society today, this new literature presents implications on a macroscopic scale for the definition of literature. Whereas German literature offers a multitude of terms, considered as a sort of addenda which enrich central German literary space, French literature essentially created a single global term: Francophone literature. Conferences, university study associations, and publications have been formed around this term.

Nonetheless, the term of Francophone literature has incurred criticism in recent years. Critics have often brought up the fact that the proximity between the term/concept of *Francophonie* and Francophone literature is a (paternalistic) way of grouping, under the banner of the beauty and love for the French language, literatures which in reality do not share anything, having us forget all too soon the historical reasons leading to the writing of these literatures in French. The expression "Francophone curse" ["Malédiction Francophone"] also the title of Ambroise Kom's analysis of the topic (2000), is certainly not too strong, as it appropriately suggests the devastating effects of the politics of *Francophonie* as associated with the development of the language and of the Francophone presence.

What the term conceals, which has yet to be criticized, is the fact that "Francophone" acts as a safety valve for French literature. The term indeed allows for the categorization of French-language literatures that French literature can then choose to exclude from its own category. The term thus becomes a practical mask, a way to classify in a single aisle all French-language literatures that are not considered part of French literature. Consequently, the canon of French literature remains untouched, unthreatened by a "foreign" literature. The presence of this third-party term, by revealing relationship and filial links (and thus referring the reader to the colonial heritage of paternity), moreover creates a certain cushion of security. As a result, the debate regarding what constitutes French literature at its core remains obscured.

But because these new writings are reflections on a literary level of the globalization and trans-culturation currently experienced by French society, they break this dichotomous balance. By creating a third *métisse* dimension drawing from a double, both African and French, heritage, they nullify all strict demarcations. The success of these authors (not to mention the growing number of French literary awards bestowed on Francophone novelists) leaves the distinction between Francophone and French literature to the imagination. The success of writers like Beyala or of the late Ahmadou Kourouma confirms the fact that new African writings/Francophone literatures have become the reference figures, thereby inverting the usual attributions. French literature no longer plays the referential role for French-language literatures. Instead, so-called "peripheral" literatures, which were originally grafted onto the center as a sort of enrichment, today constitute the central element for renewal.

On their part, the writers do not want to be reduced to peripheral label. Both through their persons and their work, they illustrate a phenomenon of daily globalization. Their aspiration is simply to be recognized as writers. Their rejection of literary engagement comes, in a way, from the compartmentalization of literary production, where the criterion of engagement was retained as the a priori characteristic of African/third-world literature. The very diversity of the narrative fabrics selected in this study marks the authors' desire to break from the usual enclaves and to express themselves through the strength of their individual voices.

Although in existence for barely fifteen years, these new voices have displayed an evolution, notably in their tone of voice. Whereas in the mid-1980s the authors' initial individual explorations essentially led to a rejection of engagement and to a disinterest in the continent and in Africans, and which led then to the conflicted exploration of displacement in the early 1990s, the voices have progressively converged towards a more pronounced interest in the immigrant African community in Paris. That does not mean that the writers have created a collectively engaged writing, but rather that the multiple facets of immigration on all its levels offered by these texts create a prism effect reflecting on literature in France, as well as on French society.

These new writings also carry implications for the African novel. Through their rendition of the identity issues affecting African men and women—mostly today's youth—and their exploration of unrealistic dreams (with regards to France in particular), they have challenged the norms. This is particularly crucial considering that three-quarters of current Francophone African literary production is written outside the African continent and that a large percentage comes from these authors who live in France. By creating a dynamic current, the novel of the African self makes room for diversification, forcing writers from the continent to rethink their own writing and objectives. Through the gaze it directs—or does not direct—towards Africa, this novel plays the role of a mirror image. Indeed, while it displays a certain disinterest in the place/memory of Africa (characterized by a quest for the past and place left behind), the novel from the continent instead marks a renewed interest in the reconstruction of a collective historic past, no longer simply through the exultation of glorious times, but also through the confrontation of past mistakes and weaknesses, and a renewed engagement with regards to today's Africa. Ultimately, the literary canon of the African novel must also be reconsidered and revised. Rather than considering the works of these authors as an autonomous whole, we should instead consider them for their implications for French literature on one hand and for African literature on the other. The texts of each invoke those of the other. Unapologetic texts encompassing us all, the new African writings of self are the reflection of a new geographical and cultural map of post-coloniality.

As writings of African selves in today's France and African writings of self, these plural voices located at the intersection of spaces and cultures speak of the possibility of a self-writing construing itself outside the cultural norms imposed on Africa and Africans by the West, and breaking on a literary level with the usual norms of the novel. Hence the emergence of the police mystery approach, but also that of various strategies of language subversion through the use of humor and derision, as in the work of N'djehoya and Bessora, and of slang and sexuality, as with Ngoye or Sami Tchak in *Place des fêtes* (2001).

Alternatively funny, ironic, iconoclastic, and occasionally violent, these new writings stir us. By disturbing us through their self-derision, their ambivalence, and the depiction of occasionally insane characters, these writings operate as eye-openers and force us to think about discourse, society, and literature on new bases.

Ultimately, our analysis of these new writings, of their visibility and of what they represent for the French novel and for the African novel from the continent, refers us to the writing of new identities on the international literary scene, to an almost tangible pulse of life which echoes James Baldwin's words in another context: "Listen to me, I breathe too. I want to live. I know very well that if you don't live, we don't live, and others don't either; it's impossible. That's what it's all about."

Notes

1. In "Multiculturalism in Europe," *Ethnicity*, eds. John Hutchinson and Anthony D. Smith (London: Oxford Press, 1996), John Rex contests the dynamic force of these absorptions, limiting them to "superficial manifestations restrained to the culinary realm." "The original majority culture cannot be considered as a culture among others. No more than it could be argued that this culture will undergo inevitable modifications through the absorption of little things here and there. There are superficial elements in minority cultures, such as those dealing with food, which will affect the majority culture, without being susceptible to fundamentally modifying the majority culture" (244).

2. In his analysis of immigrants and of the generational effect, Eric Taieb explores the dynamic value of the integration of sports and of soccer in particular: "Sport, football, discipline emblématique, facteur d'intégration à la base même, tout en fournissant aussi à des immigrés récents ou d'origine un moyen de représenter au sommet leur pays 'd'accueil'. Un moyen qui est aussi instrument de promotion sociale pour eux-mêmes, et vecteur d'identification comme d'espoir de faire la même chose pour les autres" (286) [Sport—soccer—emblematic discipline, factor of integration at its very core while also providing recent immigrants and French people of immigrant origins with a way to represent their 'host' country at the top. Also an instrument of social promotion for themselves, and a vector of identification and of hope of doing the same for others]. In parallel, he notes the double-edged emblematic value of the athletes, through the hope they carry and represent for others, but also through their role in stereotypical representations.

3. The notion of victory is essential for this point. In this regard, Taieb cites the remarks of tennis player Yannick Noah: "French" when he wins, but who is reminded of his African origins and his lack of discipline when he loses; the color of his skin varies, as he says himself, depending on *the gaze of others*.

4. Michel Wieviorka's analysis of France's dualization and of the rise in xenophobic sentiment throughout the 1990s amply proves this point.

Selected Bibliography

Novels

Baenga, Bolya. *Cannibale*. Lausanne: Pierre-Marcel Favre, 1986.

———. *La Polyandre*. Paris: Serpent à plumes, 1998.

Baker-Léandre, Alain. *Ici, s'achève le voyage*. Paris: L'Harmattan, 1989.

Barry, Kesso. *Kesso, princesse peuhle*. Paris: Seghers, 1988.

Ben Jelloun, Tahar. *Les raisins de la galère*. Paris: Fayard, 1996.

Bessora, Sandrine. *53 cm*. Paris: Le serpent à plumes, 1999.

———. *Les taches d'encre*. Paris: Stock, 2000.

Beti, Mongo. *Les deux mères de Guillaume Ismaël Dzewatama*. Paris: Buchet-Chastel, 1983.

———. *La revanche de Guillaume Ismaël Dzewatama*. Paris: Buchet-Chastel, 1984.

Beyala, Calixthe. *C'est le soleil qui m'a brûlée*. Paris: Stock, 1987.

———. *Tu t'appelleras Tanga*. Paris: Stock, 1988.

———. *Seul le diable le savait*. Paris: L'Harmattan, 1990.

———. *Le petit prince de Belleville*. Paris: Albin Michel, 1992.

———. *Maman a un amant*. Paris: Albin Michel, 1993.

———. *Assèze L'Africaine*. Paris: Albin Michel, 1994.

———. *Lettre d'une Africaine à ses soeurs occidentales*. Paris: Spengler, 1995.

———. *Les honneurs perdus*. Paris: Albin Michel, 1996.

———. *La petite fille du réverbère*. Paris: Albin Michel, 1997.

———. *Amours sauvages*. Paris: Albin Michel, 1999.

———. *Comment cuisiner son mari à l'africaine*. Paris: Albin Michel, 2000.

Biyaoula, Daniel. *L'impasse*. Paris: Présence Africaine, 1996.

———. *Agonies*. Paris: Présence Africaine, 1998.

Boni, Tanella. *Les baigneurs du lac rose*. Abidjan: NEI, 1994.

Bugul, Ken. *Le baobab fou*. Dakar: NEA, 1983.

Burford, Barbara. *The Threshing Floor*. London: Sheba, 1986.

Camara, Philippe. *Discopolis*. Paris: L'Harmattan, 1993.

Charef, Mehdi. *Le thé au harem d'Archi Hamed*. Paris: Ed. Mercure de France, 1983.

Dadié, Bernard. *Un Nègre à Paris*. Paris: Présence Africaine, 1959.

Dracius-Pinalie, Suzanne. *L'Autre qui danse*. Paris: Seghers, 1989.

Effa, Gaston-Paul. *La saveur de l'ombre*. Paris: L'Harmattan, 1993.

———. *Quand le ciel se retire*. Paris: L'Harmattan, 1995.

———. *Tout ce bleu*. Paris: Grasset, 1996.

———. *Mâ*. Paris: Grasset, 1998.

———. *Le cri que tu pousses ne réveillera personne*. Paris: Gallimard, 2000.

———. *Cheval-Roi*. Paris: Editions du rocher, 2001.

Efoui, Kossi. *La polka*. Paris: Seuil, 1998.

Emecheta, Buchi. *The Family*. Oxford: Heinemann, 1992.

———. *Kehinde*. Oxford: Heinemann, 1994.

Essomba, Jean-Roger. *Les lanceurs de foudre*. Paris: L'Harmattan, 1995

———. *Le paradis du Nord*. Paris: Présence Africaine, 1996.

———. *Le dernier gardien de l'arbre*. Paris: Présence Africaine, 1998.

———. *Une Blanche dans le noir*. Paris: Présence Africaine, 2001.

Etoke, Nathalie. *Un amour sans papiers*. Paris: Editions Cultures Croisées, 1999.

Gilroy, Beryl. *Boy Sandwich*. London: Virago, 1989.

Kane, Cheikh Hamidou. *L'aventure ambiguë*. Paris: Julliard, 1961.

Karone, Yodi. *A la recherche du cannibale amour*. Paris: Nathan, 1988.

———. *Les beaux gosses*. Paris: Publisud, 1988.

Kohnson, Amryl. *Long Road to Nowhere*. London: Virago Press, 1985.

Laye, Barnabé. *Une femme dans la lumière de l'aube*. Paris: Seghers, 1988.

———. *Mangalor*. Paris: Seghers, 1989.

Loba , Aké. *Kocoumbo, L'étudiant noir*. Paris: Flammarion, 1960.

Lopès, Henri. *Le Chercheur d'Afriques*. Paris: Seuil, 1990.

———. *Sur l'Autre Rive*. Paris: Seuil, 1992.

Mabanckou, Alain. *Bleu-Blanc-Rouge*. Paris: Présence Africaine, 1998.

———. *Et Dieu seul sait comment je dors*. Paris: Présence Africaine, 2001.

———. *Les petits-fils nègres de Vercingetorix*. Paris: Le Serpent à plumes, 2002.

———. *African Psycho*. Paris: Le Serpent à plumes, 2003.

———. *Verre cassé*. Paris: Seuil, 2005.

Makhele, Caya. *L'homme au landeau*. Paris: L'Harmattan, 1988.

———.*La fable du cloître des cimetières*. Paris: L'Harmattan, 1995.

Monénembo, Tierno. *Un rêve utile*. Paris: Seuil, 1991.

N'Diaye, Catherine. *Gens de sable*. Paris: POL, 1984.

———. *La mémoire en couleur*. Paris: POL, 1984.

NDiaye, Marie. *Quant au riche avenir*. Paris: Eds de Minuit, 1985

———. *Comédie classique*. Paris: POL, 1986.

———. *La femme changée en bûche*. Paris: Eds de Minuit, 1989.

———. *En famille*. Paris: Eds de Minuit, 1990.

———. *Un temps de saison*. Paris: Editions de Minuit, 1994.

N'Dongo, S. *Exil, connais pas*. Paris: Seuil, 1976.

Ngal, Mbwil a Mpaang. *Une saison de symphonie*. Paris: l'Harmattan, 1994.

Ngoye, Achille. *Agence Black Bafoussa*. Paris: Le Serpent à plumes, 1996.

———. *Sorcellerie à bout portant*. Paris: Le Serpent à plumes, 1998.

———. *Yaba terminus*. Paris: Le Serpent à plumes, 1999.

———. *Ballet Noir à Chateau-Rouge*. Paris: Gallimard, Série noire, 2001.

Njami, Simon. *Cercueil et Cie*. Paris: Lieu Commun, 1985.

———. *African Gigolo*. Paris: Seghers, 1989.

N'djehoya, Blaise. *Un regard noir*. Paris: Autrement, 1984.

———. *Le Nègre Potemkine*. Paris: Lieu Commun, 1988.

Ouologuem, Yambo. *Lettre à la France noire*. Paris: Seuil, 1969.

Pineau , Gisèle. *Un papillon dans la Cité*. Paris: Editions Sépia, 1992.

———. *L'exil selon Julia*. Paris: Stock, 1996.

Riley, Joan. *The Unbelonging*. London: Women's Press, 1985.

Sebbar, Leïla. *Shérazade. 17 ans, brune, frisée. Les yeux verts*. Paris: Stock, 1982

———. *Le chinois vert d'Afrique*. Paris: Stock, 1984.

———. *Parle mon fils parle à ta mère*. Paris: Stock, 1985.

Sow Fall, Aminata. *Douceurs du bercail*. Abidjan: NEI, 1998.

Tchak, Sami. *Place des fêtes*. Paris: Gallimard, 2001.

Yamgane, Kofi. *Droits, devoirs et crocodile*. Paris: Robert Laffont, 1992.

Works of Criticism

Aldrich, Robert. "From Francité to Créolité. French West Indian Comes Home." In *Writing Across Worlds. Literature and Migration*, edited by Russell King, John Connell and Paul White, 101-124. New York: Routledge, 1995.

Alloula, Malek. *The Colonial Harem*. Minneapolis: University of Minnesota Press, 1986.

André, Marcel. *La France et ses Nègres*. Paris: Edition de la Flamme Pure, 1983.

Appadurai, Arjun. "Disjuncture and difference in the Global Cultural Economy." *Public Culture 2* (Spring 1990): 1-4.

Appiah, Anthony. *In My Father's House*: *Africa in the Philosophy of Culture*. New York: Oxford University Press, 1992.

Ashcroft, Bill, Gareth Griffiths, and Helen Tiffin. *The Empire Writes Back: Theory and Practice in Post-Colonial Literatures*. London: Routledge, 1989.

Balibar, Etienne, and Immanuel Wallerstein. *Race, nation, class: Ambiguous Identities*. London: Verso, 1991.

Bammer, Angelika, ed. *Displacements. Cultural Identities in Question*. Bloomington: Indiana University Press, 1994.

Bataille, Philippe. *Le racisme au travail*. Paris, Seuil, 1997.

Baudrillard, Jean. *A l'ombre des majorités silencieuses, ou, La fin du social, suivie de, L'extase du socialisme*. Paris: Denoël/Gonthier, 1982.

Begag, Azouz, et Abdellatif Chaouite. *Ecarts d'identité*. Paris: Seuil, 1991.

Belbahri, Abdelkader. *Immigration et situations postcoloniales. Le cas des Maghrébins en France*. Paris: L'Harmattan, 1987.

Ben Jelloun, Tahar. *L'Hospitalité française: racisme et immigration maghré-bine*. Paris: Seuil, 1984.

———. *Le racisme expliqué à ma fille*. Paris: Seuil, 1999.

Bhabha, Homi K, ed., *Nation and Narration*. New York: Routledge and Keegan Paul, 1990.

———. *The Location of Culture*. London: Routledge, 1994.

Bonn, Charles, ed. *Littératures des immigrations*. 2. *Exils croisés*. Paris: l'Harmattan, 1995.

Bourdieu, Pierre. *The Field of Cultural Production*. New York: Columbia University Press, 1993.

Brah, A. *Cartographies of Diaspora: Contesting Identities*. London, New York: Routledge, 1996.

Braidotti, Rosi. *Nomadic Subjects*. New York: Columbia University Press, 1994.

Brinker-Gabler, Gisela and Sidonie Smith, eds. *Writing New Identities: Gender, Nation and Immigration in Contemporary Europe*. Minneapolis: University of Minnesota Press, 1997.

Casanova, Pascale. *La République mondiale des Lettres*. Paris: Le Seuil, 1999.

Cazenave, Odile. *Femmes rebelles: naissance d'un nouveau roman africain au féminin*. Paris: L'Harmattan, 1996.

———. "Calixthe Beyala: l'exemple d'une écriture décentrée dans le roman africain au féminin." In *L'Ecriture décentrée*, edited by Michel Laronde, 122-148. Paris: L'Harmattan, 1996.

———. "Roman africain au féminin et immigration: dynamisme du devenir." In *Changements au féminin en Afrique noires* Vol. II, edited by Danielle de Lame and Chantal Zabus, 49-69. Paris: L'Harmattan, Paris, 1999.

———. "Calixthe Beyala's "Parisian Novels": an Example of Globalization and Transculturation in French Society." *Sites: the Journal of 20th Century/Contemporary French Studies* 3, no. 2 (Spring 2000): 119-127.

———. "Vingt ans après Mariama Bâ: nouvelles écritures au féminin," *Africultures 35*, "Masculin-Féminin" (Février 2001): 7-15.

———. "Writing New Identities: the African Diaspora in France." In *Literature of Immigration in France*, edited by Susan Ireland and Patrice J. Proulx, 153-163. Westport: Greenwood Press, 2001.

———. "Francophone Women Writers in France in the Nineties." In *Beyond French Feminisms: Debates on Women, Politics and Culture in France, 1980-2001*, edited by Jean-Roger Celestin, Eliane Dalmolin and Isabelle de Courtivron, 129-142. New York: Palgrave Macmillan, 2003.

Célérier, Patricia-Pia. "De la gaulologie à l'impéritie." *Présence Francophone* 58, *Francophonie, Ecritures et immigration* (Mai 2002): 73-84.

Chatterjee, Partha. *The Nation and Its Fragments: Colonial and Postcolonial Histories*. Princeton: Princeton University Press, 1993.

Collier, Gordon. *Us and Them*. New York: Brunner/Mazel, 1987.

Davies, Carole Boyce. *Black Women Writing the Anti-Imperialist Critique*. New York: Routledge, 1994.

———. *Migrations of the Subject: Black Women, Writing and Identity.* London: Routledge, 1994.

Deltel, Danielle. "Marie NDiaye: l'ambition de l'universel." *Notre librairie, Nouvelles Ecritures Féminines* 2, no. 118 (Juillet-Septembre 1994): 111-115.

Egejuru, Phanuel Akebueze. *Black Writers, White Audience: A Critical Approach to Literature.* Hicksville, NY: Exposition Press, 1979.

Fabre, Michel. *La rive noire. De Harlem à Paris.* Paris: L Centurion, 1985.

Fall, Mar. *Des Africains noirs en France. Des tirailleurs sénégalais aux . . . Blacks.* Paris: L'Harmattan, 1986.

Fanon, Frantz. *Les Damnés de la terre.* Paris: Gallimard, coll. Folio/Actuel, 3rd ed., 1991.

———. *Peau noire. Masques blancs.* Paris: Du Seuil, coll. Points/Essais, 1952.

Gandoulou, Justin-Daniel. *Entre Paris et Bacongo.* Paris: Collection Alors, Centre Georges Pompidou, 1984.

Gaye, Amadou, Erice Faverau, and Leïla Sebbar, eds. *Génération métisse.* Paris: Syros/Alternatives, 1988.

George, Rosemary. *The Politics of Home: Postcolonial Relocations and Twentieth Century Fiction.* New York: Cambridge University Press, 1996.

Glad, John, ed. *Literature in Exile.* Durham, N.C.: Duke University Press, 1990.

Gurr, Andrew. *Writers in Exile.* Atlantic Highlands, NJ: Humanities Press, 1981.

Gracia, Eliana, Jean-Marie Marconot, Alain Hullot, Nicole Nivelle. *Migrations, Racisme et Cultures dans les Pays du Rhône.* Nimes: C. Lacour, 1993.

Grenier, Jean-Claude et Jean Jolly. *Les onze peurs des Français pour l'an 2000.* Paris: Orban, 1990.

Hansen, Joseph, and Evelyn Reed, eds. *Cosmetics, Fashions, and the Exploitation of Women.* New York: Pathfinder Press, 1986.

Hargreaves, Alec G. *Voices from the North African Immigrant Community in France; Immigration and Identity in Beur Fiction.* Providence, RI: Berg Publishers, 1991.

Harrow, Kenneth. *Less than One and Double.* Portsmouth, NH: Heinemann, 2002.

Harvey, David. *The Condition of Postmodernity.* Oxford: Blackwell, 1989.

Hiro, Dilip. *Black British, White British.* London: Eyre and Spottiswoode, 1971.

Hoffman Baruch, Elaine. *Women, Love and Power, Literary and Psychoanalytic Perspectives.* New York: New York Uiversity Press, 1991.

Hooks, Bell. *Yearning: Race, Gender and Cultural Politics.* London: Turnaround, 1989.

Ireland, Susan, and Patrice Proulx, eds. *Immigrant Narratives in Contemporary France.* Westport, CT: Greenwood Press, 2001.

Irigaray, Luce. *Je, Tu, Nous. Pour une culture de la différence.* Paris: Editions Grasset & Fasquelle, 1990.

Jean Mohammed, Abdul R. "Worldliness-without-World, Homelnessness-as-Home: Toward a Deifnition of the Specular Border Intellectual." In *Edward Saïd: A Critical Reader,* edited by Michael Sprinker. Oxford: Blackwell, 1992.

Jules-Rosette, Benetta. *Black Paris: The African Writers' Landscape.* Urbana: Illinois University Press, 1998.

Kanneh, Kadiatu. *African Identities: Race, Nation and Culture in Ethnography, Panafricanism and Black literatures.* London: Routledge, 1998.

King, Russell, John Connell, and Paul White, eds. *Writing Across Worlds. Literature and Migration.* New York/London: Routledge, 1995.

Kom, Ambroise. *La Malédiction francophone. Défis culturels et condition post-coloniale en Afrique.* Hamburg: LIT, 2000.

———. "Une littérature plurivoque; pays, exil et précarité chez Mongo Beti, Calixthe Beyala et Daniel Biyaoula." Paper presented during the third International Colloquium of the Association of Francophone Studies of Central-Eastern Europe (AEFECO), Leipzig, March 30-April 4, 1998.

Kouri, K. *Multiracial families: issues of race, culture, ideology and identity.* Los Angeles: USC Press, 1994.

Kristeva, Julia. *Etrangers à nous-mêmes.* Paris: Fayard, 1988.

———. *Lettre ouverte à Harlem Désir.* Paris: Editions Rivages, 1990.

Kuoh-Moukoury, Thérèse. *Les Couples Dominos.* Paris: Julliard, 1973.

Kureishi, Hanif. *The Black Album.* New York: Scribbner, 1995.

Laronde, Michel. *Autour du roman Beur.* Paris: L'Harmattan, 1993.

———, ed. *L'Ecriture décentrée.* Paris: L'Harmattan, 1996.

Lawrence, Karen R., ed. *Decolonizing Tradition.* Urbana: University of Illinois Press, 1992.

Lazarus, Neil. *Resistance in Postcolonial African Fiction.* New Haven: Yale University Press, 1990.

Lionnet, Françoise. *Post-colonial Representations. Woman, Literature, Identity.* Ithaca: Cornell University Press, 1995.

———. "Inscriptions of Exile: The Body's Knowledge and the Myth of Authenticity." *Callaloo* 15, no.1 (Winter 1992): 30-40.

Lorraine, Alain. *175.000 Réunionnais en France, Une communauté invisible.* Paris: Karthala, 1996.

Magnier, Bernard. "Beurs noirs à Black Babel." *Notre Librairie. Dix ans de Littératures* I, no. 103 (Octobre-Décembre 1990): 102-107.

Makouta-Mboukou, Jean-Pierre. *Les littératures de l'exil: des textes sacres aux oeuvres profanes.* Paris: L'Harmattan, 1993.

Mbembe, Achille. "A propos des écritures africaines de soi." *Politique Africaine* 77 (March 2000): 16-43.

Midiohouan, Guy Ossito. *Du bon usage de la francophonie. Essai sur l'idéologie francophone.* Porto-Novo, Bénin: Editions CNPMS, 1994.

Miller, Christopher L. *Nationalists and Nomads: Essays on Francophone African Literature and Culture.* Chicago: University of Chicago Press, 1998.

Miraz, Heidi Safia, *Young, Female, and Black.* New York: Routledge, 1992.

Miraz, Heidi Safia. ed. *Black British Feminism.* New York: Routledge, 1997.

Mouralis, Bernard. "Marie NDiaye ou la recherche de l'essentiel." *Notre librairie*, Nouvelles Ecritures Féminines 2, 118 (Juillet-Septembre 1994): 108-110.

Mudimbe, Valentin. *The Invention of Africa*. Bloomington: Indiana University Press, 1986.

Mudimbe-Boyi, Elisabeth. "The Poetics of Exile and Errancy: Ken Bugul's *Le Baobab fou* and Simone Schwarz-Bart's *Ti Jean L'Horizon*." *Yale French Studies* 82, no. 2 (1993):196-212.

———. ed. "Post-colonial Women's Writing." *L'Esprit créateur* 33, no. 2 (Summer 1993).

Mullard, Chris. *Black Britain*. London: Georg Allen and Unwin Ltd., 1973.

Narayan, Uma. *Dislocating Cultures*. New York: Routledge, 1997.

N'Diaye, Rachid. "Dans sa nouvelle maison, un nouveau roman." *Africa International* 311 (February 1998): 76-80.

Ngcobo, Lauretta, ed. *Let It Be Told*. London: Virago, 1986.

Parati, Graziella, ed. *Mediterranean Crossroads: Migration Literature in Italy*. Madison, NJ: Fairleigh Dickinson University Press; London: Associated University Presses, 1999.

Patterson, Shiela. *Immigration and Race Relations in Britain 1960-1967*. London: Oxford University Press, 1969.

Revue *Autrement*. "Black" 49, Avril 1983.

Revue *Equateur* 2. "Les Tropiques d'Eros"

Ricoeur, Paul. *Soi-même comme un autre*. Paris: Seuil, 1990.

Rosello, Mireille. *Postcolonial Hospitality: The Immigrant as Guest*. Stanford, CA: Stanford University Press, 2001.

———. *Declining the Stereotype. Ethnicity and Representation in French Cultures*. Hanover, NH: University Press of New England, 1998.

———. *Infiltrating Culture: Power and Identity in Contemporary Women's Writing*. New York: St. Martin's Press, 1996.

———. "Caribbean Insularization of Identities in Maryse Condé's Work: from *En Attendant le bohneur* to *Les derniers rois mages*," *Callaloo* 18, no. 3 (Summer 1995): 565-578.

———. "'Il faut comprendre quand on peut . . .' L'art de désamorcer les stéréotypes chez Emile Ajar et Calixthe Beyala." In *L'Ecriture décentrée*, edited by Michel Laronde, 161-184. Paris: L'Harmattan, 1996.

Saïd, Edward. *Orientalism*. New York: Vintage, 1979.

———. *Culture and Imperialism*. London: Chatto & Windus, 1993.

Scarpa, Federica. "Friualni Nel Mondo. The Literature of an Italian emigrant region." In *Writing Across Worlds. Literature and Migration*, edited by Russell King, John Connell, and Paul White, 141-161. New York: Routledge, 1995.

Schreiber, Maeera. "The End of Exile: Jewish Identity and Its Diasporic Poetics," *PMLA* 113, no. 2 (March 1998): 273-287.

Segalen, Martine. *L'Autre et le semblable. Regards sur l'ethnologie des sociétés contemporaines*. Paris: Presses du CNRS, 1989.

Seyhan, Azade. *Writing Outside the Nation*. Princeton: Princeton University Press, 2000.

Spivak, Gayatri. *In Other Worlds*. New York: Routledge, 1987.

─────. *The Postcolonial Critic.* New York: Routledge, 1990.

Stovall, Tyler. *Paris Noir: African Americans in the City of Light.* New York: Houghton Mifflin, 1996.

Stratton, Florence. *Contemporary African Literature and the Politics of Gender.* London: Routledge, 1994.

Suleri, Sara. "Woman Skin Deep: Feminism and the Post-colonialCondition." *Critical Inquiry* 18, no. 4 (Summer 1992).

Sundiata, Ibrahim K. "Africanity, Identity and Culture." *Issue: A Journal of Opinion, African [Diaspora] Studies,* XXIV, no. 2 (1996): 13-17.

Taieb, Eric. *Immigrés: l'effet générations: rejet, assimilation, intégration, d'hier à aujourd'hui.* Paris: Editions de l'atelier, 1998.

Tilliette, Bruno, et Simon Ndjami. *Ethnicolor.* Paris: Autrement, 1987.

Todorov, Tzvetan. *Nous et les Autres. La réflexion française sur la diversité humaine.* Paris: Seuil, 1989.

Tribat, Michèle. *De l'immigration à l'assimilation: enquête sur les populations d'origine étrangère en France.* Paris, Editions de la découverte, INED, 1996.

Tucker, Martin, ed. *Literary exile in the twentieth century: an analysis and biographical dictionary.* Westport, CT: Greenwood Press, 1991.

Umeh, Marie, ed. *Emerging Perspectives on Buchi Emecheta.* Trenton: Africa World Press, 1996.

Waldinger, Robert. *Still the Promised City? African-Americans and New Immigrants in Post-Industrial New York.* Cambridge: Harvard University Press, 1995.

Whitlark, James, and Wendell Aycock. *The Literature of Emigration and Exile.* Lubbock, TX: Texas Tech University Press, 1992.

Wieviorka, Michel. *La France raciste.* Paris: Seuil, 1992.

─────, ed. Michel Wieviorka. *Une société fragmentée?: le multiculturalisme en débat.* Paris, Editions La découverte, 1996.

─────. *Violence en France.* Paris: Seuil, 1999.

Wilkinson, Doris. *Black Male/White Female.* London: Schenkman Publishing Company, Inc, 1975.

Wolf, Naomi. *The Beauty Myth; How Images of Beauty Are Used Against Women.* New York: William Morrow and Company Inc., 1991.

Woodhull, Winnifred. "Ethnicity on the French Frontier." In *Writing New Identities. Gender, Nation, and Immigration in Contemporary Europe*, edited by Gisela Brinker-Gabler, and Sidony Smith, 31-61. Minneapolis: University of Minnesota Press, 1997.

Yekutiel, Gerbhoni. *Africans on African-Americans: the Creation of an African-American Myth.* London: McMillan Press, 1997.

Index

About the Author

Odile Cazenave is Associate Professor in French and Francophone literature at Boston University, and also teaches at MIT. She is the author of *Femmes rebelles: naissance d'un nouveau roman africain au féminin* (1996), its translation, *Rebellious Women* (2000, 2001 paperback), and *Afrique sur Seine: Une nouvelle génération de romanciers africains à Paris* (2003). She is the guest editor for *Présence Francophone* 58, "Francophonie, Ecritures et Immigration" (Spring 2002). She has also published many articles on issues of identity, alterity, migration, and trans-culturation.